Pieces Of Me

Through Faith, Love, Disappointment, Heartbreak, Health, Illness, Family & ViSalus

SEPTEMBER 1, 2014

JULIA ANNE SIMPSON
Anacortes, WA USA

Contents

Pieces Of Me
By Julia Anne Simpson

ACKNOWLEDGMENTS & INTRODUCTION

Through life we all come across our own trials. How were go through them is what makes us who we are. The way I look at life is that you can either let life own you, or you can own it. Too many people become discouraged, but we were given the gifts and tools to prosper in life; it is how we use them and believe in ourselves that we find that true prosperity we all seek.

I am not perfect. For 10 years I have had a writers' block due to throwing away talents because I thought I had to choose between a boy I cared for and my dreams. Then the last man I was dating triggered a part of myself I have been craving to get back. He inspired a huge part of who I am again and I have never felt so alive and in two and a half months I have written over 366 poems.

Three things have brought me here; God and my faith, love, and ViSalus. If it wasn't for ViSalus, I honestly would not be publishing today. I have always kept on my path with goals and determination. I don't believe in regrets, for I live true to who I am and do so on my own. However, watching transformations and the stories amazed me.

Life stories are what inspires others to succeed; for this reason alone I am publishing myself. 366 poems was my goal and mission to put into this book. There are 365.25 days in a year and 366 days in leap year. Sometimes you have to do a total 360 degree turn around and a little extra to find where you are truly meant to be.

Pieces Of Me
By Julia Anne Simpson

Chapter 1
Inspiring Through Faith & God

For You I Will

My love only becomes deeper
My ambitions grown stronger
For you I will

My dreams are big
But your plans are bigger
For you I will

For you I will be stronger
For you I will love deeper
For you I will dream bigger
For you I will

I will never stray
I will stay in the light
I will pray for everyone to see you in this light
For you I will

For you I will
I will dream bigger
And I will love stronger
For you I will

Faith

Have faith in all you do
For the Lord & Jesus have faith in you
Always hold your head held high
Believe in what is true
For I have faith in you

Faith is deeper than believing
Faith is deeper & true
For he has faith in you

Have faith in love
Have faith in life
And you will always know what's true

Lift your head & pursue forward
There is so much in store for you
Keep your faith in the Lord Father
He continues to have faith in you

Evil Will Fail Here

Too much faith
So much passion
No darkness will triumph
For only evil will fail here

The sun shines bright
For the Lord is the light
My journey I see so clear
Evil will always fail here

No matter the length of the mission
It will only be at my discretion
And only evil will fail here

I will shine in your glory
I conquer in your dreams for me
I will continue on your path I see
Only the season weather will ever be changing around me
But through the greater power
Failure will always be for the enemy

Heal The Suffering

Let there be peace
May we not know to suffer
Heal the sick
Feed the hunger

Jesus you are the healer
The Redeemer
There are no boundaries to your love

Heal the suffering
Let them feel peace
Let them feel love

You are the redeemer
The healer from above
You are capable of all things
All things maybe touched by your hands

I pray that those who suffer
Suffer no mor

His Name Is Jesus

Born in Bethlehem
Son of God
Our Heavenly Father
Born to lead & heal
He rose again
After sacrifice for our sins
His name is Jesus
Our redeemer
King of kings

Through his amazing grace
We have been set free
His unconditional love
Continues to have faith in all of us
His name is Jesus
His faith restores us

Healer of all things
Almighty king
Son of God
You have saved & inspired me

His name is Jesus

Dream Of Heaven

Do you ever dream of heaven?
How glorious it must be
Flowers too beautiful to touch
Waters so appealing
Will there also be trees & mountains
What a site we will see

To be reunited with ones we love
What a perfect life that will be
Do you ever dream of heaven?
And how glorious Jesus will be to see

Money & status won't matter
What matters is thee
Do you ever dream of heaven?

The beauty & perfection
I can only imagine what we will see
What a home it will be

Deliverance To Hope

There is true beauty here
So much for you to believe in again
His love delivered us to him
He gave us hope to truly live again

Unconditional Love
Deliverance to Hope
Incredible Faith
We will live again

He fought our fight
He conquered death
He redeemed us
And hope was delivered
Love continues to grow

Unconditional Love
Incredible Faith
Deliverance to Hope
We will live to honor him

Dear Father

No one will ever know me better then you
You created me, you molded me
You know my heart & soul
You accept me through good & bad
No one else can know me like you do

Dear Father
I am proud to call you Father
I only pray that you truly know
How much you mean to me
Thank you for accepting me
And loving me unconditionally

Dear Father
No one could know & love me better
Dear Father
I am forever proud to call you Father
For no one could ever know & love me better then you

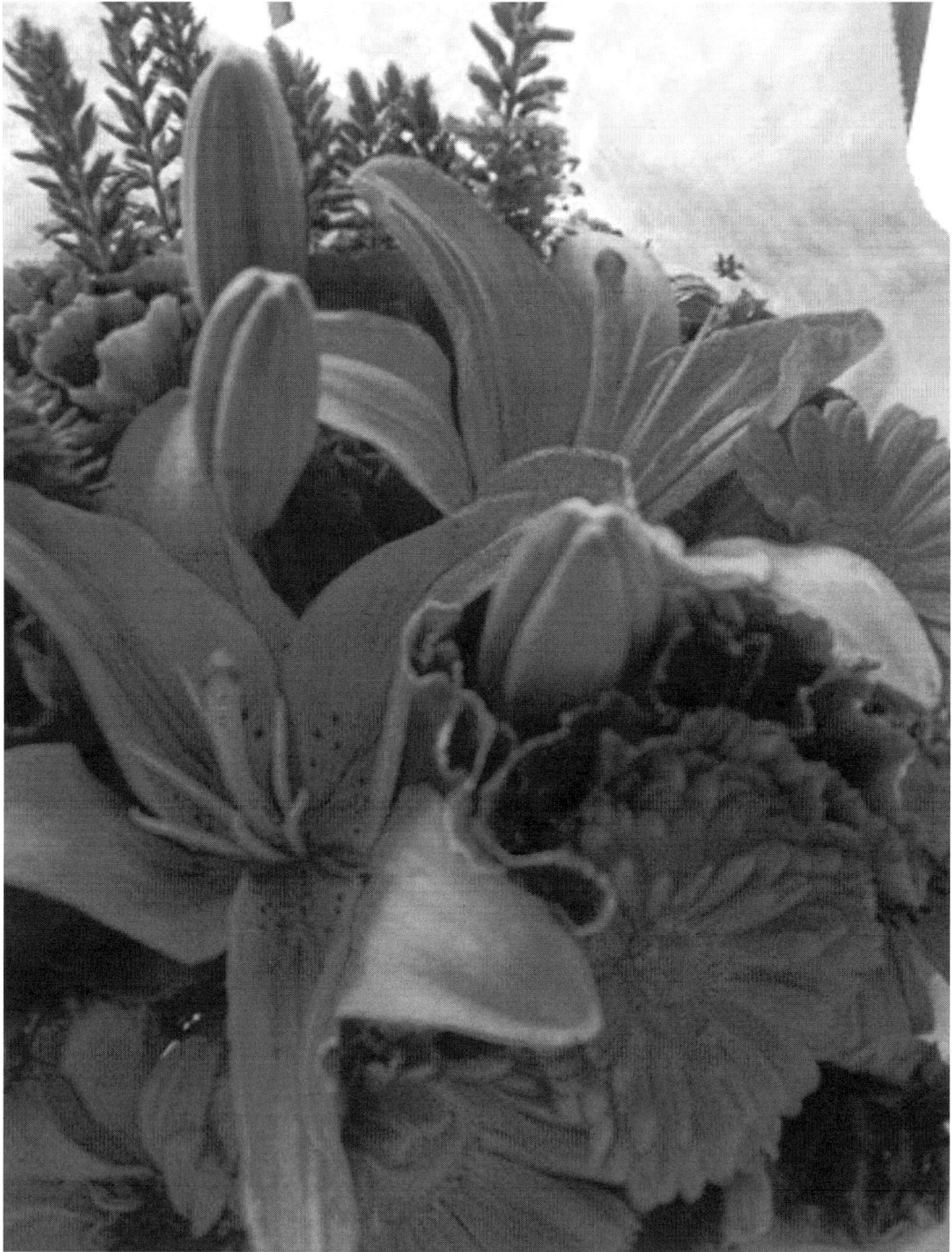

Count All Yours Blessings

So much love to be seen here
So many blessings
So much life
Our Lord continues to fight

Love your family
Love your friends
Love thy enemy
And your life will make better sense

Count your blessings
Jesus gave his life for you
Where his life ended
He rose in you

Count all your blessings
You have already won
For those around you
Believe your path has only began

Count all your blessings
Know true love
For you are very loved by him

Believe

What is proven in believing
Seeing isn't always true
To truly believe is to really feel what is true

I believe in the Heather Father
I believe in all the wonders
I believe in his love is truth
Through the innocence
To the believers for you

Miracles don't just happen
They happen in you
I am a believer in something deeper
I have faith & know you are true

I believe in a father so amazing
So amazing so true
I will always believe in you

Truth

What's truth when you don't believe
How do you see when your eyes are blind?
How do you feel when you're numb?
How can you believe in what is real

What is truth when you have no faith?
What can you believe is real
When only negatives & fear control your life today

It's so much better is the positive light
It is so much warmer when you aren't numb to life
So much more beautiful when the darkness is bright

To believe is to know what's true
Truth is to have faith in what is real
Truth

To know truth you must believe & have faith too

Storms

The whirling wind
The crashing waves
The clouds hovering about

The storm is getting louder
No fear I pray
You are much stronger
Your love never fades

Storms come and go
But you never stray
No storm will ever scare me
For your love is the most amazing grace

So bring on the rain
I will not drowned
You father are my strength

Another storm is coming
Lightning may strike
But I stand firm
The storm won't take my faith
For I know your amazing grace

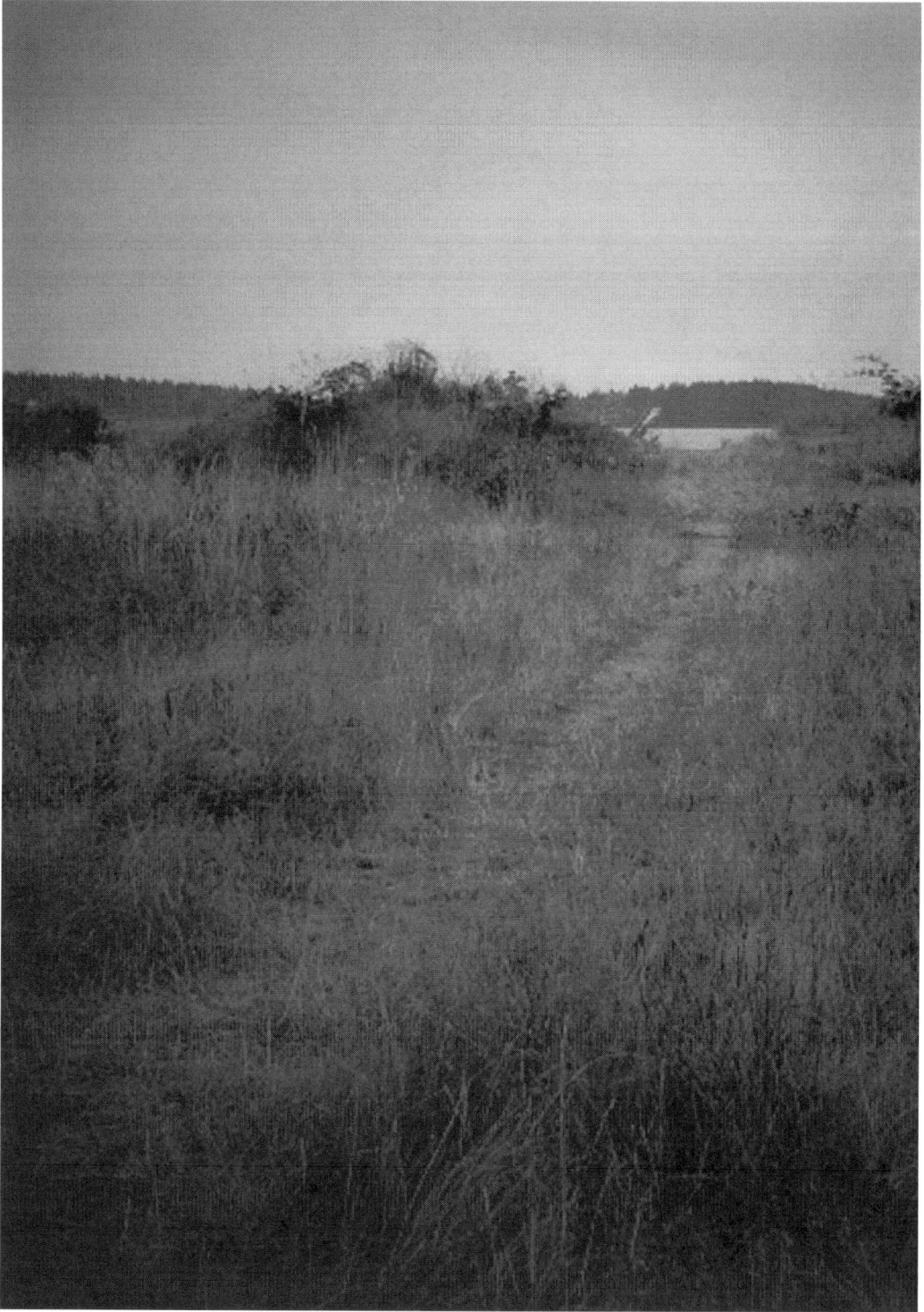

Perfect

Unfailing love
An amazing faith
Jesus gave us a greater gift

Perfect life
A deeper love
A bigger plan
God's only son

Jesus is perfect
Unconditional Love
An inspiring faith
Unfailing presence

Perfect brother
Amazing son
I'm proud to know you
He is perfect
Jesus is Perfection

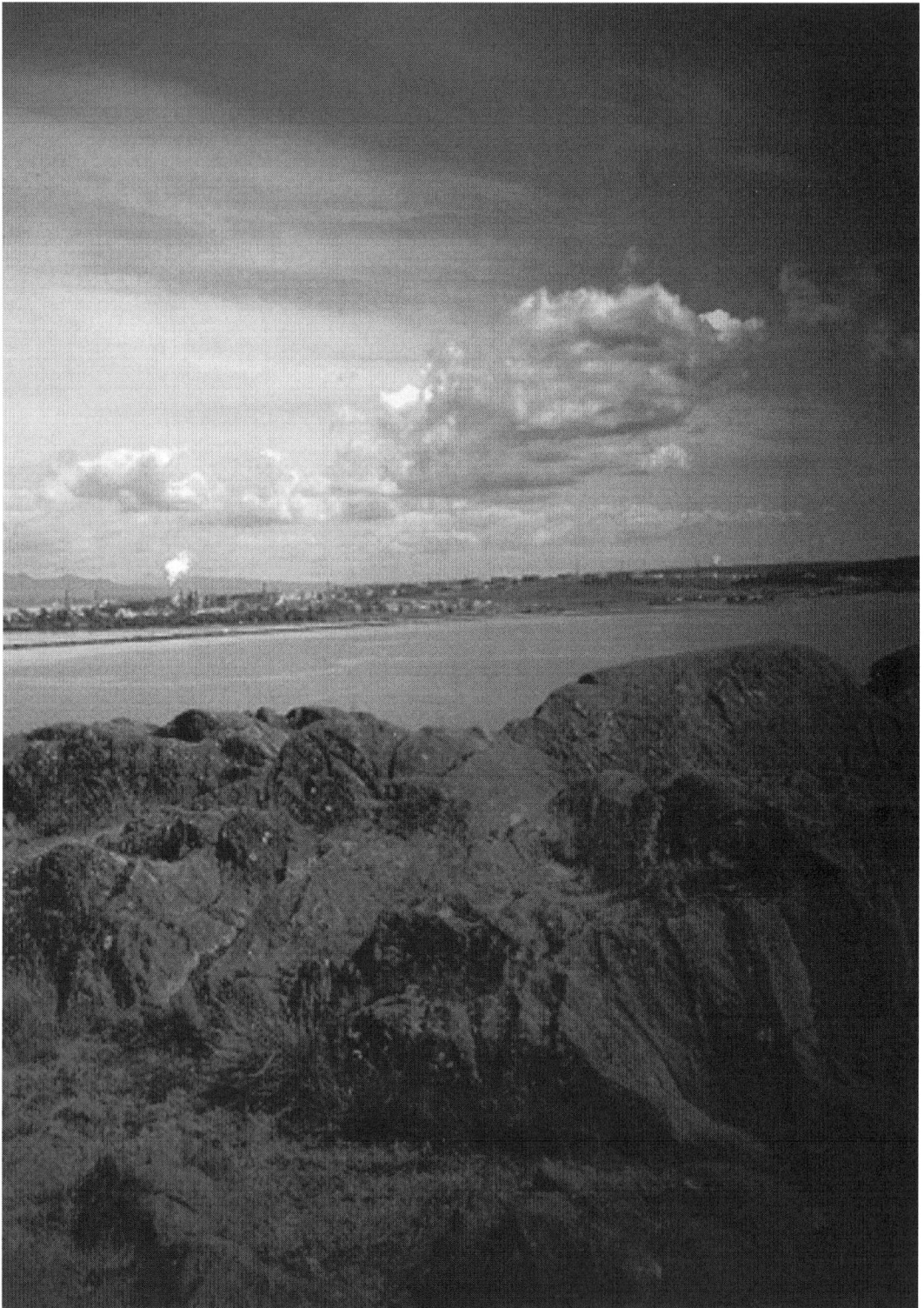

No Matter

No matter what you do
No matter how bad you try
Jesus will always be at your side

He will never leave you
His love is forever unconditional
Don't try to run away

All things are possible
His forgiveness is unfailing
He is never the one to fear
His love will never stray

Stop your running
Get on your knees and prey
Its time you live with his presence
In your heart is where he wants to stay

No matter what you do
Jesus will always see you through

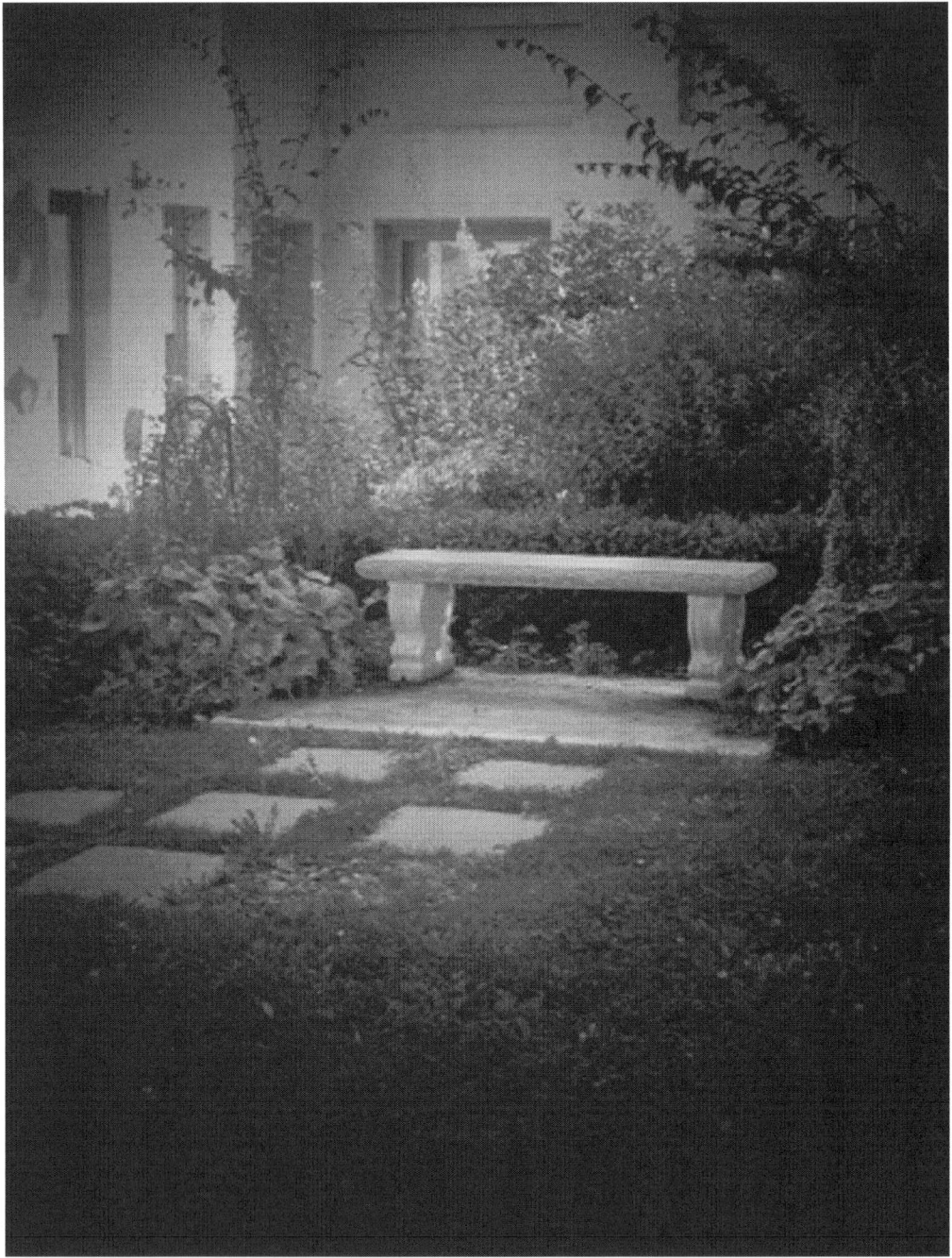

Never Alone

Through my journey
I am not alone
I may endure suffering, struggles & heartbreak
But they do no define me
I am not alone

I am not afraid
My Heavenly Father is always with me
I am not alone

I feel peace & love through my difficulties
And will push forward with a smile
I am not alone

I will conquer any & all things
I lift up & pray
May faith will carry me through
All things are possible
I am not alone

I am not alone
For I always have you

Life Without You

Life without you Lord
I couldn't imagine
A true love that runs deep
My life without you will never be seen

My strength & faith
Are the commitment from your love
You have taught me to only always rise above
And be true with love
You are my Heavenly Father above

With love so true
I will never abandon you
I could never imagine
A life without you

I See You In Me

There is a deeper mission
More than the eye can see

This journey is just beginning
There is no denying that we are winning
I see you inside of me

Use me through this journey
Give me strength through the greater mission
Let them see you shine through me
I will see you through victory

I am not strong enough
Tough enough to succeed
With a deeper love & compassion for humanity

This journey is my destiny
Through faith & love & the determination
I see you in me

Another Hill To Conquer

Hard times may come
But they will pass
Just keep believing
And continue to push forward
Nothing ever lasts

Another storm
Another mountain
The road will continue on

What you will find
When you follow through
It's only other hills you conquered through

Keep your head high
And your eyes open
It is your only solution

Don't give up
Don't let it conquer you
Know no defeat
There is more strength in you

When you follow through
It will just be another hill to you

Your Love Makes Me Stronger

I have weak moments
For my life has been a journey
But your strength is my destiny

I have loved & lost
I have triumph & fought
But through much hurt
I have been guided through you

For your love makes me stronger
Your loves carries me through
Destruction is weak before you
And only your love makes me stronger
With you I power through

With faith & strength
I will rise above
The world needs your greater love
For passion & truth
Is what I behold in you
So much faith & so much love
I will always rise above
For it is your love Lord that makes me stronger
With you I power through

Much Love For You

Deeper than the ocean
Higher than the mountains above
So much love can't hide
So much love given from the Lord above

Clearer than the air I breathe
Thicker than the ground underneath me
So much love he has for me

Much love is so beautiful
Much love is worth more than everything
For his love is much more than anything
He has so much love for you & me

His Only Son

Can you only imagine
Giving up your only son
To redeem a world of hatred
For an unconditional love so strong

Can you only imagine
What the Lord has done
For you & me
To watch your son be tortured
To watch his son die on a cross
For the sinners sins to be washed

His only son
Is our redeemer
Proof of his unconditional love
Jesus had risen to only prove this redeeming love

Can you truly imagine
A sacrifice this strong
He believes & loves faithfully
Be true to the grace of God

Continue To Strive

I strive through this life given
Though it has not been easy
But the Lord created me to survive
He is my salvation
For him I continue to thrive

He has been my salvation above
Creating me to be a survivor in on earth
For him I strive faithfully through each day he gives me
Always continue to strive & thrive for God

I continue to strive
Each & every day I try
To help those achieve the peace & beauty created
Every day I am alive
I continue to strive in you

He Is On Your Side

Have you ever just stopped and looked
At all the beauty God created
Have you stopped and gave thanks
For all the amazing blessings

He is on your side
Even if things are hard to see
That is when he is truly working
Just say his name
And believe in him
Keep your faith
And soon you will see

He is on your side
Jesus is working not only on the inside
Don't lose faith
You will get through anything

God is on your side
He will help you get through
Jesus walks beside you
He has more faith in you

Goodbye Darkness

I am finally here
The darkness is not near
It is so clear to see
I believed I would arrive
No more darkness
I have survived

Goodbye Darkness
I have arrived
In the light is where I survive

Through faith & determination
Struggles & suffering could not last
It is finally so clear to see
The light here is overwhelming to me

Goodbye Darkness
I have once again found me

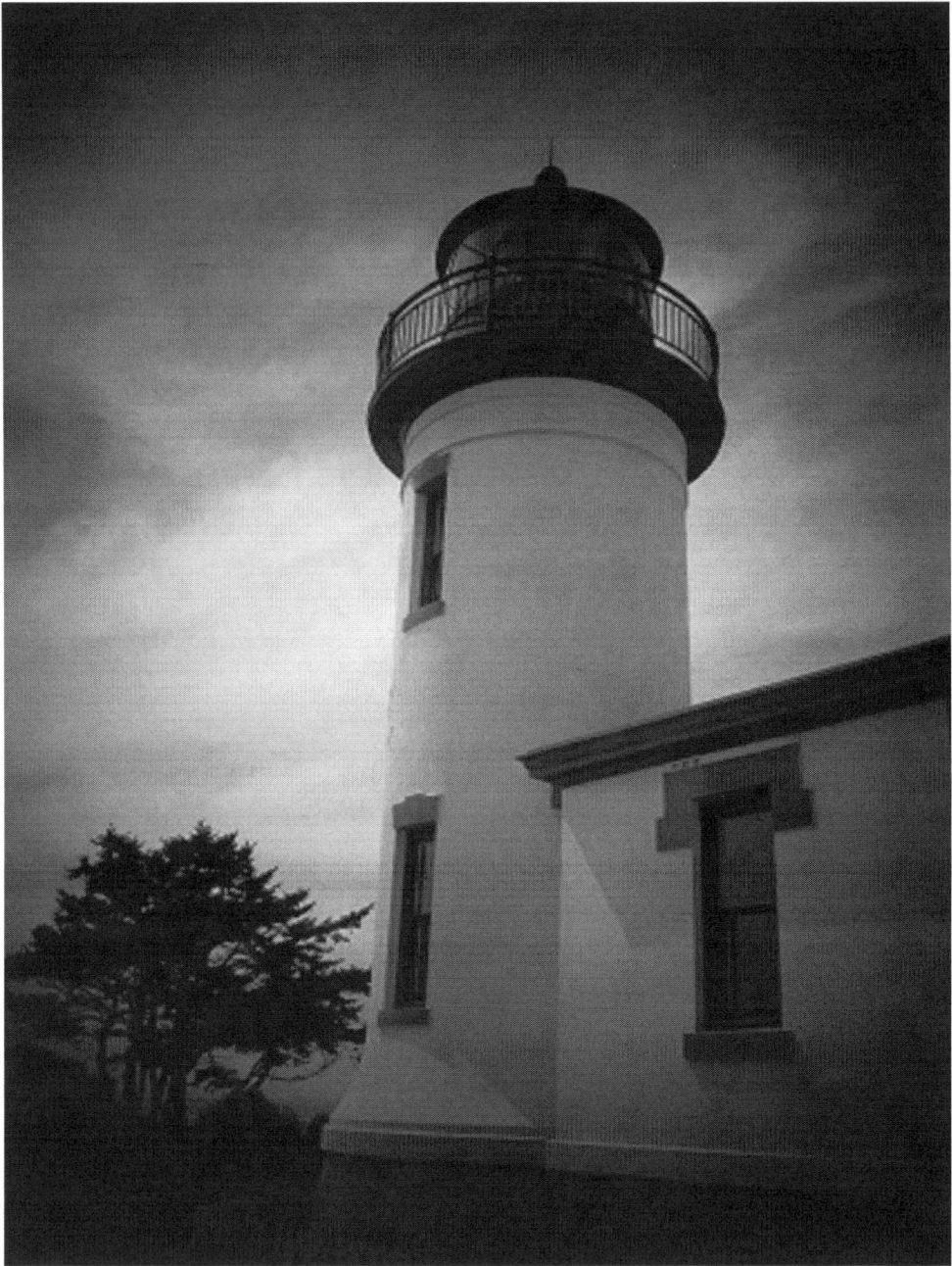

Consistency

Another night in the city
Too many tall buildings
Can't even see the moon & the stars in the sky
But I know they are above tonight
Like clockwork; consistency

Just as I know the Lord is above
I have always felt his love
Just because you cannot see
He continues to love and watch over you & me

Consistency in loving and believing in us
Our father never loses faith
Continues to love us
Always unconditional & true

So always remember
It is not what you see
Faith runs much deeper
Then the eye can ever see

True consistency

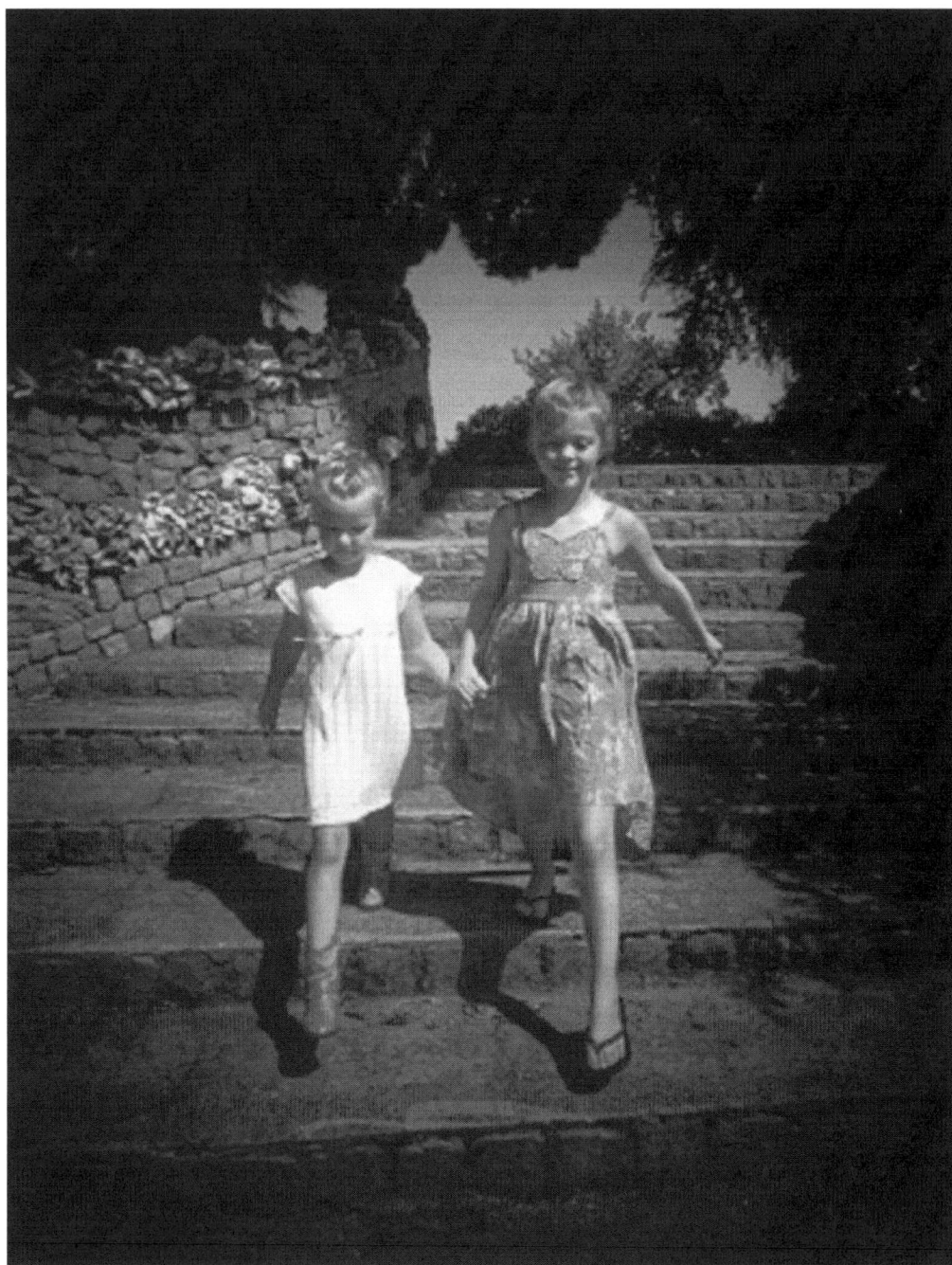

We Are Children Of God

We are the children
Of the king of all kings
He created all humanity
Our Heavenly Father above
Of heaven and earth
He created us through his unconditional love

We walk the walk with Jesus
He is our brother
The son of god
His love and devotion
Sacrificed his life for us

We are his children
How gracious & glorious is he
His love & faith in us
His true children are we

Our Heavenly Father above
Continues to unconditionally love
Forgives us our sins
Cleans us new again
And shows us the path
To prosper in righteousness

We all are the children
Of the king of all kings
Our Heavenly Father reins
For he created everything
We all are the children of God

Bigger Mission

In each day you learn more about yourself
Through poverty to success
The Lord continues to work through us

Believe and have faith
Trust the Lord each & everyday
There is a bigger mission
In the blessings and struggles among us everyday

Every day is a gift from God
Tomorrow isn't promised
So keep faith and love in Jesus
Let him continue to work through you
He will never betray or leave your side
He is with your through night & day

You are the mission
Allow the Lord to work through you
There is always a bigger mission before you
Never lose faith
This is what I pray for you today

Beauty In Everything

There is beauty in everything
For God created something more amazing
There cannot be light without darkness
There is no grass without rain or water
As there is no success without knowing failure

Open your eyes to see such beauty
Such a wonderful path has been given
For I shall dance in the rain
And conquer in the storm again

So beauty & love created here on earth
May we stay humble I pray
To see beauty in each & every day

Shine in the sun
Conquer each storm
Feel peace in the rain
There is true beauty in everything

While I Lay Down To Rest

Now when I lay down to rest
I pray to my Heavenly Father above
To keep me safe
May I dream of your plan for me
So I can wake up with inspiration to succeed

For if today was my last
I hope I made you proud
Through the journey given
It is for you Father I lived today for
I stayed true to my path

I only pray my life I leave behind
May be a story to guide
May my faith inspire those who seek to see
Let them strive in motivation
To live each day on this road to heaven

Now as I lay down to rest
I pray to my Heavenly Father above
Help me to dream the dream of truth
If I wake up tomorrow
May I stay inspired by you

For one day I will walk by his side
And I know that he knows I tried

Water At My Feet

This is my destiny
Fate has found me here
With the waves of water
At my toes & feet
I feel safe & free

Such a blessed peaceful feeling
Where I have found my life
Beyond the waters
Is my path to Christ

The water at my feet
Reconfirms me here
My fate is near the water
As I was baptized & blessed

Water glorifies this life
Here is where I feel you most
I arise feeling more alive
You Lord make me whole

The water at my feet
Gives me strength
And gives me peace

Until My Last Breathe

Until I take my last breathe
I will be true to myself
I will not live with regrets

Because of Jesus
I have been forgiven
Because of God's love
I know a greater life to live

I will not stray
I pray each & everyday
I learn to be better
I yearn to know more always
And live with the gift of his love

Until my last breathe
I will not stray
I will keep my faith
I will live true to myself
I have been forgiven
I have found his unconditional love

My faith can never be betrayed
Until my last breathe
I live for my Heavenly God
And my brother Jesus

Trust In The Lord

Your journey is your own
I cannot walk your path for you
You must rise up
And believe in yourself
You can get through it with God

Trust in the Lord
With all your heart & soul
He will guide & protect
Through each one of your storms

It may not be easy
You will have hard times
Just keep believing
Trust in the Lord
Jesus is walking at your side
Trust in the Lord
At all times

Time Will Tell

Time will tell
Where your heart has failed
But the Lord will continue to have faith in you
For his love with never fail

It is never too late
To your last breathe he will wait
He will forgive your past
His unconditional love will not fail

His love runs deep and true
In both me & you
Where your heart has once failed
Forgiveness always will be fulfilled
If you cry out & seek the Lord

Whatever your journey has been
He will always lay within
His love never strays
And it is never too late

Time will tell
The Lord will always prevail
Seek him & all will be forgiven once again
He loves unconditional

The Lord Is My Anchor

It is on the ocean I feel free
On the calm water
With waves crashing around me
My sail maybe pulling
But it is you who holds me still
It is always smooth sailing
Through here is where I feel whole

The Lord is my Anchor
The anchor to my heart & soul
Through any storm coming
Or calmer waters to thrive through
It is where my anchor defines me
For in him I survive as a whole

To know not where the wind will blow me
Through him I know I will thrive
There is nothing more peaceful then the water
This is where I feel most alive

Strength In God

I have loved & lost
I have turned & tossed
This road did not make me weak
But showed me my strength in God

I have grown in knowledge found
I have made my family proud
I stand firm in a mission
To follow through with the Lord's decision

Through life I have learned to grow
I have lost and loved
But my faith could never fall
This road did not make me weak
But proved my strength in God
He has seen me through it all

Song In Me

I have a song in me
Created by his majesty
I will find the strength to sing

A song has much power
His song is the key
Wisdom, courage & religion
Are the existence in the song in me

How powerful is his love
My faith is true
I pray that my song
May speak to you to

I sing for a vision
Of peace & love combined
Created to be shared down here
Heaven will always rein & rise

Our Father sings
He has truly blessed me
Through suffering of the heart he found me

I sing for my Father above
For his true unconditional love
He strengthens me with courage & wisdom
I have the song to sing
It is a song in me

Soldiers In You

We are soldiers on a mission
We search to seek prosperity
Only those who seek it pure
Will prosper in the Lord

To those soldiers who seek for more
Will never be able to fully endure
There is much more beauty & glory here
Through honor & faith on our journey alone

We are all soldiers on a mission
We search to seek true prosperity
I pray that you seek it here pure with me
So you can truly endure what it means

I am a soldier of God on a mission
I seek more than to prosper
For its much different to prosper in the Lord
There is much more than glory to be given
I yearn for a better seat in heaven

So Amazing

So amazing
God's unconditional love
The beauty of what he has created
Paradise is awaiting all of us

There is beauty everywhere to be seen
A flower, a tree
A mountain, the ocean
Beauty in his love
We must agree

His love is much higher than the skies above
So much beauty deeper than the seas crossed

So amazing
So true
His love & beauty
That live in you and me too

So amazing
God's unconditional love for all of us
So amazing is he

Power Beyond

You can be strong
But you are powerless without faith
There is power in knowing
And believing in his great name

Power through faith
Will keep you above anything
You will succeed with his love & grace

If you truly believe
You will not know defeat
His love is everlasting
And powerful is his glory for you always

Indulge the power in you
He will follow through
Praise his holy name
Seek the power of truth

You may be strong
But he is the power beyond
You will never know true strength
Until the day you love and praise his great name

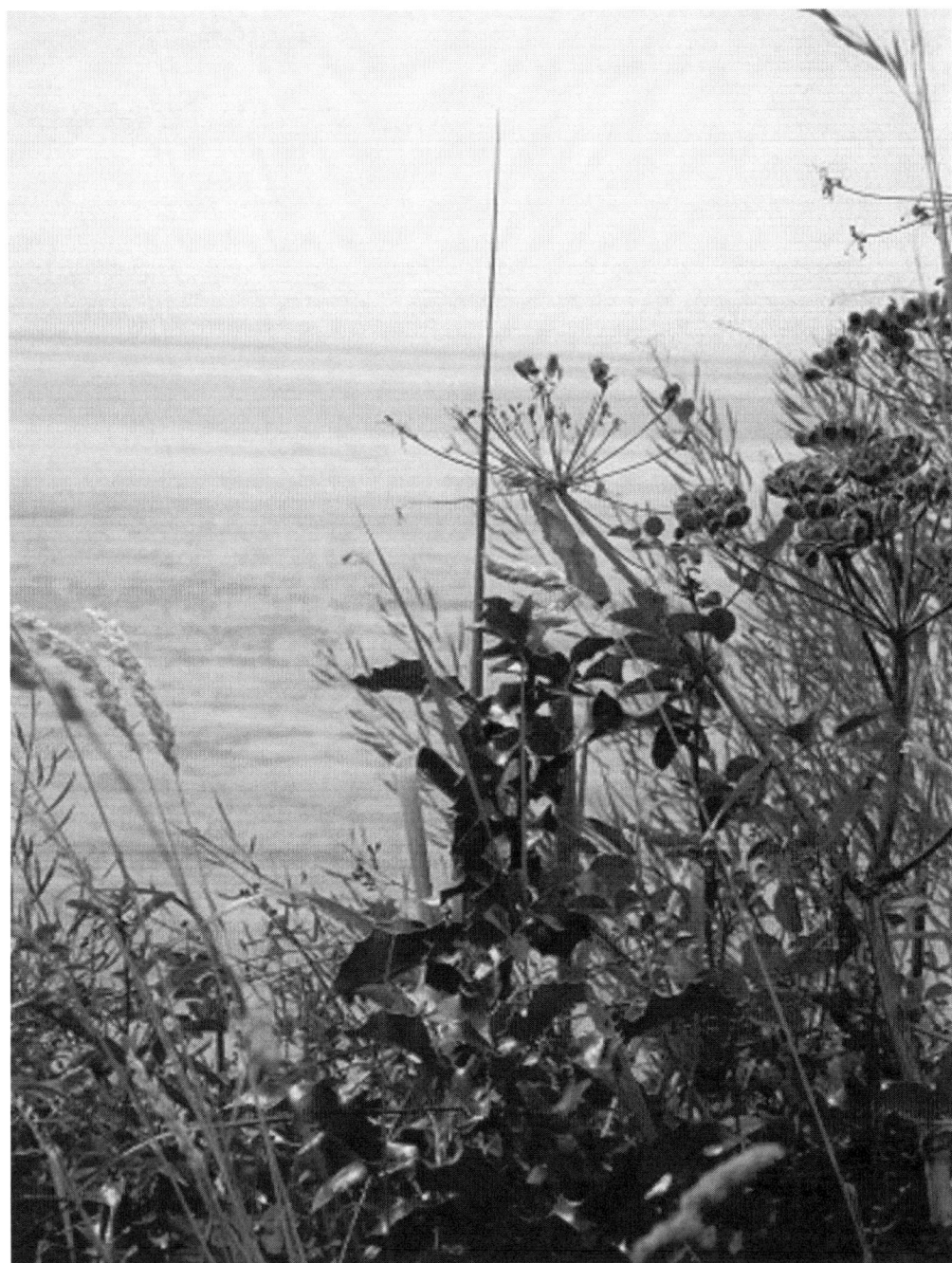

Only God Knows

Only God knows
The road ahead
If there will be happiness
Before I am dead

A crazy life we must live
Blinded by love
When real love can only be blessed by God

I keep walking this life given
Praying for this mission
In a life I haven't yet reached
Only God knows if and when for me

Only God knows
My path for me
It hasn't been easy
But I keep faith in him

I keep my faith
I pray each day
Talk to my Heavenly Father above
Only God knows
How much journey will happen
So my story continues on

Only God knows

On Broken Ground

I stand here on the broken ground
He will not let me fall
But stand firm & tall

Pieces of this world have been broken
But his love & guidance are true
He will not allow you to fall through the cracks
He will keep you strong & firm
As he is always walking beside you

If you take his hand
He will walk you through
The broken ground is only path to conquer
Another journey to continue to walk through

There is much sin down here
But I do not fear
My home is in Heaven
My journey on this broken road
Hasn't been fully conquered just yet

Light Beyond

There is light beyond the darkness
You just have to believe and have faith
You can pass this darkness

It may not be easy
But fear can make you lazy
There is more life in you to be had
So you will be glad to continue the path

Rise up & carry on
You really are more strong
Can you begin to see the light beyond
This darkness will not always carry on

Life Is The Beginning

Everything I have
I achieved for
My life hasn't been easy
But I continue to stand firm

Trials can mislead you
But I have been faithful
True on the path to you Lord

Things are not easy
But in these times I see more
All around me
Who pray to be inspired

My journey has been difficult
I have to admit
But you have guided me through

Life isn't easy
But never forget
We are always meant to be better
To rise up
Life happens
But it's only to start a new beginning
He is not finished with us yet.

Life is only the beginning.

Jesus Is My Lighthouse

A shining light
In the darkness night
You lead me to safety

Through twists and turns
No matter the storm
He will guide me though always

For Jesus is my lighthouse
No darkness can dim his light
He will stand firm
And guide me through

The darkest hour may arise
But in him I have grown stronger
My path only shines brighter
Jesus will guide me through always

He is my lighthouse
He is my path the whole way through
His shining light will guide me
As the storm surrounds me
I will never fear you

For Jesus is my Lighthouse
And his light will always guide me through

Inspired By God's Grace

I sit here
In aww of all god's grace
Inspired by song
Music & faith

Inspired by love
Love of family
Love of friends
And in love with so much more deeper to be seen

It is love that makes life worth living
True love is unconditional
The Lords greatest gift and lesson
To be inspired by love
Not hate
This is God's true grace

I sit here
With a full heart
And deeper faith
For inspiration through God's grace

I Want To See Through Your Eyes

You Lord know me deeply
You know my heart
And hold my soul
You have the power to see life as I do

But I yearn to know you more
I want to see through your eyes
What a vision that would be to behold
To see what you see in and outside

I'd love to see how you see me
That would be more inspiration for me

You are amazing Lord
Your love for this world
Truly incredible
What a sight it would be to see
To see what all it is you see
You are amazing

I Pray

We all pray for peace
From struggles and suffering
We all pray for the sins may be erased
And forgiveness for the lives we may have lived today

But I pray for a deeper relationship
With our Heavenly Father above

We pray for family & friends
We pray for financial freedom
We pray to succeed & prosperity

I pray for the tools to help others
I pray to inspired
And to continue to be inspired
Through his faith & unconditional love

We pray for relationships
To heal from heartbreaks

But I pray for you and I

I Dream Of The Day

I dream of the day
I stand before Jesus' face
Face to face with his all forgiving grace
The unconditional faith he keeps in you & me
I dream of looking into the true eyes of grace

You have blessed us
You have redeemed us
You have loved us with no conditions

You are the King of all kings
Hold true to the highest majesty
I dream of the day I stand before Jesus' face

I dream of the day
I will see you rein on the thrown of paradise
Heaven will stay true
For God & Jesus too

I dream of the day
When I can see his face
Then will truth be proved

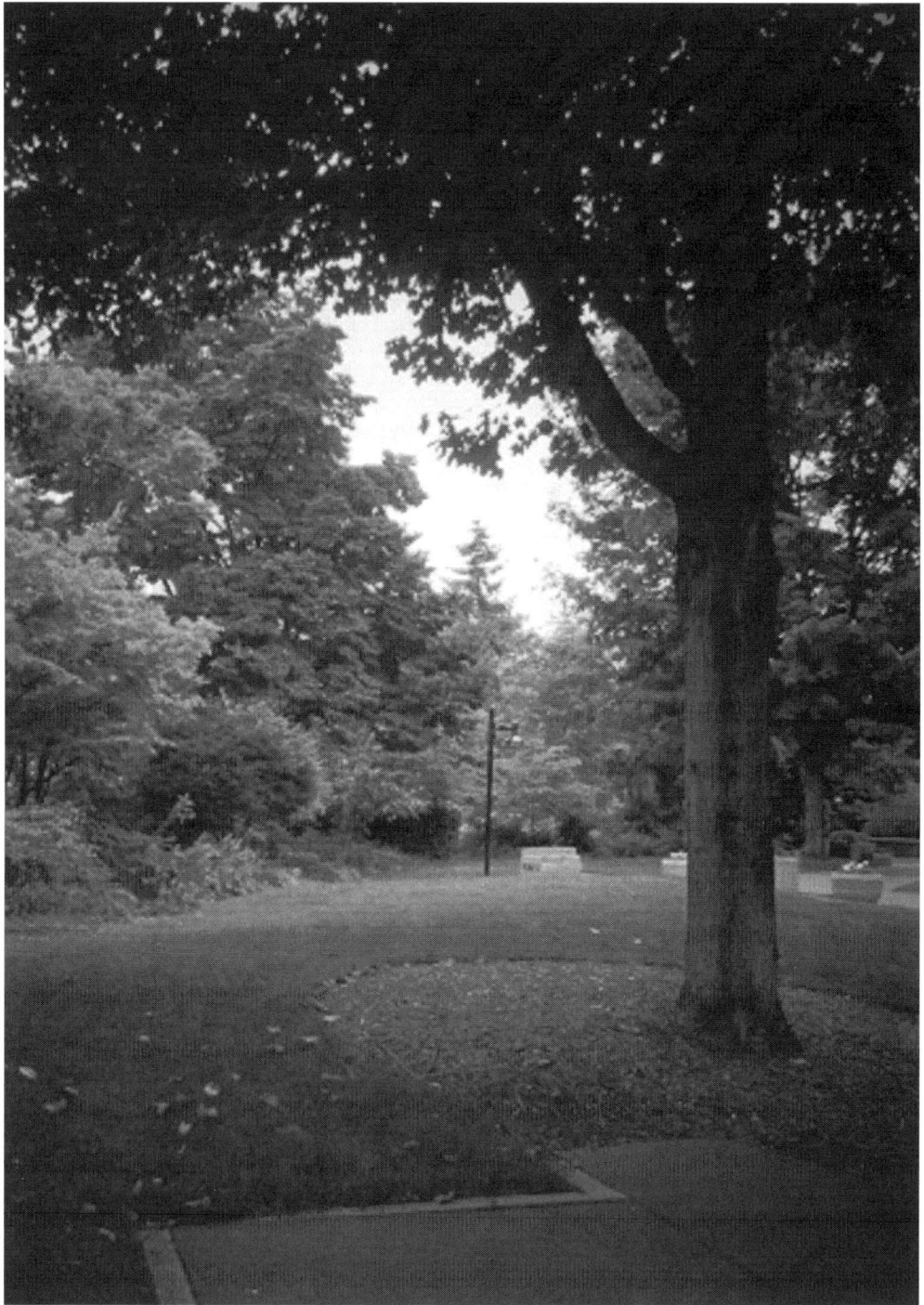

I Am A Survivor In You

I know strength
And the power to succeed
I believe all things to have a purpose
A faith so limitless & true
For I am a survivor in you

I strive to survive
With a stronger mission
I continue to survive in you

Devotional faith & Faithful love
For all is true in the great heaven above
He will always survive in you

Peaceful peace & Unconditional love
The determination to thrive
As we continue to strive to survive
With the greater power we will succeed
He is the survivor in you & me
With the Lord
We will achieve & succeed

For I am a survivor in you.

I Am New

You made me new
Let me start over
Forgiveness has been blessed
By the sacrifice of Jesus

I pray we be worthy & true
To show our true love & faith in you
Life is not easy
But it is meaningful with you

I a new
I am set free
Blessed & forgiven
For sins I have too made

Your love is strong
Unconditional & true
Forgiveness is pure
I pray I am worthy of you

I am new
Because of Jesus
He believes and forgives you too

Pieces Of Me
By Julia Anne Simpson

Chapter 2
Inspiration Through Love

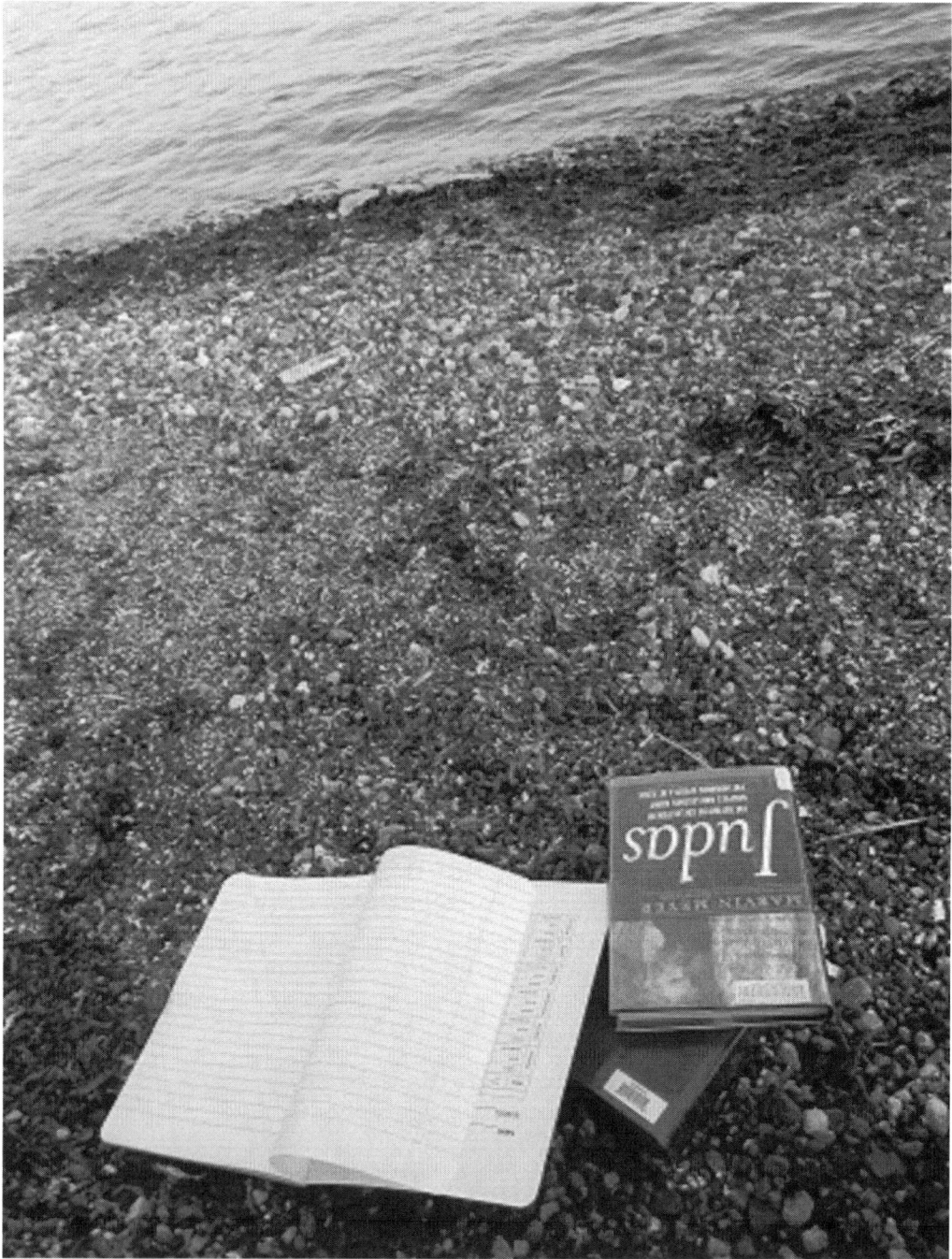

I Yearn To Know Him

Drawn like a magnet
I cannot hide
Nor do I really want to
With this feeling inside

I yearn to know you
To have to be by your side
I want to learn you
It is so hard to describe

I yearn to know him
What makes him feel so alive?
His face, I just cannot erase
Enticed by his mind
Drawn like a magnet
This intense feeling has arisen inside

I yearn to know him
And it is to no surprise
I yearn to know you
The man I see deeper inside

If Your Only Knew

If you only knew
The secrets I am ready to share with you
Maybe then you would see
A deeper side of me

If you only knew
It has always been you
My heart has been on reserve
For a love so true
Only for the man I see in you

If you only knew
How crazy my love is for you
Unconditional & true
Only wishing good things come to you
If you only knew

If you only knew
I am crazy in love with you

Here By Your Side

Looking in your eyes
Face to face
I know inside
We are just right

Weak at the knees
I swallow my pride
When I am at your side
For with you is where I feel most alive

I pull you in
All I want is a kiss
No other place
Have I ever felt like this

Face to face
As I look into your eyes
I swallow my pride
I feel most alive
Here by your side

Alive

His brown eyes compelled me
It was that night
I began to fall

He was everything I ever wanted
All rolled into a man who is strong & tall
He saw deeper in me
I could hold back nothing
My heart pounding

The moment I fell in love
Is the moment I found myself
You made me feel so much more alive
Helped me breathe again inside
A deeper love to behold
Since he was brought into my world

Kiss

Your lips, your touch
I love you so much
Your kiss is my true bliss

To my knees I yearn for you again
So tender to endure
There is so much in a kiss
But it is your kiss I can't resist

Your lips, your touch
I need you so much
You kiss has unleashed too much

To my knees you make me weak
There is nothing more
I want to endure
Then your lips on my lips
I yearn to kiss you more

It is your kiss
Your lips
Your touch
I need you here
To kiss me again

A Rose

Our love is like the beauty of a rose
Comes in layers
Blooming can be overwhelming
But the thorns are sharp
We may bleed to hold such a beauty

So delicate to touch
But hard to hold
I am so drawn to this rose

Inspired by the life it holds
But pierced & scared by the thorns of this rose

Just as our love
Such beauty to be had
But boundaries set in place
Protection to the beauty
Layers of passion
Blooming to perfection

Can this love be held
Or will the beauty welt

What beauty in love can hold dearly
Love hurts
But the thorns won't hurt as deep
As walking away from a love strong
Will our love carry on

Our love is a rose
Beauty waiting to bloom before us

Much Love

So much love here
Attention is needed
I need someone who can challenge me
And show me life in a new way

Someone to trust
To be able to run to & confide in
I want to feel at home once again
I have so much more love to give

Little things mean the most
Texts & calls on the phone
I don't desire money
Just a man with passion
And a deep soul

So much love to give
But attention is a must
To feel an equal amount of love

LOVE AS STRONG AS WHISKEY

You are a whiskey man
I am a martini girl
But when we are together
It is much stronger then alcohol

Your lips taste so sweet
As you kiss me so deep
Your love is as strong as whisky to me

I am a martini girl
You're my whiskey man
Enticing love for what we can
Alcohol isn't as true as for my love for you

I am a martini girl
But I can handle the love of a whiskey man

I Will Be Your Martini

We love our martinis
Sweet yet strong
With sugar around the rim
Leaves such a sweet taste on your lips

Let me be your martini
I will treat you sweet
And will love you strong

You inspired me
Your sweet lemon drops
Now I am your martini
May have a hint of sour
But the sweetness consumes all

Let me be your martini
With love so sweet and strong

You Are Enough

I lay here looking into your eyes
Only wishing you could see the amazing man you are inside
You are man enough for me
I really wish you could see
How much you inspire me to be me

The love that you possess
Is the love I most cherish
I wish you could see & believe
You are man enough for me

The chemistry we share
The moments we get lost
Are more real then what is real when we are apart
There is a deeper side I feel and see
He is more than enough for me

He is the only one who makes me happy
Let's me be the true me
He inspires a much deeper part of me
You are the only man for me
Stay & be the man you were meant to be
You are enough
Enough man for me

You Awaken Me

A feeling inside
I feel more alive
You awakened me

There is so much more
That I have had to endure
But you brought me back to life

I have never felt so alive
You gave me a deeper passion inside
Now I only strive deeper to survive

You awakened me
You made me see
A mission has arrived
There is much more then you see
This passion in me
Has a deeper power to succeed

I feel more alive
You have awakened me

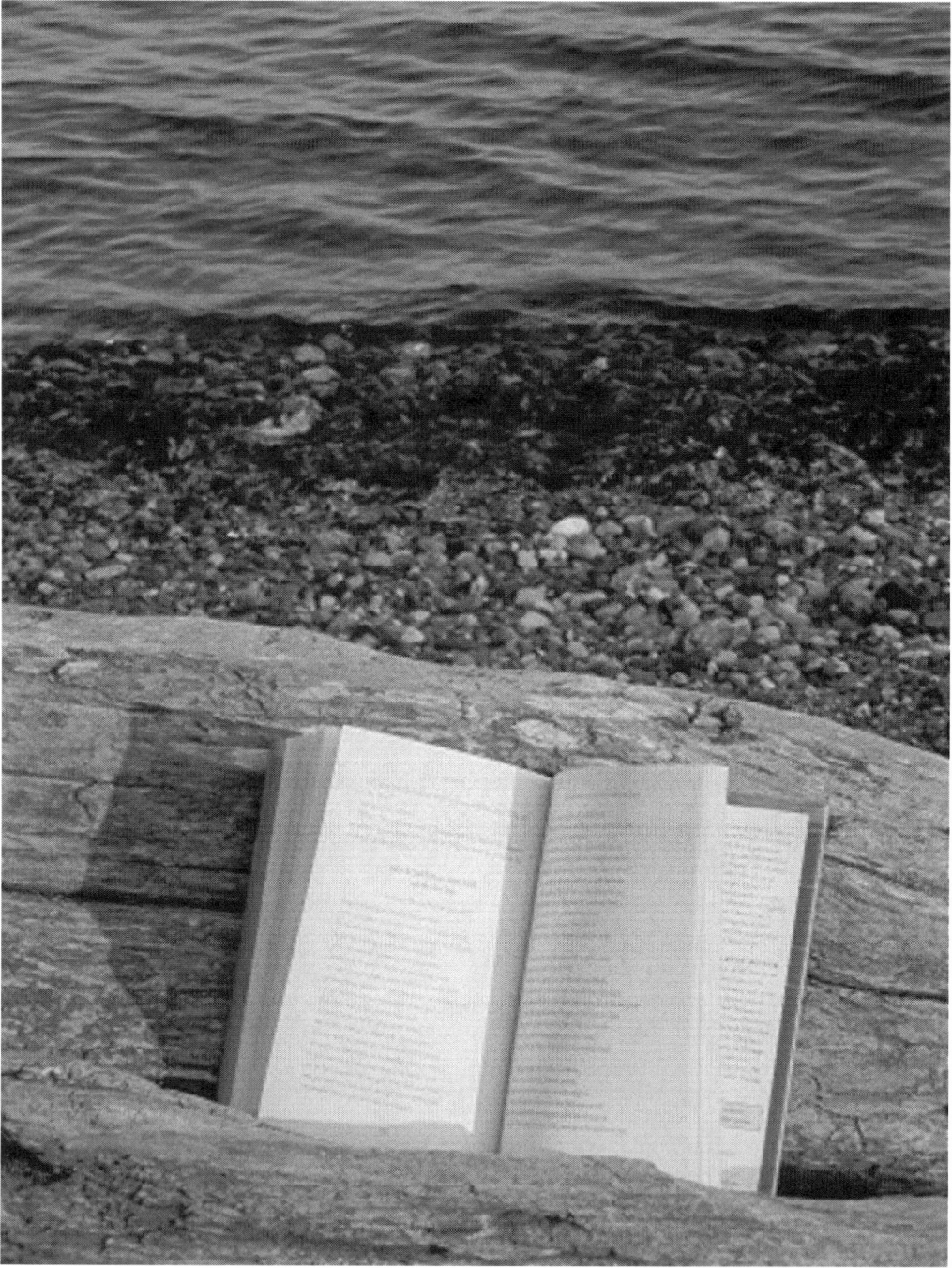

Tell Me Your Story

Tell me your story
So I can see the real you
I only want to understand
And know the truth

Tell me your story
I truly care to know
You can whisper if it's hard to say out loud

I yearn to know you
I cherish you more than you know
So tell me your story
My love is unconditional

I believe in the man I see
I only want to know you more
I want to understand
Why this can be so hard
How can you be so unsure?

So tell me your story
I need to know what's true
Tell me your story
I don't want to judge on you

I love you more than you know
I only yearn to know you more
So tell me your story
I want to understand you more

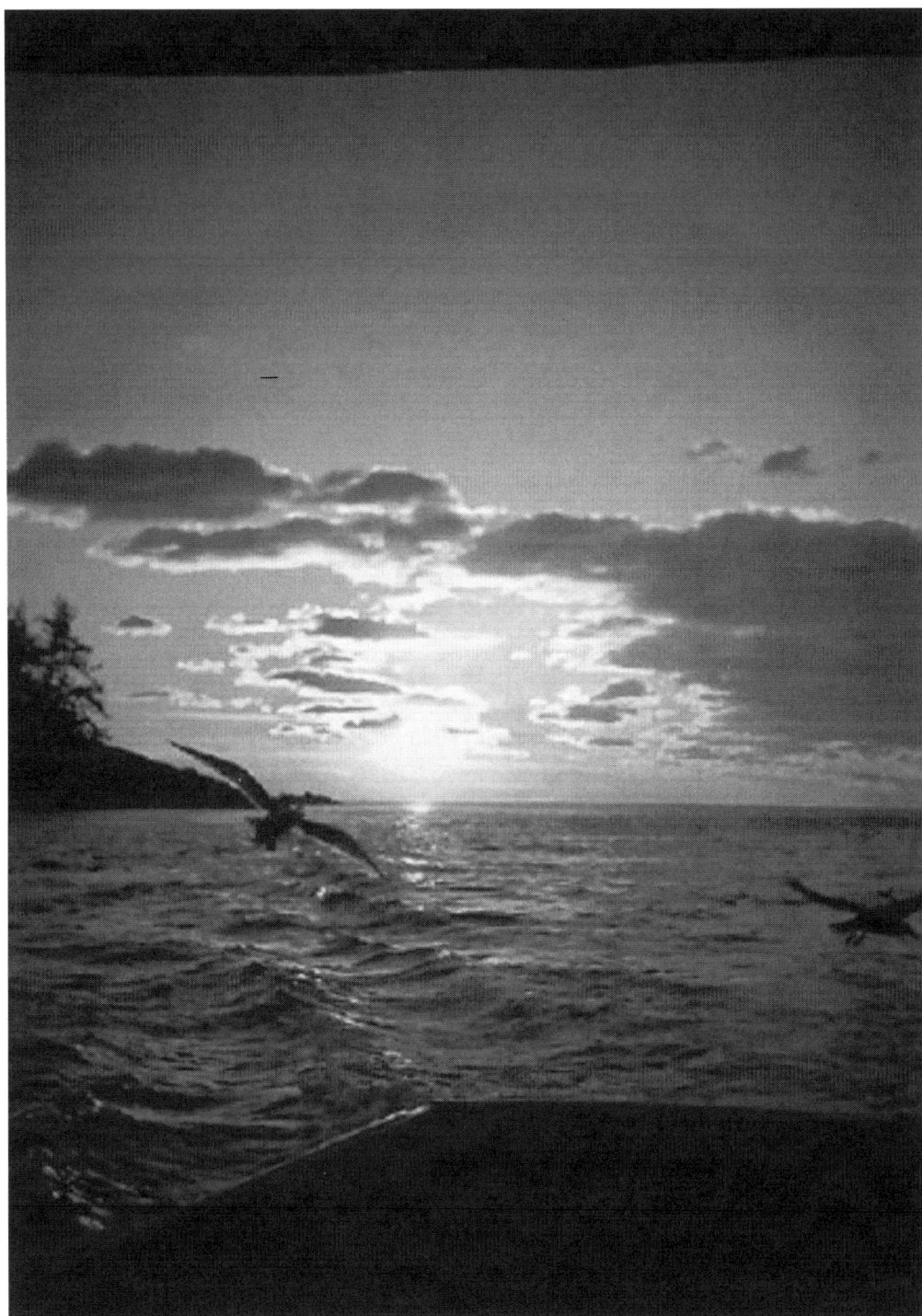

Let's Give This A Real Chance

We have another shot
Time is giving us another chance
Let's do this right this time
We deserve this to ourselves

This feels so right
Let's give is a good fight
Fate seems to be on our side

Let's give us a real chance
Give the romance a shot
I will give my all
If you are ready to take my hand

We have another opportunity
Let's give this a real chance
Time has brought us back
Gave us a real chance

Time is on our side
Just say the words
And I will forever be at your side

Perfect Day

A perfect day
An amazing memory
So much love & passion
On the ocean we lay

Your presence lingers still
Can this really be real?
This love for you I bare

Such a perfect day
We were meant to share
My heart feels reborn
I thank god I found you

A perfect day
Such a peaceful place
As we drift with the waves
Your arms hold me close

An amazing memory to behold
Of a perfect day on your boat

On The Cliff

As I sit on the edge of the cliff
Remembering the time we had
Missing every moment spent

This world is so big
Yet it feels so small to me

Standing on the edge of this cliff
Taking all in around me
Standing firm in what is yet to come
Staying true to who created me & you

I kneel on this cliff & wonder
Will we meet once again?
What this journey will endue
What will rise & fall
What will be conquered?

I know the Lord will see all things through
But will we meet once again
Where will our journey end?
What will this world bring us?
On this cliff I ponder...

I sit here believing you were sent to me from above
On this cliff I stand believing in all that's true
On this cliff I never stopped loving you

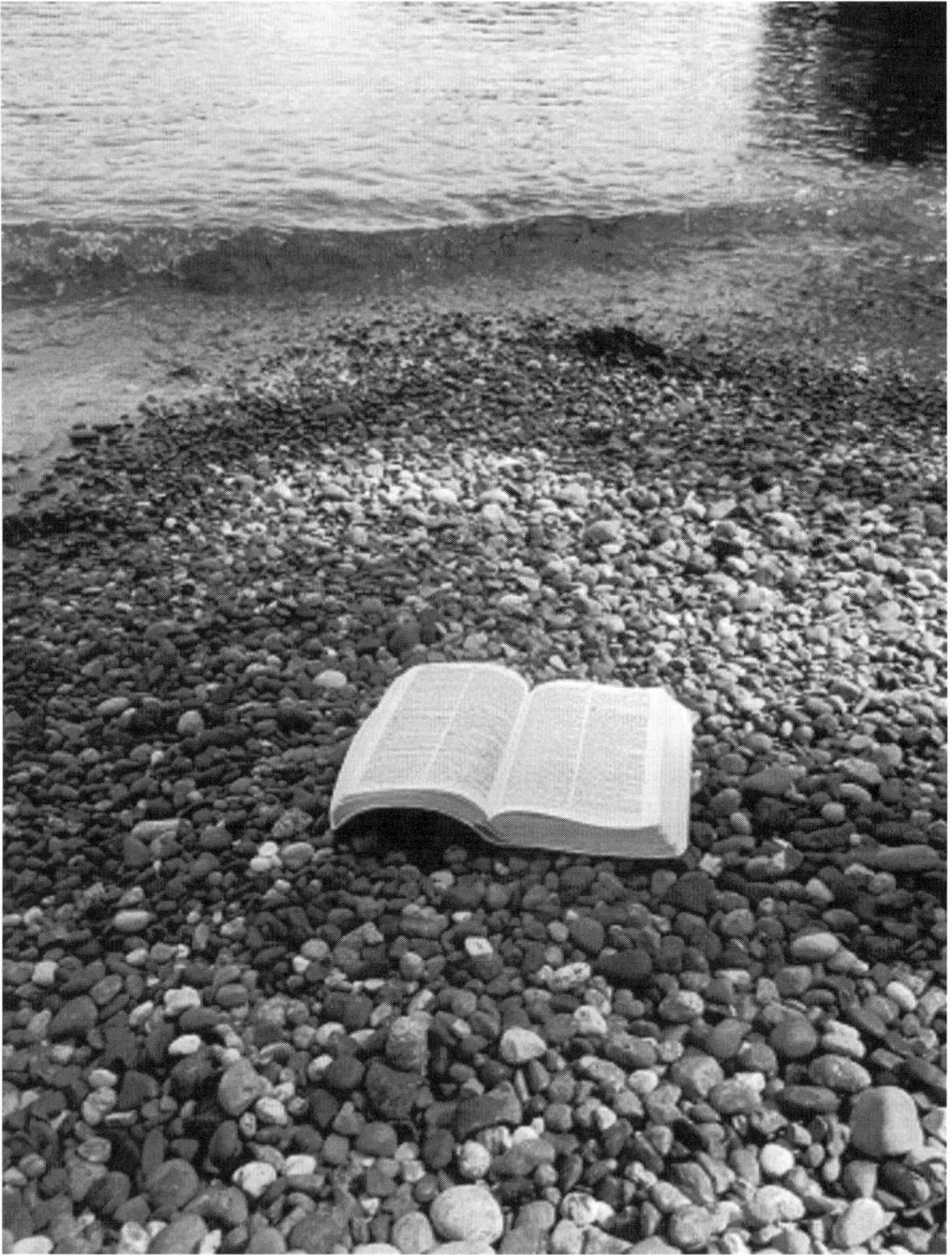

Powerful Love

Life can be tricky
There can be many tricks
But living faithfully
In the moment deep within
Is definitely not a sin
To listen to your heart
That's when it's true within

God created you to have passion
To love unconditional
To be true to your faith
But also be true to you

Jesus loves you
He wants you to be happy
Ignore the haters around you
Your heart is what matters
Not the negative surroundings

To love the Lord above
And to yourself be true
Then you will live a powerful life too
With a powerful love in you

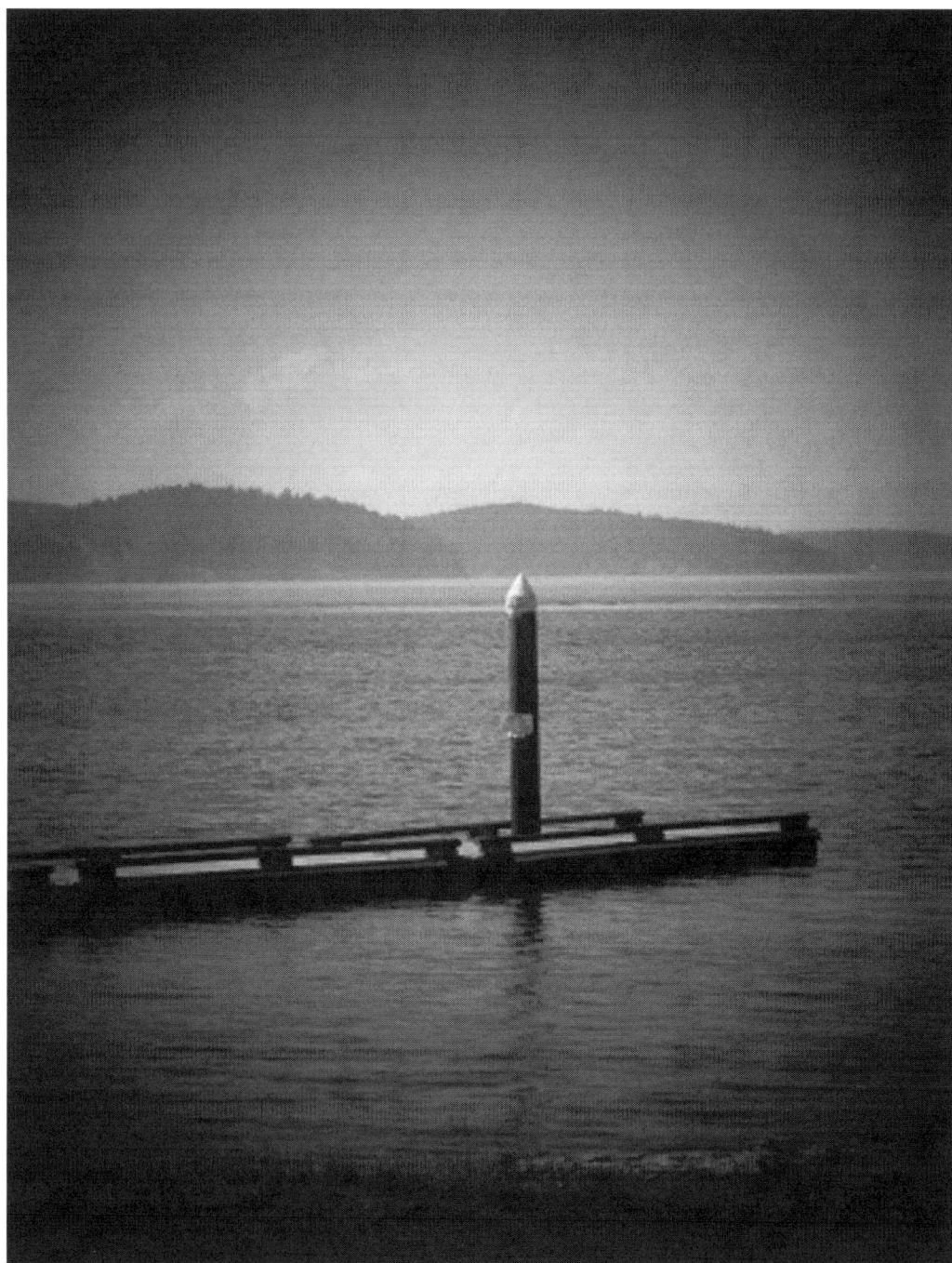

Second Chance

The beauty I see in you
I see to be much deeper & true
I pray each & everyday
That we can move forward

Together we can grown
With you is where I want to growl old
I accept your past
And look forward to our new beginning

I will love all of you
I promise I will adore you son too
I hope this is real
The feelings I have for you are true
I pray that you do love me too

The beauty I see inside
Is the man I wish would arise
Our future is in your hands
I am giving you a second chance

Start Over

I believed we could rise above
That you had so much more love
You inspired me
Challenged me even
Completely won me over

Mind and muscles combined
I never thought that I could find
A man who can keep up with me on all levels
You were a hard man to find

I believed we could rise above
With this overwhelming love
Your inspiration & knowledge within
I still believe we can rise above this situation

To start over once again
I need you here
I miss you
You are my home
I have never felt so alive
Then when you are at my side
I still believe we can
Start over again

All Or Nothing

I am here for the long road
Or I will disappear & be gone
I am an all or nothing kind of woman
One that will stay strong

Loyal, passionate & determined
I am ready to give my all
Or else I am ready to be done

Give me your all
Love me completely
And I will give you all of me
This is what I seek
Together our love can truly set us free

Put nothing out
You will receive nothing back
Little texting doesn't mean a thing
When you are holding back from me

I told you I am all or nothing at all
I won't waste your time
I have so much to offer
But such little time for a crime

I will not wait & wonder
If you can't give me your all
It's a crime to waste
If you don't truly love me
What will be our fate?

All or nothing at all

All or Nothing
I have nothing to hide
Not if you really love me
You would not run & hide

For all or nothing
Maybe it's time to step aside

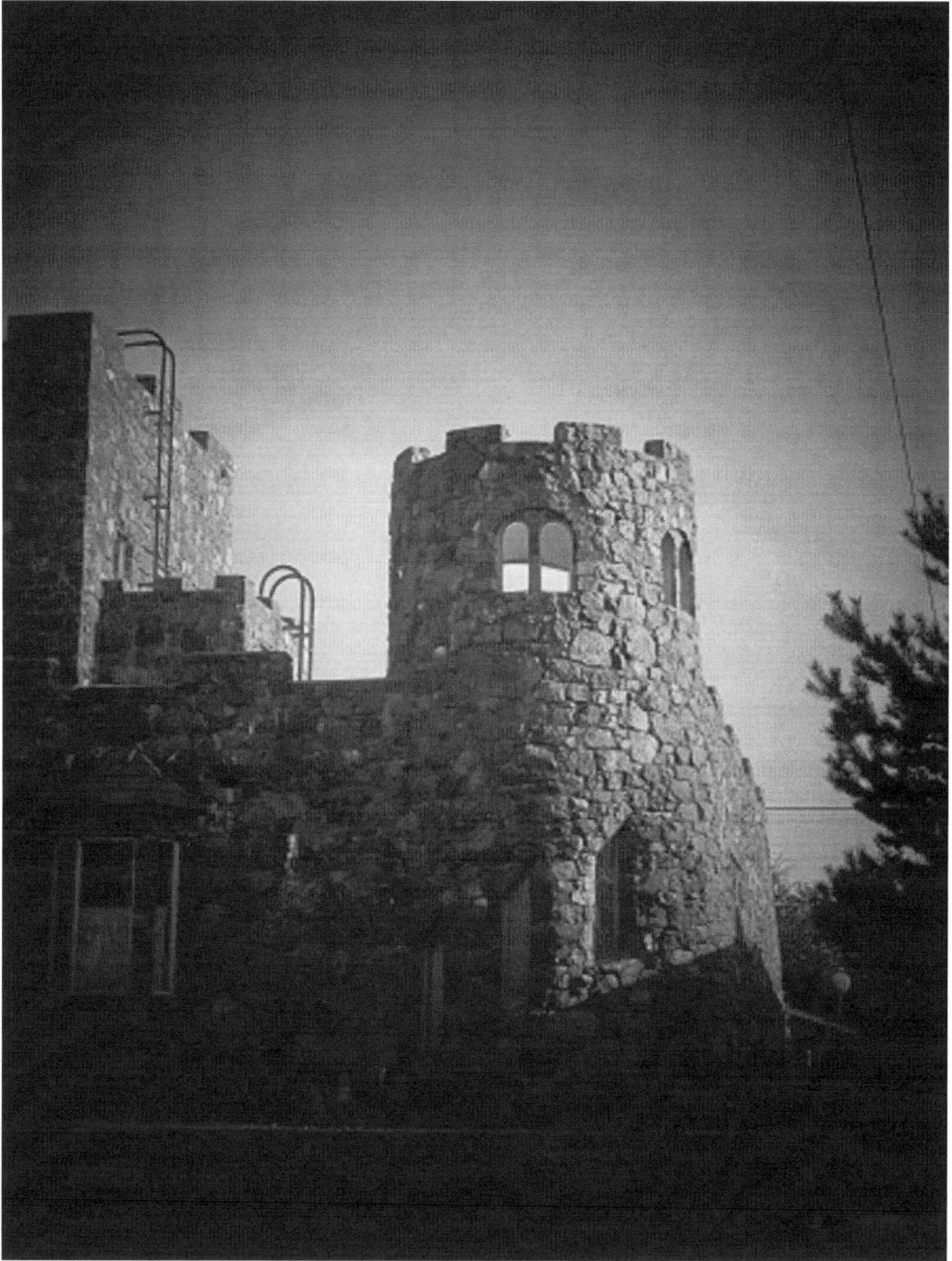

Deeper Love

I don't want a prince charming
I want something more real
I need a deeper love & companionship
I am ready for so much more still

I need someone to keep up with me
I want someone to challenge me too
I don't want just another sweet talker with a pretty face
I want someone genuine and real

I know there is so much more
I trust God's plan with my heart
I want a deeper love
I need someone to grow old with
And I won't settle for anything less
Only deeper love to be had

Faith, love & something more worth waiting for
I trust in the Lord above
I know there is someone out there
I want something real
A deeper love to be had

BEAUTIFUL MAN

So much passion
So much faith
So much beauty when I look at your face

I wish you could see what I see
I wish you knew what you mean to me
You are a beautiful man
From the inside out
You are a better man
Then I have been told about

You have a soul I admire
And a heart I believe in
You make me feel so alive
You are a true hard man to find

I wish you could see what your smile does to me
I have felt like you could be my destiny
Inside & out you are truly beautiful
And you should know I love you
The beautiful man I see

I wish you could see what I see
I wish you felt the same way for me
My life is God's journey
And only he knows if this beautiful man is truly for me

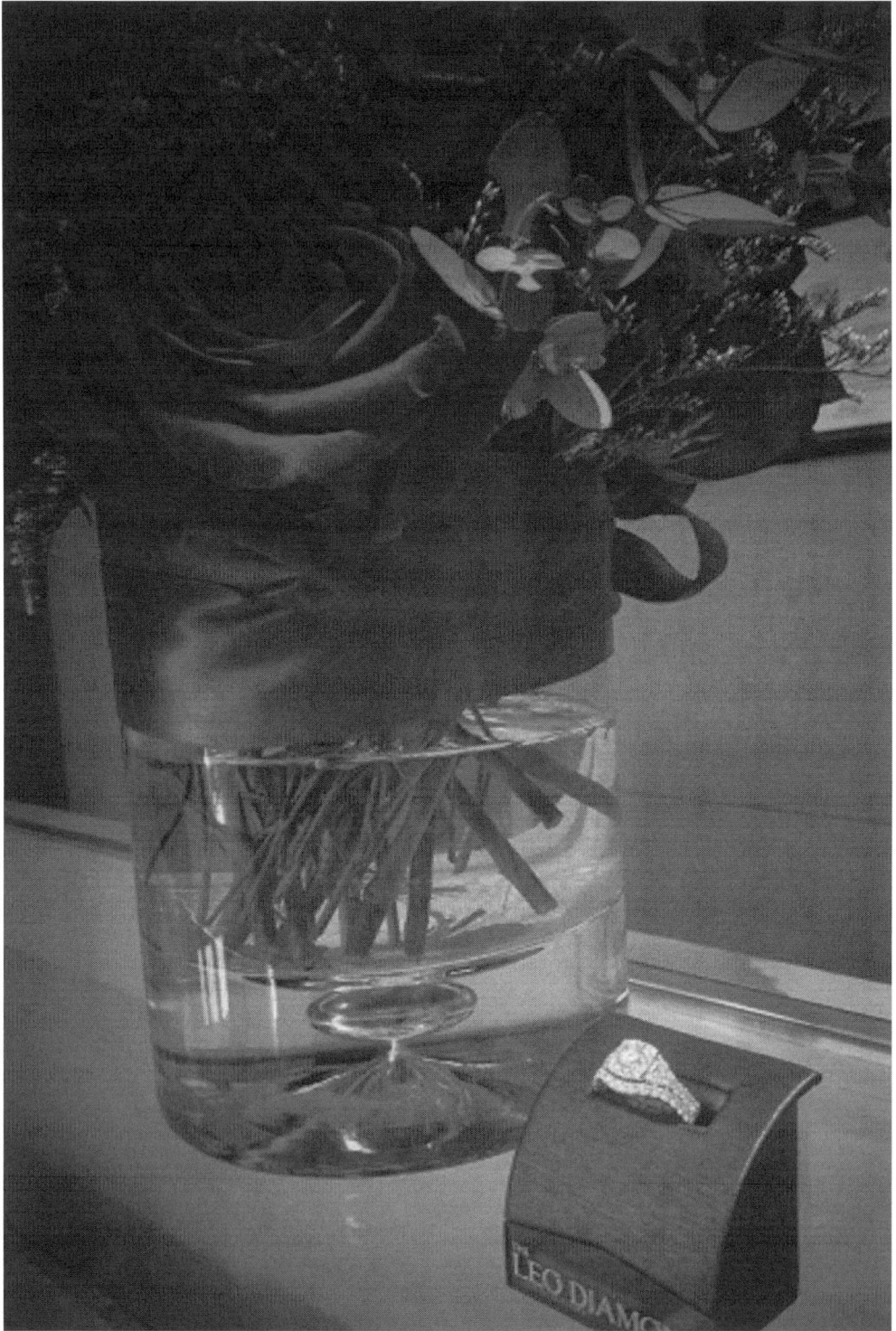

Companionship

I seek something much deeper
Deeper than lust or love
Truly unconditional love
With a deeper companionship is a must

A deeper connection
A better friend
A match on every level
The companionship bond through love

I want much deeper
Then a romantic gesture
Someone who inspire me
Guide me to who I really am
And let me in completely
A deeper companionship of love

I want a companionship
And all the above
Inspiration
And unconditional love
I wait for my match
The man I share a secret bond
The true companionship with a deeper love

Committed Faithfully

Devotion & love
I continue to be faithfully committed to you
A deeper love
A stronger strength
My path only continues to grow closer & true
For I will always be committed faithfully to you

Faith & belief
Love & devotion
Are the bindings to be seen
Unconditional love inspires me

His passion, his mission
His strength, his devotion
He is committed faithfully to me

So pure & true
I continue to strive in you
I will always be committed faithfully to you

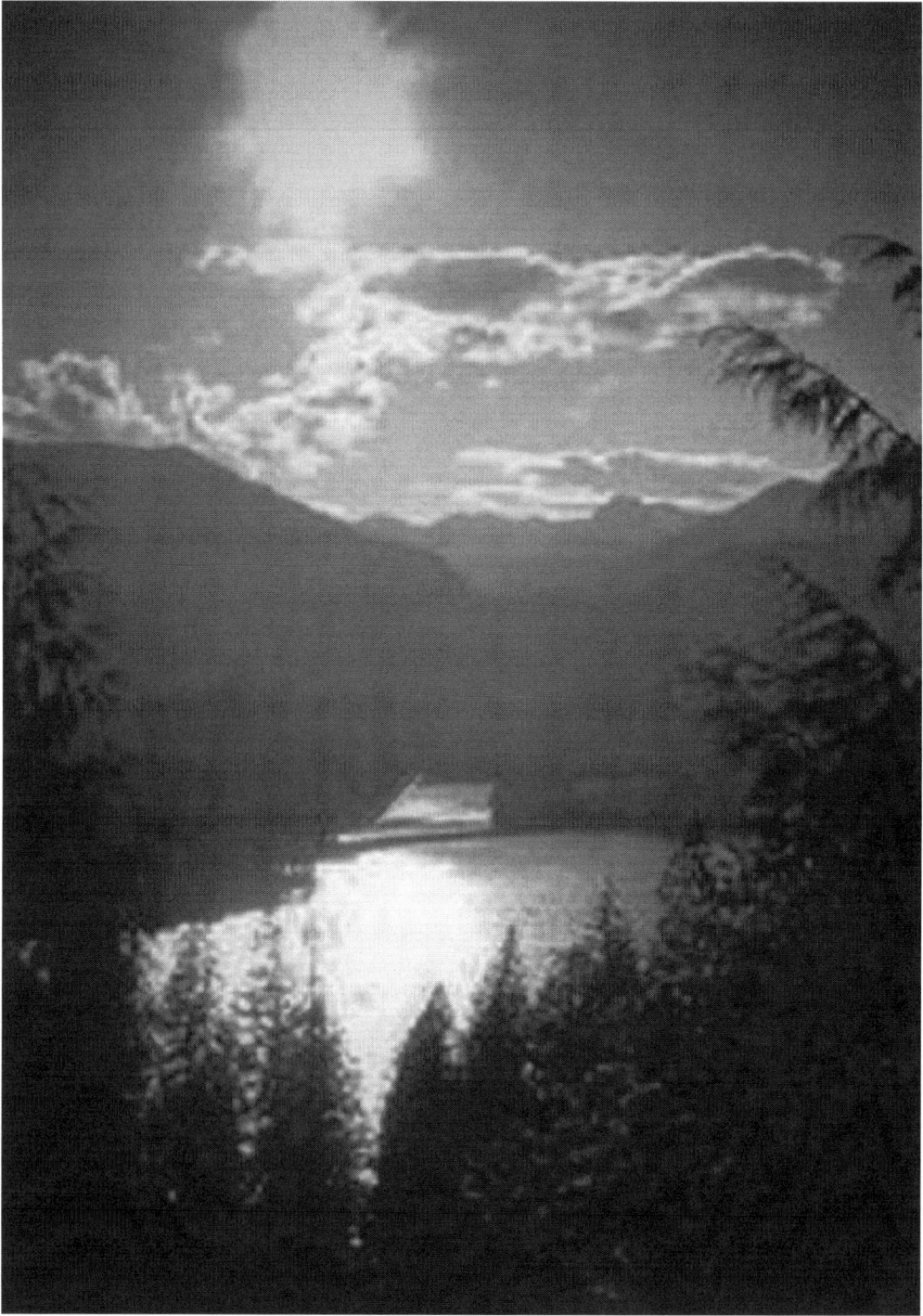

Inspired To Inspire

You have inspired me
I found the me I love most
And I found a deeper passion then I knew

So let me inspire you
I pray you see the man I see in you
The man God created you to be faithful & true

Let me inspire you to see
The beauty of your journey
So beautiful to behold
I pray you see what's true
What you inspired in me
Aspires in you too

I pray you inspire more
With the passion of God
I continue to see in you

How Amazing God Made You

When you look into my eyes
I truly wish you could see what I see inside
You have a beautiful soul
An amazing passion for life
How truly amazing God made you
I wish you could see what I see

Your heart & mind overwhelm me
You are a true match for me
Yet you hide from yourself
And choose not to see the truth
You are created with so much to offer
How amazing God made you

You are intelligent, beautiful & kind
Beautifully created for so much more to find
How truly amazing the Lord created you

I only pray for you to see
You were created to be so much more
Only if you could see through my eyes you'd see
Maybe you would believe how amazing you really are to me
How amazing God made you to be

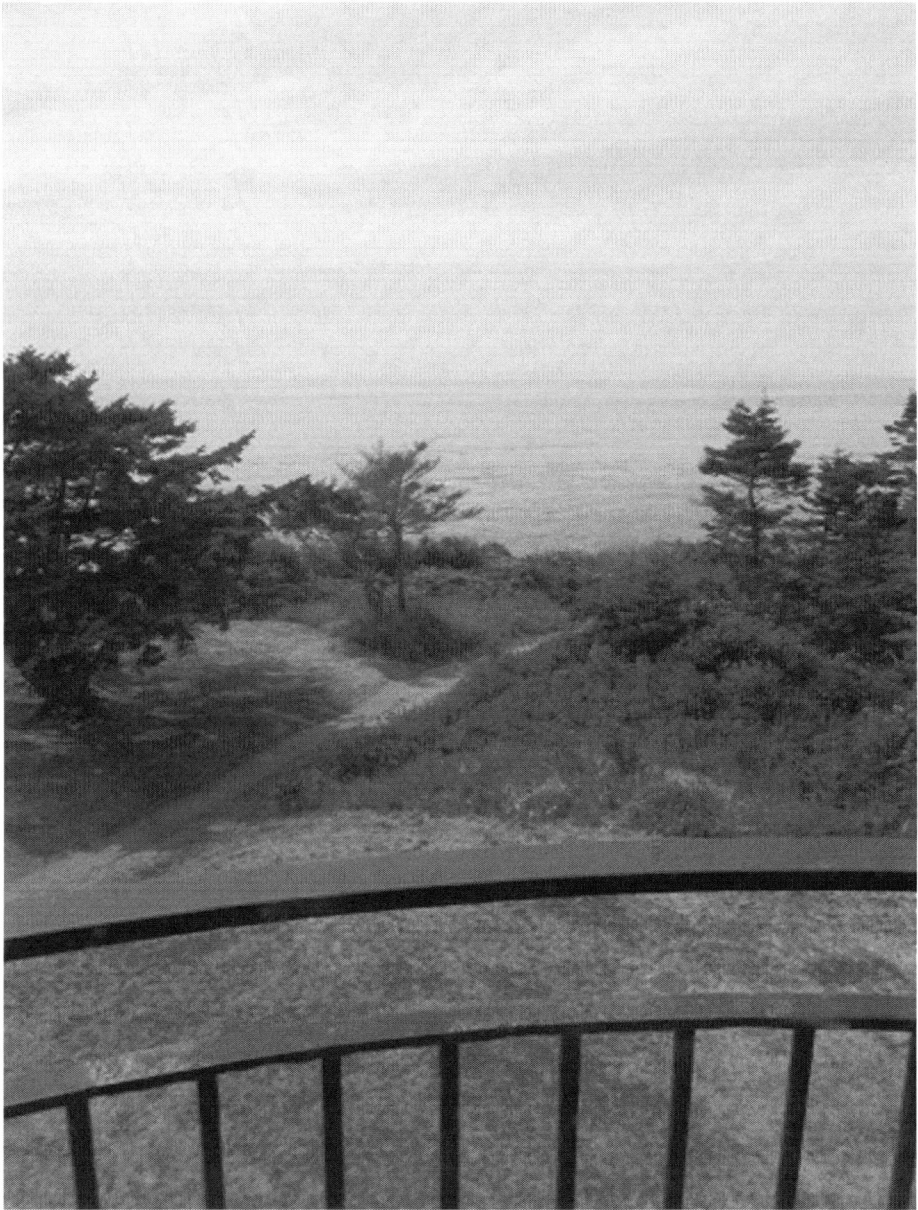

Our Paths Will Cross Again

I'm a believer of fate
For we all have a purpose
A journey
I believe our paths will meet again

What's meant to be will be
In his timing is perfect
We are mold to become better
Through paths, trials & continued faith
Our paths will cross again

Our time is in his hands
And all will happen again
Love, loss & a bigger purpose
Our paths will cross again

There is a greater purpose
For all things true will happen
We will meet again
If not here on earth
Our paths will cross again in Heaven

There Is Peace In Love

Take a deep breathe
There is peace to be had
Peace within his love

A greater gift to be bestowed
So breathe
And let the peace unfold

Unconditional love
Is bestowed onto you from above
Believe in his truth
You will the find peace within you

There is peace in love
True love is not tainted
It is pure & true
Unconditional
It will find peace in you

Breathe
And let the Lord above
Show you true peace in love

Unconditional Love

A love so pure & true
No boundaries, no boarders
Limitless & over powering
His unconditional love for you

Only those who accept him
Can feel the peace of love of grace
The limitless wonders
The millions of stories of faith

To know & accept true love
For God is love
To know him is to know unconditional love
You must know his love
Unconditional love will change you

He has made my life better
He has showed me how to love unconditionally and true
I never found life to be so pure & true

He loves us unconditionally
He believe in me & you

Pieces Of Me
By Julia Anne Simpson

Chapter 3
Heartbreak & Disappointment

Lost In What Is True

So much to be heard
But don't know what is really true
And yet I still love you

If they could only see
The man I know
The man I see him to be
Would they let us live in peace

Or can what they say be true
Are you a fake and a woman beater too?
I am so scared and unsure
I don't know what to do

This year has been too much
But I wish I wasn't in love
I don't know what is real
You sweet talk me and I melt

Lord, I need you
I am so scared and unsure
I am an all or nothing kind of girl

Should I believe him?
Or leave him completely
Does he love me or doesn't he

Such a mess
I am so lost
Single or taken
I don't know

More has to be proved
Not from me, but from you

I am scared
I have been here once before
9 years devoted to an unfaithful stranger
I won't do that again
So be a better man
I do love you
So be the man I have always seen in you

I don't know what real anymore
So much betrayal
It would be easier if I never loved you
But I do and my love is true
So be the man I see in you

Scared?

Are you really so blind to see
What you really mean to me
How deeply I care for you
Why are you so scared to see what is true

Why are you so scared
Scared of loving me
I never took you for a coward
But you vanished with no word
Leaving me broken hearted

Are you really so blind to see
How much you really do mean to me
Why does my love scare you so much
When I only have believed in who you were

I was so scared to let you in
And now that I have
You are gone

What scared you from being here
When all I did is believed and care

Thinking Of You

I still sit here thinking of you
I pray you are thinking of me too
I really do miss you

I don't know what happened
I don't know how to believe in love now
Did you ever care for me?
Have I really been so blind to reality?

So hurt & confused
For I truly have loved you

I still miss you
I continue to believe in you still
The memories of you I have do feel real

I do pray you are thinking about me to
Because I sit here
Thinking about you

When You Kiss Me

I miss that feeling
The feeling that only you gave to me
You made me weak at the knees
But made me fly with wings inside

When your lips touched my lips
You make me so happy inside
When you kiss me
My whole life makes sense once again

I wish you could see how much you mean to me
Do you feel what I feel
When you kiss me

I miss that feeling
When your lips touch mine
When you kiss me so gently

Hatred

So much hate risen from this pain
Love hurts
And I am so ashamed

Hate is powerful
It can control your life
And consume you inside

Hate is the dark side of love
You cannot hate those you don't care for
Only those you love can hurt you more
Hate through love can be so cruel

I still love you
But you have deeply hurt me
I am not over you yet
I don't want this hatred

Hit That Point

So much has happened
We have lost and gained
But I don't know if we will ever be the same

I love you deeply
But we have hit a point
Too much has happened
Either we move in together
Or move on

So much has happened
I don't know quite how to carry on
Can we move forward
Or move on

I love you deeply
But so scared and unsure
We have hit a point
Where we can only move in together
Or completely move on

Hard To Be In A Relationship

"It is hard to be in a relationship"
But you miss me
And you are crazy about me
So you lead me to believe
Turns out you were not true to me

You want to be alone
So be alone
Do not message me
Your sweet talking means nothing

It is hard to be in a relationship
You make me laugh
You just were not man enough for a girlfriend
And being with a good woman

Obviously you were scared
Don't be this coward
Be something more

It is not hard to be in a relationship
When you are true
And really love someone
You should have been only here

How Did I Get Here

How did I get here?
What did I do?
For another heart break
I need peace within you

So hard to breathe
Everything happened so suddenly
This pain continues to arise
Can they see it in my eyes?

How did I get here?
This path is broken
How could I be so blind…
Is this my fate?
He was my bate
Was it all a lie?

How did I get here?
Help me more to understand
I must move forward
I am wounded
I need you Lord

How I got here
I don't know
But I need to move forward
I need you Lord

Hurt

Where I was felt adored
I now feel ignored
You make me come alive
But now I am truly hurt

What one can do
When his feeling aren't true
A coward can't win
And now I am hurt again

I was loved & adored
Then like nothing
I was ignored
A new beginning lost
A broken road I must cross

My heart is heavy
Hurt & confused
I found the true coward in you
The truth does hurt
But at least I know what's true

How Do You Feel Now?

You ran away
When my life fell apart
How could you have such a little heart?

Such a coward to know
The reason why we fell apart
I love you & you ran
Was this your all along your plan?

Was I an opportunity?
Or a mission?
To steal a love of a good woman

What did you prove?
The true coward in you?

I believed you to be a better person
I saw a better man in you
But you only know how to hide
I no longer know
How you truly feel inside

How Do You

I wish I could trade places
I wish I felt your feelings inside
Maybe then I could understand your pride

How do you live…
When you walked away from faith
How do you love…
When you walked away from god's grace
How do you know…
When you are scared to pursue
How do you?

How do you have so much pride
When you aren't happy inside
How do you live?
How do you…
When you are just a complicated mess

How Do I

How do I love thee
For your love consumes me inside
But you are not here
Not even near
How do I...

How do I
When you can't be the man I need
How do I move on
From this love that's so strong in me
A connection I have only prayed for
A man I have but only dreamt of
How do I...

How do I continue on moving forward
When every moment
You're in my thoughts
You're in my heart
How do I...

How do I find strength
When I miss you already
You inspired me
But won't stand beside me
How do I...

How do I love you?
What happened to you and I?
How do I move on
And find peace inside

Gone

It is too late
I have given up on you
I am gone
You weren't the man I saw in you

No regrets
I am just moving on
I should have been cherished
Not treating like I meant nothing at all

I won't live with the hate
The denial of lies
It is too late

I already dried my eyes
I am gone somewhere you won't find
My hearts been locked
And only God holds the key of mine
He won't let you in again
You lied
I should have meant more to you
You shouldn't have made my heart cry

You knew I deserved better
Instead of being true
To the man I saw in you
I loved you and you treated me so small
I am now gone
For you let me go

I have gone
It is too late now
And you must live you fate
I wish never to know you after today

I am gone
Forever gone away

Games

I hate the games you play
You open up
Unleash my love
Only to run away

It is a cowardly game to play
To capture my love
Pretend to care
Then never really want to be here

I am not that girl
Who runs away
I do not play with hearts
When I say I love you
It mean you are where I want to stay

Don't unleash a love so true
Pretend to open up
And then run the next day
I hate these games you play

Fighting For Truth

I continue to find to know the truth
Which path am I supposed to choose
I am getting so lost in all that is around
Fighting for a truth that can't be found

I do not know where to go
For my love in this life is real
I continue to fight for something deeper
Captivated by a life I yearn for every day
I am still fighting for you

I am here, I don't give up easy
When I love, I love with everything God gave me
I am fighting for what true
But don't know if the truth will find me

I am lost
Fighting to breathe
Yearning for only the truth to see
But I feel blind is me
I fight for everything
And it should not be a fight to see

I am fighting for the truth today
Scared and unsure what the truth may bring

Farewell – Goodbye

Farewell.
Goodbye.
It was fun while it lasted
But I am done
You have really become pathetic

Your lies & betrayals
Put me through hell
My heart couldn't stop breaking

So farewell, goodbye
I am done with your lies
You never respected me
You rejected my love
While my feelings were true
So now I gladly say
Farewell to you

You are not worth another tear
Or a second look at most
I met your ugliness inside

It was fun while it lasted
But I am done
So goodbye

Faithfully Devoted Scam

If he seeks to find me
I am no longer here
Time has come and gone
And he left me here behind

I do not wish to see him
My wounds are meant to heal
He may no longer have my heart
I wish not to know him still

If he comes to see me
Do not let his tears fool you
He fooled my heart inside
I wish not to see him
The punishment is not mine

I loved him faithfully
I devoted myself to a love
I believed him to be much more
Then the lost soul he has become

The fault is my own
I wished not to see the truth
He was someone much better
But he lost himself when I lost my daughter
I lost them both

But I do not miss him
I no longer know him
I stand better on my own

Evil

I met evil today
He couldn't even look at me in the eye
Evil will not let you in
A coward who only knows how to hurt
Only will be a sin

So much pain
You will never feel the same
When evil deceives you by name

You cannot run & hide
But stand up to evil with pride
For evil is weak
So love yourself & rise

I met evil today
Thought I saw something much deeper
So I pray

Evil won't look you in the eye
It is coward less
Worse than a lie

Don't Lead Me On

Don't lead me on
My love is fierce
It runs deep & true
It can be a curse

Don't deceive me
Don't lead me on
It will be your curse
Karma can be cruel to find you

Don't let me love you
If you don't love me too
Don't lead me to believe
You are crazy about me too

Don't lead me on
I have been a good woman to you
I have nothing to prove
My love has been strong & true

If you don't plan on staying
Leave now, just don't stay
Don't lead me on
We have nothing more to say

Don't Crush Me

I will be crushed
If this is a lie
When you are the one
Who makes me feel alive

What else can I do
I do believe in you
A Christian man is who I see
I pray that he is that man you will always be

I will be so crushed & hurt
Do not lie & pretend
You are the man I defend

Do not deceit
But believe & trust in me
For I believe in you to be the better man
I see so much more in you

I will be crushed if you are untrue

Do You

Do you love me
The way I loved you

Now I am gone
Do you choose to remember the truth
The truth in what you really lost
Now that I am gone
Do you see what you really had
The love you had lost

Do you think of me often?
Do you miss those nights you lost?
Remember acting as I meant nothing
But could not bear to look in my eyes
As you lived a lie

What was real
You lost
Do remember
Do you miss me?
How much do you love me
Now that I am gone

Do you love me
The way I loved you
And are you ashamed of what you did
Do you miss what we really had?

Do you…?

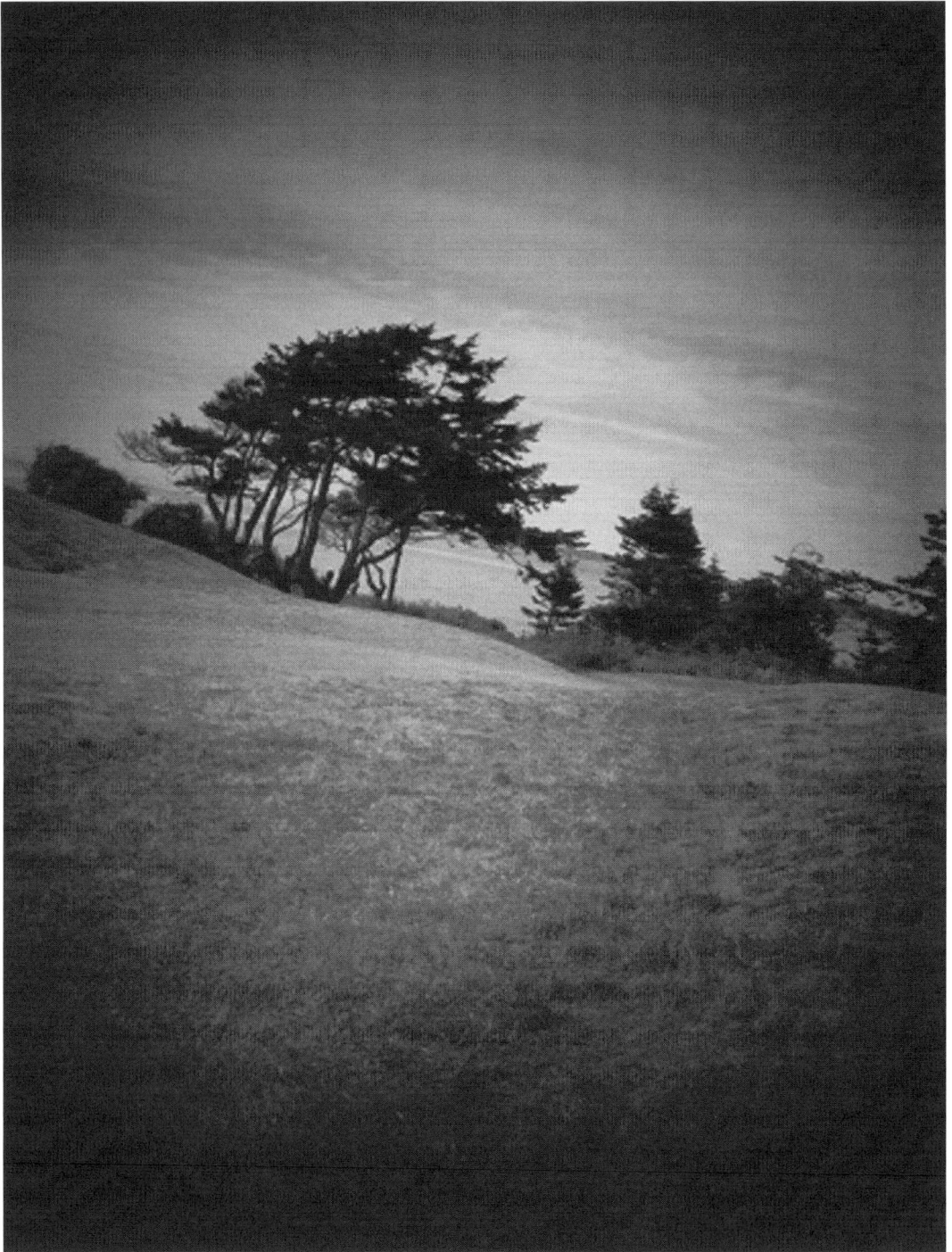

Do Not Deceive Me

My emotions are going crazy
I do not trust easy
And I am trusty you to be true
To be the man I see in you

My emotions are going crazy
Do not run again
I believe honesty always will win

Be true
For I have loved you
I do not wish to hate
I am trusting you deeply

I do not trust easy
I pray you are true
To the man I see in you
Do not deceit me

All I have asked from you
And all I have prayed
Do not deceit me
For I will love you always

Distraction

I no longer know what is true
I was distracted by a lie
The lie was you

I only wanted a new beginning
With a man I loved more than anything

For a future & family
But it seems I may have been distracted by a lie
A man I knew and thought was wise
I yearned for a future at you side
With you is where I was even more inspired
For you were my home
But I loved you more

So happiness we both felt
But to my surprise
I was only a distraction from your lie
As you were a distracting lie

I thought we had much more
Love to me was shared
The future I yearned for
We were only a distraction
I need so much more
It's not a distraction I yearn for

Deceit Is A Crime

I hate gossip
I despise lies
If this is a disaster
It will be to your own surprise

Do not deceive me
I have only been true
I deserve love & respect
That is what I have given you

I hate gossip
And drama too
I despise lie
I respect those who are real
Deceit is a hearts true crime

Could've – Should've

If we could start over
If our lives were different
When our paths finally met

Things could have been forever
We should have had no boundaries
No lies, No limitations

Could have, should have
Life would be so different
In another time

You are all I ever wanted
The only man I ever needed
But the past is behind us
You build a barrier
And wouldn't let me in

I love you still
I miss you more
Could have – Should have
We had something more

We should have been our new beginning
We could have had the life we were yearning for
Could haves – Should haves
What would have been

Could Have Been Friends

This did not have to be the end
I could have still been your friend
If only you didn't stay away
You should have never lied to me
I am not your enemy
I believed in the man I see

This did not have to end
I was in love with you then
But we still could have been friends
You should have been a better man

You should not have stayed away
For you I continue to pray
I only asked for you to be real with me
We could have been friends at the very least

Only if you didn't let this end like this
As if I really meant nothing
We then could have at least been friends

Condemned By Love

I feel condemned
For a love I confessed
True & faithful I was to you
But with a stronger love
Made you fear
That's when you condemned my love for you

My love is pure
It wasn't lust
My passion rose much deeper than that

We inspired each other
To be true to ourselves
With you is where I felt most alive
But my love was too much
Once again you ran scared

Betrayed & condemned
You ran away & wouldn't stay
Condemned by a strong love we shared
And no my love is imprisoned
Condemned by my faithful heart
Strayed from my love
You condemned me here

Broken

I feel broken
It is true
When I am without you
I don't know what happened
I do not know why you are gone

I feel broken
Deep within, it hurts
So sad yet confused
For I still continue to love you

My heart has been broken
Once before, but not like this
Little did you know how much I loved you
Or did you know when you left

No more drinks
No more wins
No more messages that made me grin
No more starring at the man within

My heart has been broken
You broke me deep within

Blocked You

I finally blocked your number
And deleted pictures of you
I chose to move on forward
From your games I found to be true
We both know I am better than you

Could have been so much more
There was much potential to be had
But instead
Your true colors bled through
And I choose not to know you

The emotions were hurtful
I really believed I knew you
It is time I finally blocked you

Betrayed By A Man

I will forgive you tomorrow
But today I am ashamed
I loved a coward
And believed in a lie he gave

It is because of you I cry
You should be the one to feel shame
For your cowardly heart
Should feel the pain you caused today

It is God you must answer to
For woman were created for man
To be loved, not betrayed
You should be the one ashamed

I had faith in you
And you were untrue
Unconditional love taken for granted
I loved you & love you still

I will forgive you tomorrow
But today I stay ashamed
I love a coward
But hurt by the lie he gave

Betrayed By A Kiss

Betrayed by a kiss
For you I could not resist
I didn't see the evil
But it seems to exist

You betrayed a love
Took for granted once again
God gifted you with a new beginning
And like a coward
You ran & hid

Betrayed by a kiss
Where I felt bliss
But did not see
You are where evil exists

How beautiful I found you
Pulled in like a magnet
I couldn't resist
A lie unfolded
And I was betrayed with just a kiss

Beside Me

I wish you were here beside me
It was where you were meant to be
I only wish your eyes could see

I miss you here beside me
It was where you made me happy
Did you know you inspired me?
Next to you is where I felt most alive

I wish you were here to walk beside me
To stay at my side in the journey I prayed
You left me here standing
Inspired & spared the truth instead

I wish you were here beside me
To be the man I saw in you
I continue to walk through this journey
Deep down I wish it were with you
But God will always see me through

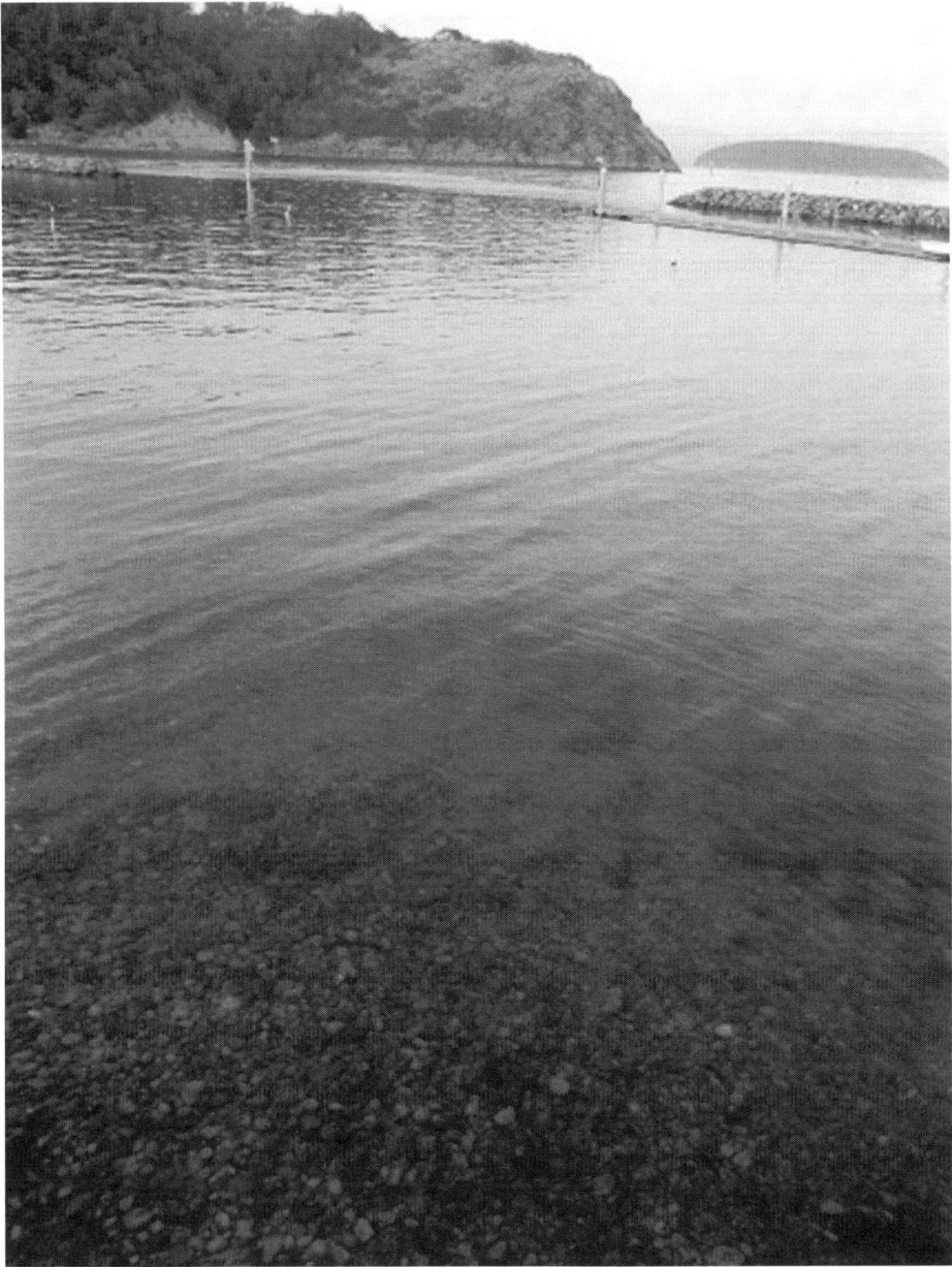

Another Day

Another day come & gone
And my feelings for you are still so strong
As time passes
I only miss you more and more
It isn't getting easier
I only feel so torn
My love for you stays strong

Another day come & gone
Looking towards the future only hurts me more
To find someone who completes you
And to know that are now gone

Another day come & gone
I continue to carry on
But I really do miss you
You once made me happy
And now that part of me is gone

Another day come & gone
Still I carry on
I can't let them see
What you did when you left me
I must keep a smile
Hold it all in and stay strong

Another day come & gone
You are really gone
I must continue to carry on

Another Chance

I believe in you
Believe in me
This is our new beginning

Another chance at a new start
Flaws & baggage are not an excuse
Your past should not own you

I love you for you
And all that comes with that
I believe in you
I have faith in the man before me

Only struggle here
Is you allowing me near
I believe in you
I have faith in us and our love
Do you believe in me?
This is where were we are stuck

I believe in you
Another chance
A new beginning
Don't let me fall apart
Why make this hard
We have another chance
This is our new start

Afraid Of Others Knowing

So afraid of your name
For your privacy you claim
How dumb do you see me
What a stupid boy you must be

You inspired me to write again
Thought you loved me too
And saw what lies deeper within you

Through an act of love
I believed & had faith
I only then mentioned your name
As my man with love
For the man I saw inside you

To my surprise
A coldness arised
No heart for me
My feelings even meant nothing

Only privacy you wanted
As I really did mean nothing

A Magnet To Your Disguise

Drawn to your disguise
I felt like a magnet to your side
A deeper passion would arise
But only to your disguise

To believe in your touch
I thought you believed in our love
I fell at despair
For you are no longer there

I saw you to have so much faith
To be the man I saw in you
I was a magnet to you disguise
But the truth has only aroused

I believed in you
And all you had been given
I don't know what happened

I was blinded by your own disguise
The disguise of a deeper passion
I saw you to be so much more
For what I believed
God had truly blessed you for

The disguise of who you were meant to be
I was a magnet drawn to his side
To his disguise I fell in love
But it wasn't what I expected

I was pulled to you like a magnet
But was only a magnet to your disguise

A Lie You Can't Hide

No words can erase the pain you caused
I feel lost in the lies that deceived me
I love you unconditionally
And I continue to pray for you always

But betrayed and deceived
I will never stand by your side
You chose and created your life
So come clean
You weren't the man you pretend to be

You live a lie
No longer can you hide
I am embarrassed to have loved the lie
A lie you can no longer hide

A Hard Man To Love

You are a hard man to love
Texts never calls
And you always keep up a wall

A constant distance
The closer you let me in
The quicker you seem to run

But you always get me
It is with you I feel at home
I feel most alive
The time we have together
Truly mean the most

Quality not quantity
You make me whole
But you can't be here
When I always need you the most

You scare easy
You make me question everything
And what this really means
So unsure & scared you make me

You are a hard man to read
A harder man to love
We are crazy for each other
But you only send text messages
Never a call on the phone
But sometimes you just make me feel so alone

You are a hard man to love
Yet here I am
Crazy for you still
But for how long

If you can't let me in
I am afraid this will soon end
I am crazy for a man
Who is afraid of letting me complete know him

A Deeper Love For A Stranger

I fell in love more deeper
Only God knows the truth
How much compassion & love
I have for you

I fell in love with your knowledge
The passion of your history & mine
From the excitement of your mind to share
It was my heart you didn't realize you inspired

It was your integrity
Your playfulness & outgoing life that kept me here
Your mind & spirit still entice me so deeply
It is what lead me here

I fell in love much deeper
With a deeper part of you to find
I truly had a deeper compassion & love
A deeper love for a stranger
I have come to find

Your talents go unnoticed
And your heart stays tucked away
I am no in love with a stranger
You are too far away
But are not the same today

9 Years

9 years devoted
To a love I thought would last
But you betrayed me
And all I believed was good
Really was not

So weak & heartless
The coward your mirror has come to know
I wish not to know you
But I do pray you find the Lord

9 years I loved you
Faithfully unconditional
Still I love you now
But not as I did before
Only as my past
And the dad to my daughter

So much had changed
The man I knew inside
A coward was released
Our love you will never find

A Broken Boat

Stuck on a broken boat
The motor nowhere to be found
And no sails to tie down
Only two paddles found

I began to paddle
We keep going only in circles
If you can't take your part
We cannot move forward
I refuse to continue these circles
We are slowly sinking
Our love is being pulled apart
What were you thinking?

Were you wanting this journey?
Or are you a true coward at heart
Was this journey always a failure?
Did you ever love me at all?
Before we ever pulled away from the dock

Now we are stuck on a broken boat
I am the only one doing my part

Your Truth

I only wanted answers
I cared & lost
For it was only a game to you
To me, a love lost

People talk
Gossip occurs
But there are sides of each story
I asked you for yours

The truth would have set you free
But it looks like I meant nothing

From the beginning all I wanted
Was pure honesty
Instead you lead me to believe
In a man who mean a lot to me

Now all I hear is talk
Gossip does hurt
When the man I love is always the punchline
For my love for you
Was true & pure
But only a joke to you
Will I ever know the truth?

As much as the truth may hurt
I deserve the truth from you

Your Plea

I was only the one you wanted
When you were alone
It made sense while you were fishing
But now it is reality I see
I really meant nothing
Just the fling that you seek

How blind & in love I was
The man I saw to be above
The game was really on me
You made me see so clearly
That my love truly meant nothing
Why wouldn't you just leave me be

You are free
You can no longer message me
I was once weak
But no longer am I blind to see
I now see I really meant nothing

Leave me be
You really did hurt me
Lies or not
You let me love you
Then betrayed me

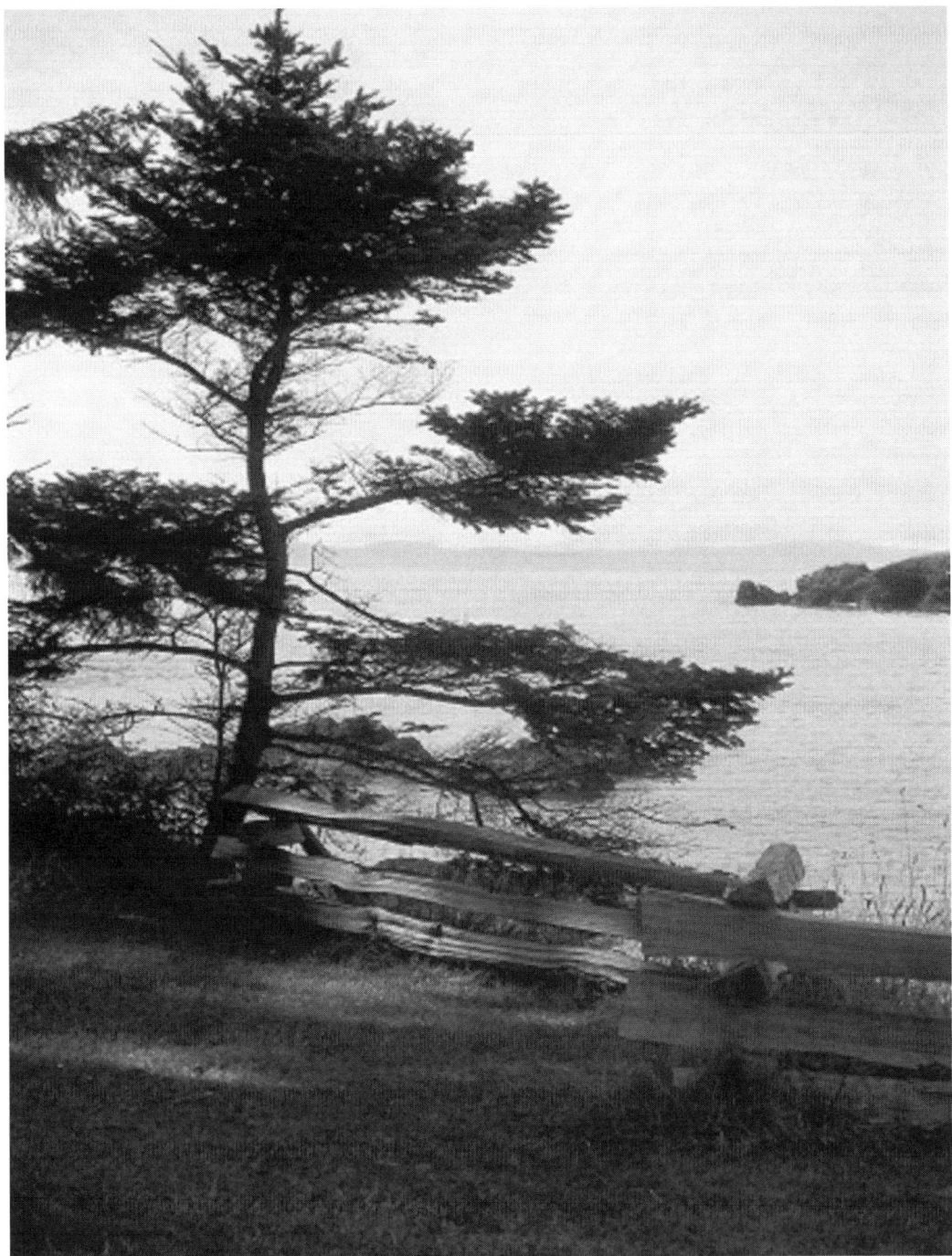

Your Lips

Never should have unleashed a love
When you weren't able to keep up
If you could not handle what it meant
You should have never let me fall in love

Never let a woman fall in love
When you never plan on loving her to
Love her first
Before all the sweet talk
Don't live the lie
Just be yourself
It would have been enough

I can forgive
But never forget the lie
You will always be a stranger
From all the hurt & lies

I forgive
But wish not to know you
I can't believe anything from you lips
Those lips I once loved to kiss
Too many lies exist

You Told Me

I opened up & cared
You told me you cared
And I was so scared to love you
But you told many so many things
Promised to show me everything
Then you weren't there for me when I needed you most

You were going to teach me to shoot
You were going to take me on the water with you
You wanted to take me to my first concert
And now you have disappeared
Like I really never mattered at all

I was so scared
And you reassured me you would be here
You told me many things
And I opened up & cared

You should have told me goodbye
You should have told me why
Because you told me you cared
You should have been true to your word

Why Care Now

What do you care?
You are the one who left me here
Cold words were spoken
Then you were gone
You left and I let you

My world was much better
The day you left me here
Positives grew
When the negatives left with you

Things come & go
But I am strong as you know
Don't worry now
You didn't care then
When it mattered the most

Why care now?
Don't be scared.
We are now strangers
It no longer matters
And I am stronger then ever

What Happened

So much potential
So much talent
So much smarts
Have been abolished

You turned away
From your Faith inside
And ran away from your gifts he gave

You were created to be so much more
Yet act like a victim
Such a shame

I am baffled today
For what you have to say
As you sit & do nothing
You are not the victim you play

He believes in you still
And it is never too late
You're not a victim
You are your own fate
Your destiny lies in you always

What happened?

Unjustified Lies

Lies cannot be justified
They are still lies
And they came from your lips
Don't wait & hesitate
As if this anger will lift

You let me love you
When you were untrue
And my kisses meant nothing to you

So run away
As you continue to play
The lies you live are worthless

You let me love you
Betrayed what that meant
Then condemned me for it
Because of your own mess

Did you once have a heart?
Or was it just all for just a moment
I will never know
Unjustified lies
You hurt me the most

Too Late Now

It is too late
You let me fall
In love with a man
Who couldn't even call

What a mess I am in
Such a predicament given
When I saw him as my angel from heaven

So much passion
So much love
But it always ends through his ignorance
And he can't seem to rise above

It is too late
I already fell
He could not catch me
He would not love me
I really know now

Life is crazy
But definitely too late now

Time To Walk Away

I wish you could truly see me
I wish you would let me in
I am crying & screaming
Your sin is being blind to what is really lays within

Pushed & pulled
I have had to be bold
Still you can't let me in
My sin is loving a man
Who can't see the woman I am

I am exhausted & hurt
Betrayed by reality
It is my turn to coward away
It is time I walk away

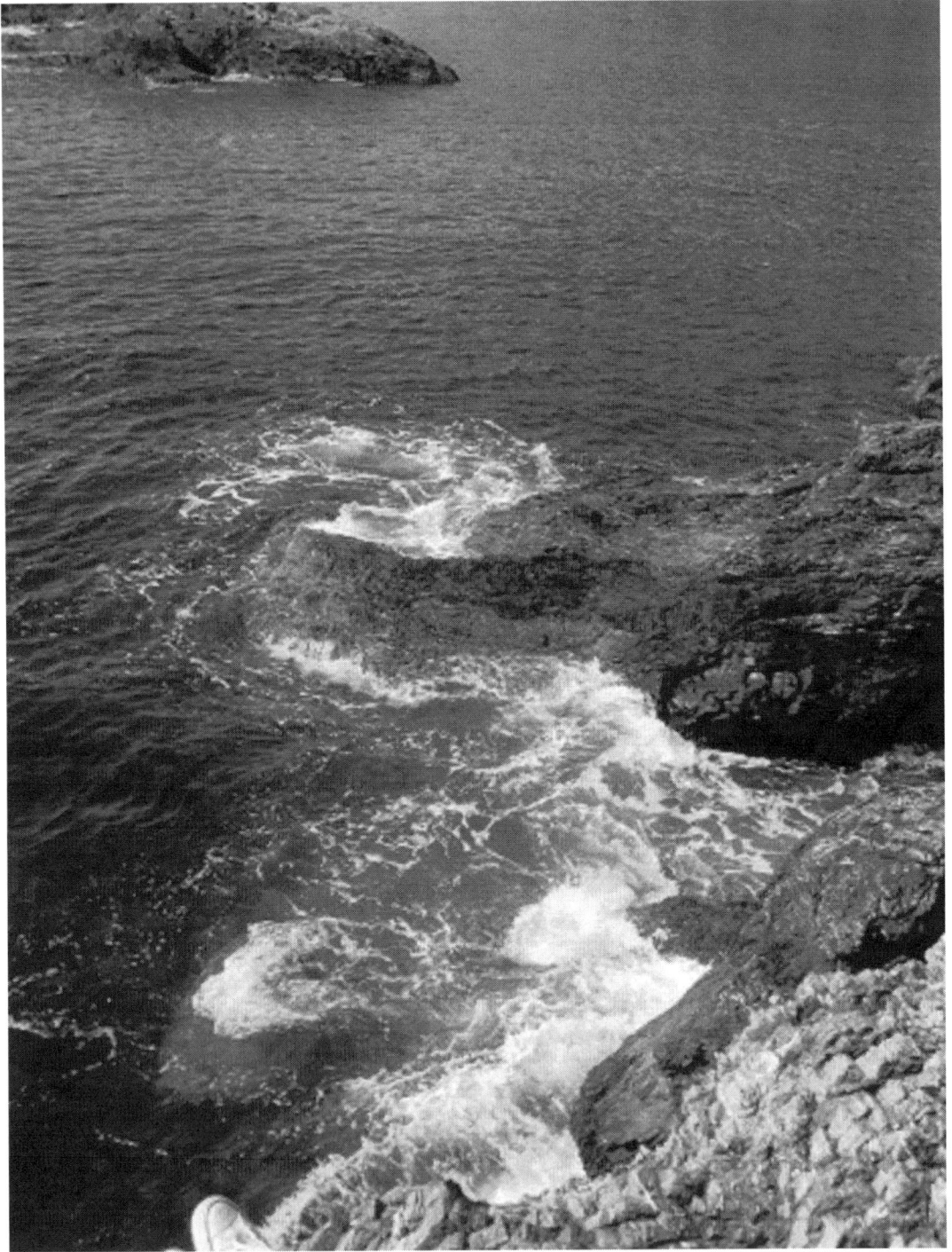

The Truth

I just can't sleep
Hurt by all the deceit
I loved another man
Who wasn't a real man to me

I saw you to be better than most
But it was a lie & you cheated yourself
Got caught & left

You were with her
As I confirmed that I loved you
If I only knew that you lived a lie
Everything turned to be untrue
You deceived me deeper than you knew

Now I can't sleep
And she is having your baby
Were you ever planning on telling me the truth?
All I did was love you

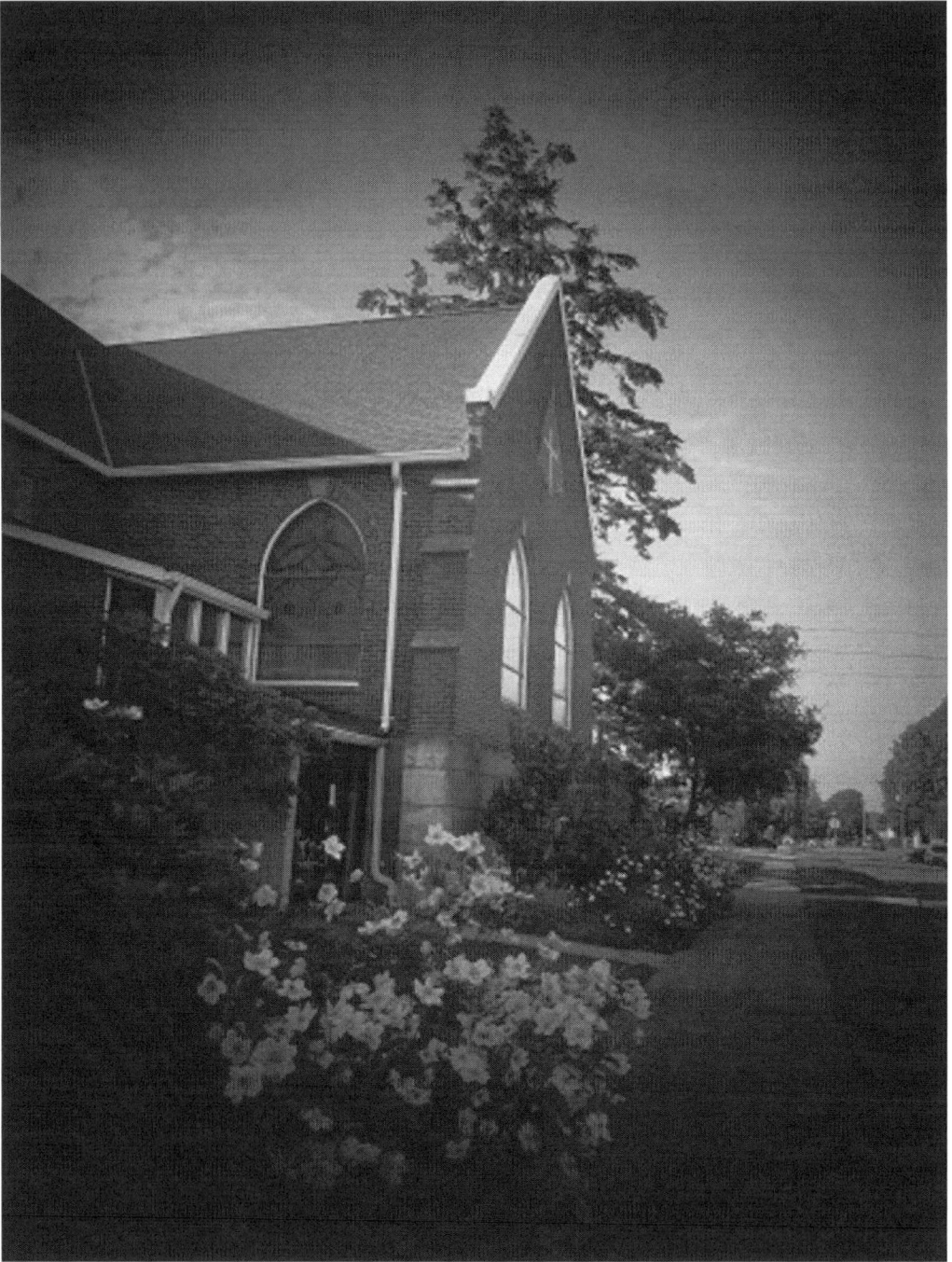

The Man I saw

I saw you to be so much more
I actually believed you cared
But to my surprise
You only live a lie
Now I fear
I never knew you at all

I saw you to be so much more
A Christian man with morals & dignity
I saw a beauty in your soul
A good man I thought was true

I saw you as so much more
A passion through faith & god
A love for history
But morally misleading
Untrue to the man I saw in you

Stupid & Naïve

Was I really so stupid & naïve
Or are you really that weak
When loves stares you in the face
You decide to turn and run away

A coward at heart
Or a boy playing games
Either way
You left me here in tears
And you had nothing to say

A coward of a man
So weak, he ran
Love staring him in the eyes

What really is pride?
An excuse to run scared
Only a coward makes a woman cry
And can't explain why

Was I really that stupid & naïve?
To believe the man I believed you to be

Story Of My Life

I meant so little
When I let myself care so much
Story of my life
That is just my luck

I did know better
Just had more faith
Thought you were better
Then you proved to be today

So much pain caused by meaning so little
I warned you not to deceive me
I called it upfront
But you lied & hurt me
Story of my life

I was ready to give it all to a stranger
Thank god he showed me the truth today
Just my luck
To love a lie
Story of my life

Should Have Been Proud

You should have been proud to be my man
Be happy I chose you to be at my side
Hold my hand with nothing but delight
Comfort me during all the hard times
And at night

Celebrate whenever we could
For the deep love we shared
You should have been proud to be my man
While you had the opportunity
You should have been more of a man

Now you can't
You have to live with the regrets at hand

I loved you most
Believed in you too
You should have been proud
Been the man I saw in you
Let me in & showed me you loved me most

You should have been proud
To be my man

Run Away

If you only knew
The truth that lays inside
Would you continue to be
The coward on the outside

If you knew what lies deep within
Would you continue to run away
Would you be hidden still

The love & faith that you seek
The path the Lord has given
A new beginning to unfold

You still run
But pray
And preach to many
If you only knew
What is being given
If you could only see the truth…

Do you really want to run away?

Respect You

Talk is cheap
Sweet talking means nothing to me
Prove yourself true
Then I will respect you

I don't ask for much
Just honest & truth
If you don't love me
Then leave me
I will be happier without you

I don't need sugar coated lies
I yearn for the deeper story
What lays underneath
Honesty & truth
That is how I will respect you

Talk is cheap
Prove it to me
Without honest
There is no me

Respect me please
And I will respect you

Relax

Relax
So easy to be said
I am not even home
Not even in my own bed

Too many memories
Lies & deceit
You never truly loved me
Only lust you had for me
When I loved you unconditionally

Relax they say
But if they only knew
There is no relaxing
Only memories of you

I cannot relax today
Maybe tomorrow
Too many memories here
Bring only pain and sorrow

It is time for a new journey
Maybe then I can relax & breathe
To relax and be happy is what I truly seek

Ready To Walk Away

Speak to me
Before it is too late
Say something
I am ready to walk away

I am giving up on you
You are not there for me
And I no longer know you
It is time to leave

I feel so lost
I don't know what happened
You made me feel so small
And heart broken

Speak to me
And tell me why
Before it is too late
You already made me cry

Speak now
Say something
I am ready to walk away
I was ready to give you my whole life
Instead you said nothing to make me stay

I don't know what happened
Speak
Just say something
Before I truly walk away

It is now too late
I am gone
I have moved on
You could not speak
So I walked away

Part Of Me

Now that you are gone
A part of me is missing
I miss my phone buzzing
I miss seeing your face
I miss the smallest things the most
For they were the most meaningful to me

Life continues to go on
But the excitedness has faded
When my heart would race before
That is when it breaks more instead

Just another heartbreak
And I know I am strong
For I will always continue to carry on

But part of me is missing
Now that part of me is gone

Now & Then

Now & then I ponder our plan together
A new beginning we both yearned
The names of our babies we had
Then you left for work

The dream of marriage & babies
But being a dad sooner was more important
So you left me to have a baby with only a stranger

Now & then
How different it has become
And now I am treated the same way from another

Now I pray for the day God erases you both
From my heart & head
Now and then
I have always deserved better then you both

Nothing More

There is nothing left I would do
To want to be anywhere near you
Your actions were cold
Feelings untrue
I will never want to be with you

Nothing I would do
To even be your friend
The hurt runs deep
And I never really meant anything

I have done enough
And even went above
I have no regrets
I forgive
But I don't forget
There is nothing more I want
So there is nothing more to do

Nothing more with you

No Chances

You told me you regret our time spent
As if I meant absolutely nothing
During the months I thought we had something

Words do hurt
Actions run deep
I cared for you
And you made me feel cheap

I don't regret anything
Only that it ended this way
There are no chances left after this

No chances to be had
Time has gone
And the past will live in the past
I have no regrets
But no chances are left

Not This Time

Do you realize you are really losing me this time?
The benefit of the doubt
No longer applies
Too many broken promises
I am beginning to feel everything is truly a lie

So much disappointment
How can you be surprised?
It was only just a matter of time
I would leave your side

You didn't have to lose me
Just be honest & try
If you didn't really love me
You should have never wasted my time

No Backbone

You have no backbone
You continue to live a lie
What is real in the moment
Isn't a healthy life

You get push & pulled
Such a strong man always having to prove
While allowing everyone to walk over you
Too proud to be the true you
There is no backbone to now be found

So weak to what may be said
The life you wish to seek
You already had

To blind to see
What should have and could have been real
Now may never be found
When you continue to lay down
No backbone to be found

Never This Heart Pain

So much I have had to choose
But never wanted to choose between me and you
You are not my first love
But I have had a deeper love for you

Never did I want this heart pain
From the man I have seen so much in
From the man my heart adores
You are not my first love
But I love you most

I am so scared
I know you love me to
When I barely get to see and hear from you
But is love really enough

I need so much more
My life has always been hard
Too many disappointments
No one knows all of me
Only God

I didn't choose to not want you
You just won't let me all in
Or give me all of you
So loving you hurts the most
Never this heart pain
I wish our love was enough

Never Mattered

I don't know if you have messaged me
But I don't know what you can really say
You continued to let me love you
And told me you were crazy about me too
But now I don't feel I have ever mattered to you

Today was the end
Proved to show me what I have really meant to you
Instead of being proud to be my man
You told me you have no girlfriend

Saying we were together
Really meant nothing to you at all
Just pillow talk
Like I meant nothing
Never mattered at all

Never Forget

I can forgive
But I can't forget
There has been too much negative

I will not live a lie
I can no longer stand by your side
I don't know what happened
But my pride is over your love
And what life we could have had

I can forgive
I don't want the hate
I will walk away
I won't live the lie

I can never forget
How it hurt
What little you said
So I say goodbye with my pride
You will never find me again at your side

I forgive you
But I will never forget with you did

Miss You Like Crazy

I have been missing you like crazy
Wishing you would call
After a month of silence
You now write me back by text
You can never call

I am still so agree
You left with no word
But I miss you like crazy
And now don't know how to feel
Or act at all

I wish you felt my pain
I wish your felt the same way
I miss you like crazy
I pray for you every day

Mislead My Heart

With this year
And all the difficulties
I have had to continue to endure
You still persist to hurt me more & more

Don't pretend to care about me in anyway
You are fake & now I see
You only misled my heart
And I believed

Such a mess
When all I did was love and believe in you

You mislead my heart
And pretend to be Christian

Mind vs. Heart

My heart & mind are at war
My mind tells me to move on
I deserve to be adored
I deserve a man who truly loves me
Who will stand by my side
And who won't cowardly stray

But my heart misses your face
In your arms is where I wanted to stay

I am at war with my heart and my mind
Why can't you be the man I see?
The man God created you to be
My man who truly loves me

Your cowardness has brought you to stray
And now I am at war
Because of my heartbreaking pain
From a coward who betrayed me

Meant So Little

I hear from everyone but you
Everyone else cares to check up
But still no word
No call or message from you
I guess I really did mean so very little to you I see now

The one person who meant so much
Really doesn't matter at all
How could I mean so little?
After all we shared & been through so much

I must have never meant much of anything
To hear from everyone but you
My nightmare of you has come true

Love Left Behind

I was in love with more than just your face
Your gentle touch & sweet embrace
It was your mind & heart which intrigued me
Captured by the smile on your face
That made me weak at the knees

I was in love with the wonder of your mind
Yearning for the knowledge behind
Your heart was enduring
I wish I could only find

I know I believed in you more than others
Unconditional love for only you to find
You read to find knowledge
And seek to find passion

My ambitions were blinded
By the weakness of my heart
Pulled like a magnet to someone deeper than I could have imagined

Only if you would seek the truth before you
You wouldn't have left a greater love behind you

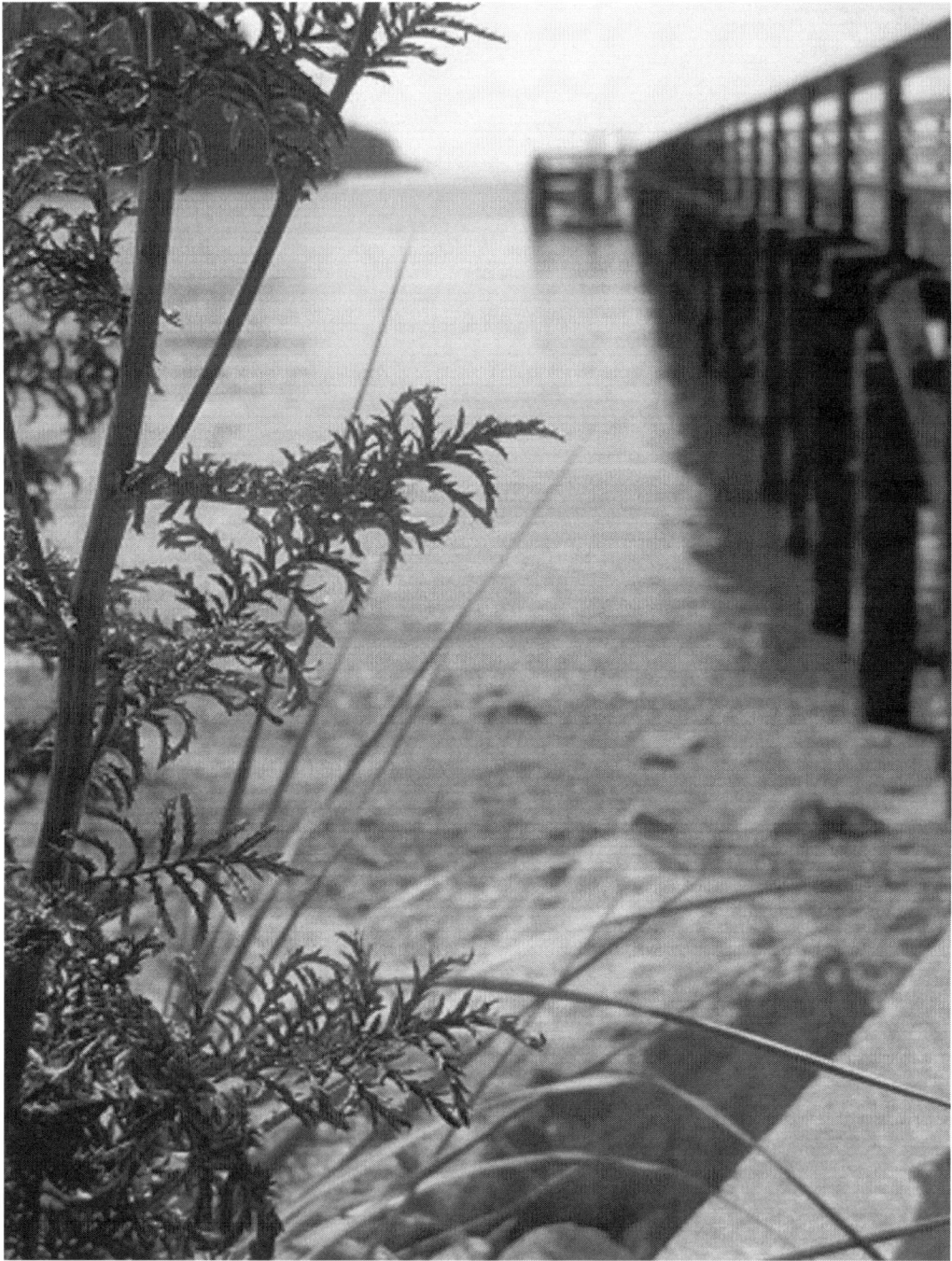

Lied & Lost

You lied & lost me
But you only did it to yourself
I don't need or want a lie
You should have been more true
To both me and to you

I deserve something and someone more real
Not live a lie
That's how you lost my love

What a joke
Felt like a game
But you are the punchline
You should have never lied

I loved you for the man I saw in you
Not the lie you live
Do you not even know the man
You were meant to be
Not the joke that you let people see

You lied & lost me
Your feelings should have been more true to me
Such a disaster this has turned out to be
Now you really know
Because you lied
You really lost me

Let Me Be

Just leave me be
I need to feel free
I want to be alone

I have no home
Only hurtful memories
You have shown

I will arise
Even though all I have sacrificed
The Lord is on my side
I will strive with pride

But today let me be
You should have stood by me
I continue to live for my Father
God in Heaven is who I call on
He is all I need

So let me be
You proved only to be weak
I don't need you here
You live in negativity

Let me be
I need to feel free
I was made for more
And more I will strive to be

Ignored

I told you I was done
Because I was done being ignored
Done feeling like I do not mean anything
To the man I love & adored

Life is crazy
It keeps me thinking
To love & to lose
I don't know whatever was really true to you

You allowed me to completely walk away
You have done nothing to show me you cared in anyway
That hurts the most

Realizing I really meant nothing
I told you I was done
Because I was done being ignored
And now it's over
As if it all meant nothing at all

I deserve so much more

I Would Have

I would have followed you
To the end of the world
Stood by your side
Through each and every storm
You didn't love me
So now I must go

Faithful & true
I believed in you
Never got to see all of me
I didn't know you to be this weak

I count my blessings
That I know now
The boy is not the man I see
You were not real with me

You lost something real & true
By your game tactics
You lose
Your karma is just beginning to unravel
You should have been true

I would have stood by you through each storm
And followed you to the end of this world
But you were not faithful & true
You couldn't be honest even with the truth
So I have gone and left you for good

I have loved you
May have forgiven you too

I Will Never Know

Maybe I am wrong
Wrong about being wrong about you
But I will never know
Because we are through

I may have meant something
It could have been everything we dreamt it could be
But who knows
I will never know what I meant to you

You pushed me away for the last time
And I need all or nothing
You would not be the man I saw inside
Not for me
Not this time

I will never know who you really were
Or what I really meant to you
Who knows what was really meant to be
Right now I just see a lie
So deeply hurt are we both deep inside

I will never know the truth
You wouldn't let me in and know all of you
All or nothing
So I must leave
I will never know
Only know you hurt me

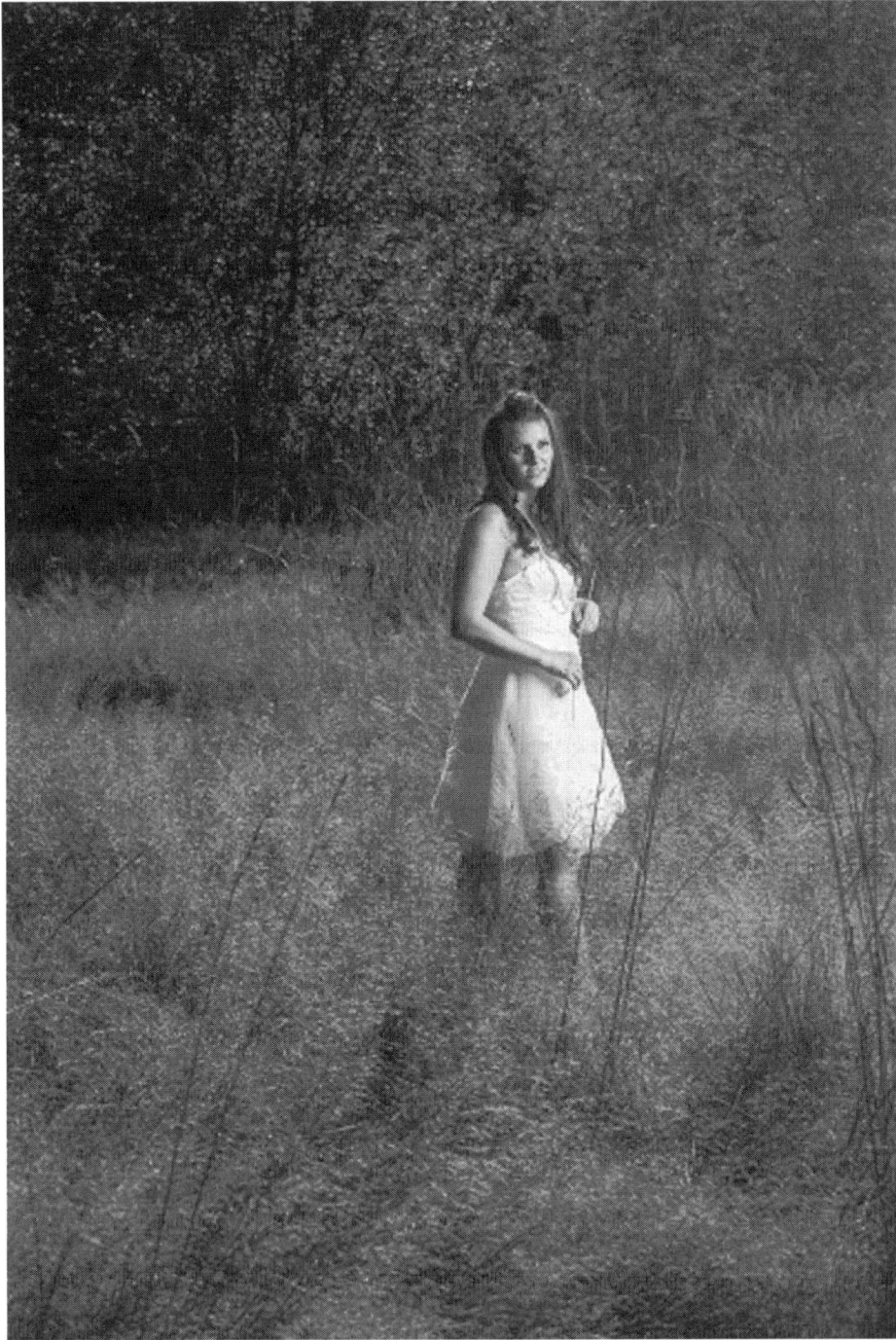

Release My Pain

Hate, anger & disappointment
I despise all your lies
I thought you to be someone better

A true Christian
You only pretend
Only to be a distraction
For a lie you live instead

No more sorrys
No more lies
To our Heavenly Father hands
Is where your future lies

Do not cry to me
It was all pretend I see
You betrayed my heart
But Jesus walks alongside me

I release my pain
To my was Father who reins
You have lost me now
For I have truly been found

Release my pain
My heart will no longer ache
A new path
Another journey awaits
I am at peace
My pain has been released

Sometimes Love Hurts

To love
Sometimes means to lose
This hurts more then you knew

Heartbreak can break us
So much we can lose
Sometimes love hurts
Hurt by the ones we choose

To love comes a greater purpose
Without heartbreak we cannot be found
Without hurt true love would not be unconditional
Without heartbreak
You wouldn't know true love or yourself

Sometimes love hurts
More than we can take
But God's love is stronger
It can never be faked

Incoherent

Drunk and high
So incoherent to live
Alcohol helps you numb the life you live
Incoherent through being drunk and high
Feelings can only be numb for a moment in time

High from the weed
You try to hide from me
It is no longer you I seek

Incoherent makes you weak
Ignorance is now all I see
You no longer know what to believe

You blame the Lord
And the world for all you have lost
It is mind over matter
All you really lost is yourself

It is not too late
To change your fate
Forgiveness awaits
When knowledge & wisdom is what you pray

Put down the bottle
Turn away from the drugs
Look in the mirror & learn
Seek the Lord above

Jesus only awaits
He has never lost faith
To him you must pray
Then you will find your way

Incoherence is a choice
Forgiveness can be your fate

It Didn't Matter

What does it matter
You are now gone
You may miss me
But you could not love me
So what does it matter now

I believed in you to be a better man
I love you faithfully
I loved you true
But you didn't want a girlfriend
And regretted our time together too

So what does it matter
You didn't love me enough
So many lies
And many tears
But it didn't matter to you

So what does it matter now
When I am now gone

The truth is you have never been true
Let me be in peace
For I never mattered enough to you

Layers

I have a tendency of pushing people away
Too many layers to keep me strong
There is more to me than the eye can see
But you truly have inspired me

You broke though
But you did not see
How perfect you were for me
So you left me here
With layers open to see

There are boundaries around my heart
Layers too hard to part
But you inspired me and broke through
However didn't see a deeper side of me with you

I wish you saw the real me
And how you inspired me
You brought me back to me
Hidden in the layers of truth

Pushed Away

I keep wondering every day
If I was the one who pushed you away
I told you I had this
Not to worry for I am strong
But the truth is I needed you to see past me
To know me deep within
To hold me close & stand by me
Instead I pushed you away

I have been through so much
Strength is all I know how to be
Strength has always been my destiny
It is easier to push people away and it just be me

Strength is also my weakness
I needed you to make me feel safe
For only with you am I home

I never wanted you to leave
I needed you to stay
Instead I was scared of the emotions which came
And now I feel betrayed
But not only by you
But the weakness of my strength
That pushed you away

I Now Laugh At You

If I only knew
It was only the alcohol speaking
You weren't that man
And I am not this woman
So I am leaving

Martinis are nice
Movies too
But you are fake
So I am done with you

If I only knew
All the sweet things said
Where only alcohol induced
And you were really worthless
I would have left long ago
You wouldn't have a chance

I believed in your words to be true
I saw a man way better in you
I quit, I learned
Through a status change
The hurt & anger grew
As I met and saw the real you

How quickly I am gone
A stranger I love
A lie I miss

But I laugh as I ponder
All the reasons
So many lies
And unmeaningful gestures

I still have my dignity and pride
You can't break me
You only live a lie

Another Photoshoot

Photos all over the world
Faces & landscapes to be shared
There is art in photography
More than meets the eye
What beauty the camera can find

Another photo lies a story
It can speak to you
Let it inspire you to

Another photoshoot
Pieces of me intertwined
What will the camera find?
Another side to me to see

Another photoshoot
A new version
What will unravel?
We will see in time
Can they see the pain you caused inside

Too Dark To See The Stars

Another day ending
So dark you can't see the stars
So quiet
I can't erase the memories
I miss you here
And I miss your smile

Once you let someone into your heart
You know you have to with the consequences
Now I am alone
Wishing for your call
Wishing you to just show up
But it's another day ending
And it's too dark to even see the stars

Only God knows what happened
Only God knows what is meant to be
It is just another day ending
It is so quiet
I can't tune out these memories

I miss you here
And your smile too
But it is too dark
I can't even see the stars

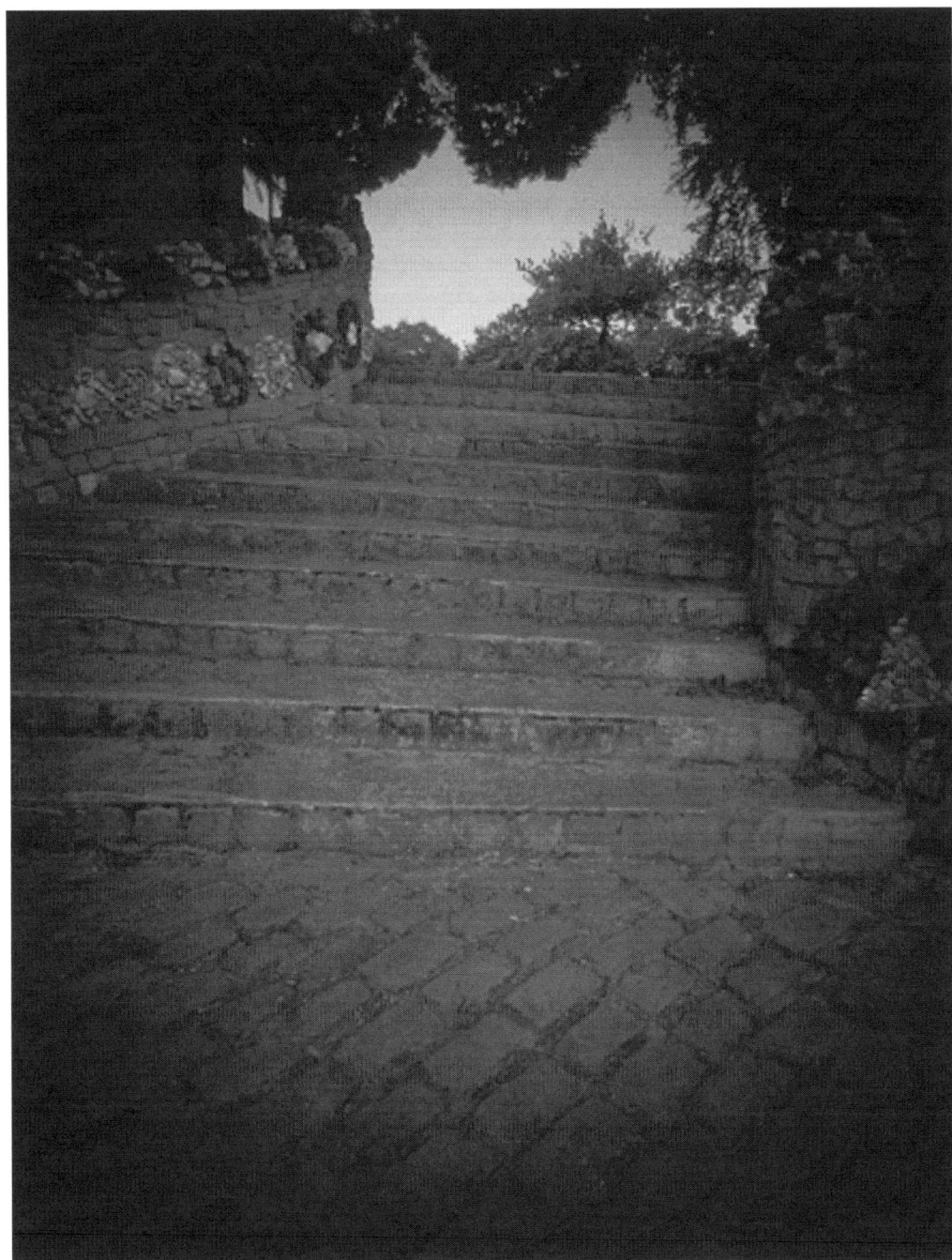

Scared & Unsure

I am scared
And unsure
I cannot be hurt once more

Rumors & gossip
Are torture to my heart
When you are not here
To prove the truth of your heart

I love you dearly
But hurt once more
By rumors & gossip
Make fear & unsure

I need you here
Be true to your heart
For your word means more to me

So do not deceit me
I cannot be hurt once more
Love or leave me
I am scared & unsure

I Lied

Time only knows what is meant to be
Only God knows what happened
But you are still the only man I think of always
I lied when I told you no longer was I in love with you

I lied when I only wanted to be your friend
In your arms is where I wanted to stay
All I ever wanted was a man like the man I see you to be

All I ever wanted was you by my side
For you to be the man I see with pride
But you left and hurt me here
When all you had to do was communicate
To make sure I knew you cared

So I lied
I have never stopped loving you
I have never stopped believe that what we had was true
The truth is, I belong with you
For I am still deeply in love with you

Pieces Of Me
By Julia Anne Simpson

Chapter 4
Through Illness & Recovery

No Fears & No Tears

He who created me
Built a greater path for me
Through weakness & pain
Has brought me a bigger gain
I will not fear for he is by my side

There is bigger plan given
Another mission, another lesson
Do not fear & do not shed a tear
For my journey doesn't finish here

There is much more to be had
But much more to be given
More strength & more wisdom
So do not fear or shed a tear
I am not finished here

It's not about what I serve
Or what I have lost
There is something bigger in a mission
Do not fear or shed another tear
There is much more deeper in my mission

Breathe

Just breathe
For each breathe will keep you blessed
Knowing the Lord is working for us

Breathe & keep breathing
You have a bigger purpose
Keep calm & keep peace in every breath
Just breathe

Just breathe
It is a key to your success
Breathe
You have truly been blessed
Let the air calm you
And lift your spirit all around you
Just breathe

Life is sure to test you
It will push & pull you
Just breathe through it all
God is right beside you
So just breathe

Let Go

Let go & breathe
Find comfort in him
All your worries
All your fears
Let go & believe

He won't let you stray
He will never abandon you
When life looks grey
Have peace knowing he is working through you everyday

So let go
Pursue your dreams
Let go & believe
For he is with you
He knows you eternally
Let him in & let go

He is beside you
He will carry you through
For he truly loves you
So just let go

Take My Pain

So much hurt
So much loss
So many struggles I have had to cross

I bow down & pray
Lord please take away my pain

Another push
Another shove
Another disappointment from love

I fall to my knees & pray
Please take this pain away

The mission from above
Is a path we may not understand
But through faith & love
I will bow down & pray
For pain is no longer hurt
He will guide me to be stronger
As he takes my pain away

They Won't Break Me

Whatever the future holds
They won't shake me
They won't break me

They can push & pull
But I will stand strong
I will stand firm in you
They will not break me

My strength & courage lies in you
Whatever the future holds
I will continue to carry on
For my courage & faith are strong

They will not break me
For they aren't that strong
My faith in you only carries on

No pain or illness
No heartbreak or disappointment
Can destroy the path I am on
They won't break me
My faith is too strong

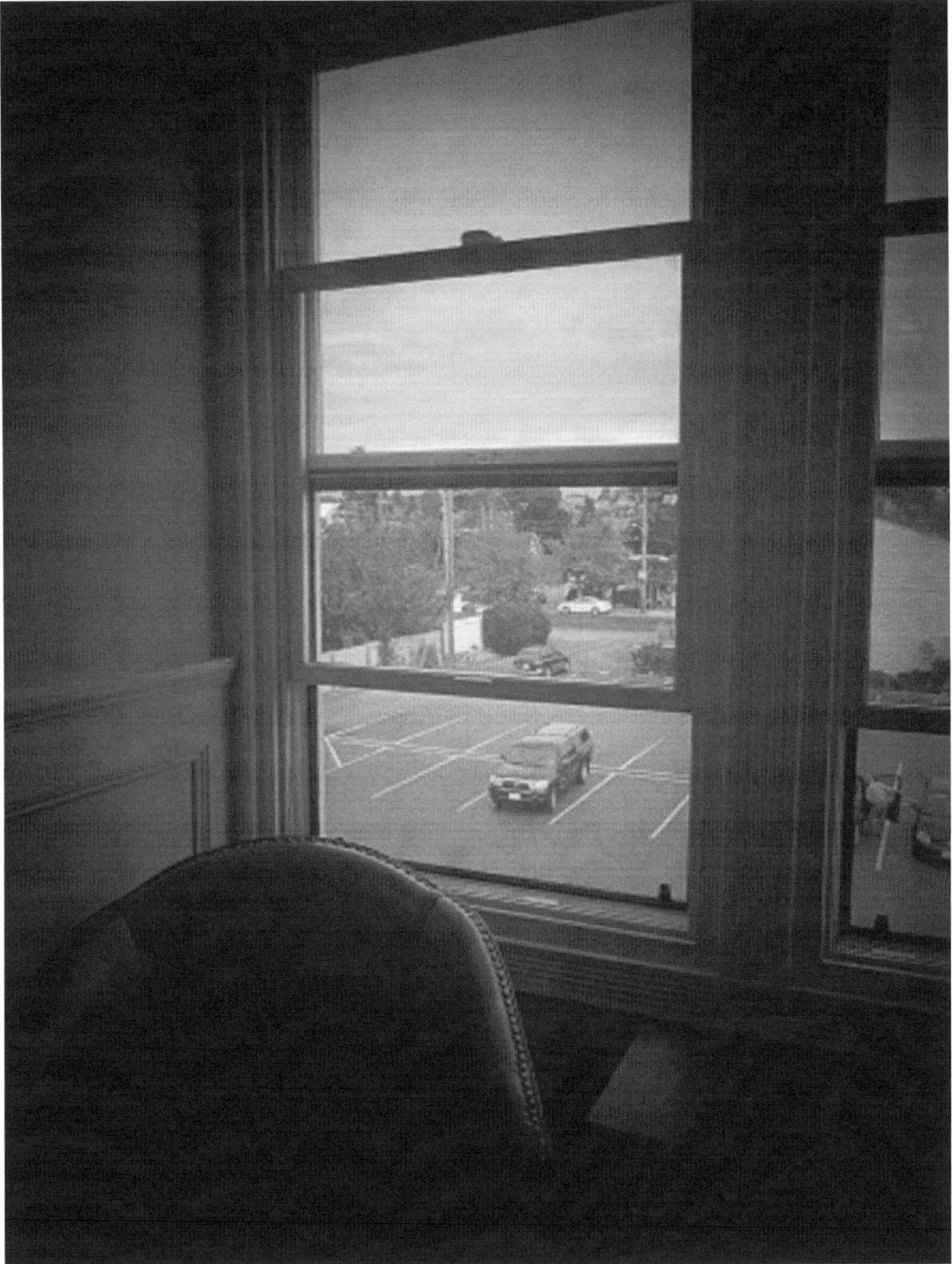

Turn The Fan On

It is so hot here inside
Harder to breathe
Harder to live my life

Turn the fan on
Cool me down
So I can live my life

Let the air cool me down
Let the wind let me free
It's getting hot here inside of me

Turn on the fan
Set me free
All I ask
Is to let me breathe

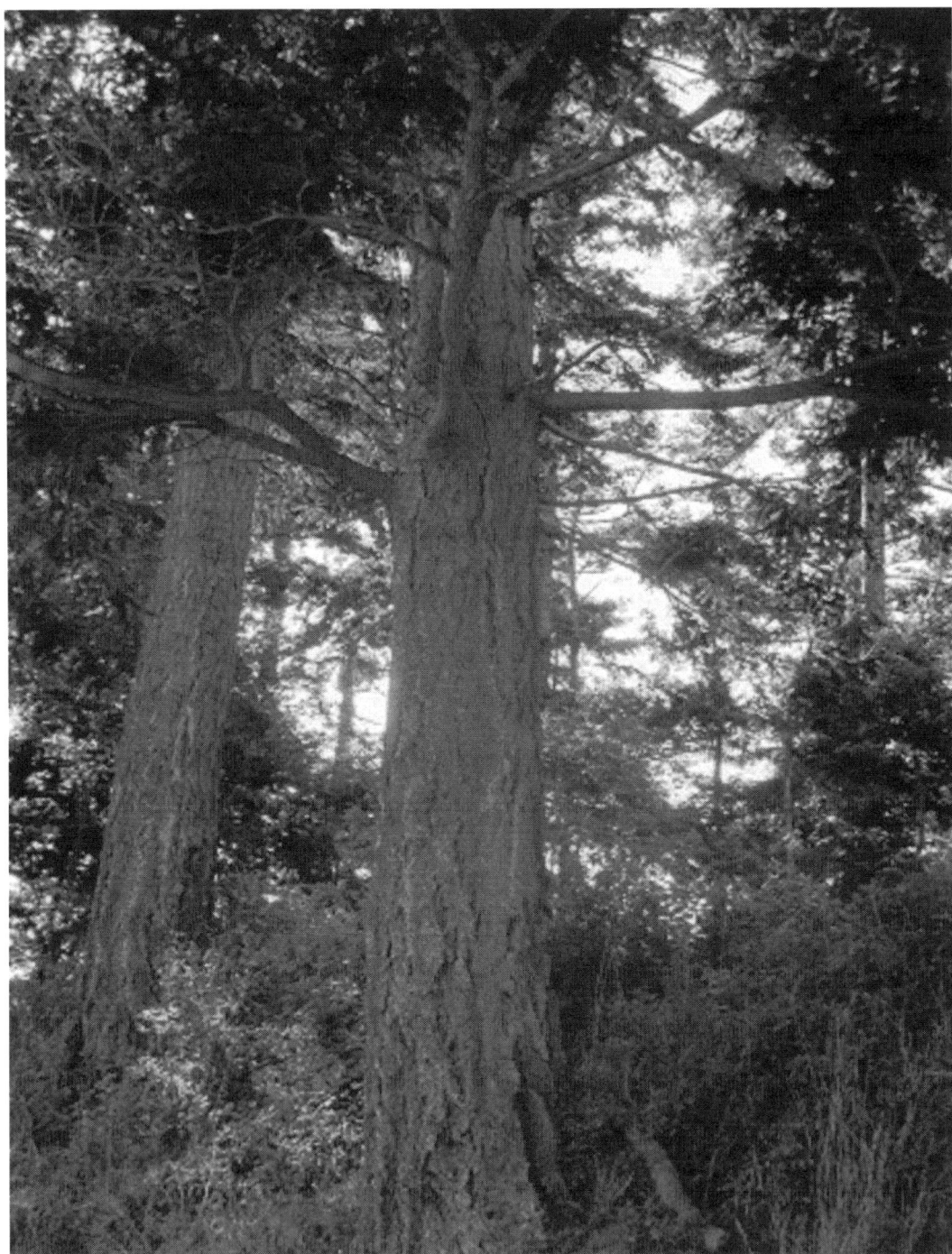

This Is Not My Life

This is not my life
This was not what I sacrificed
Hard times only continue to rise
And here I am broken hearted and lost
This isn't who I am inside

My strength & fate remain strong
I continue to push on
When will I awake?
From this dream gone wrong

This isn't my life
It's not me I see in the mirror before me
This is not my home
This isn't where I am meant to be

Lord help me rise above
Lead me through your love
Help me to the right path
Set me free to complete who you created me to be
This isn't my life
I was created for so much more

I Am My Miracle

I pray for a miracle everyday
Take away all my pain
I seek help
To my surprise
I am told I am the miracle
From a stranger at my side

Inspiration from above
A precious angel on earth
I am my own miracle
I am beginning to see

I am trying so hard to succeed
Just by being me

I pray to have the tools I need
I am told I am the miracle
The tool needed is me

How can this be?
So many praise money
When I just need to breathe
To have peace
And to inspire those around me

I need & plead to have a miracle
When others are looking to me
I am my own miracle
I never give up
I only achieve.

So Much Has Happened

So much has happened
In this year alone
My life is upside down
And only God knows where I am going
It is him I turn to most

So much has happened
I have been good throughout my life
And now I don't know what is longer real
Or who is really good

Life is crazy
Surely didn't see all this coming
So much has happened
I would really run away if I could

No one really understands me
Really knows the girl I am
I push people away
Because it's the only way from getting hurt

So much has happened
I have been there for so many
Now when it comes down to it
No one understands or knows me
I push them away
So I wouldn't get hurt

So much has happened
In this year alone
I must reevaluate
It is much easier to be alone

Disappointment Through Determination

Dear Father in heaven above
Help me through this journey down here
I am exhausted and don't know what to do
All I want is to get through
I know I am strong and true
But I am exhausted
I do need you

Help me through this life with a mission
Keep me inspired to do better
I will not give up
I live for you and that's not just talk

This year has been such a struggle
Every level of my life has fell apart
I continue to push and follow through
Through you is all I wish to get through

Such disappointment through my determination
Don't let me get lost in this mess down here
Please Heavenly Father above
Help me be the woman you see in me

Help me get through the disappointments
Through all my determination

Bumps In The Road

The road lies a path
There may be bumps, hills or even mountains too
But they are small bumps with God

No matter the situations that may arise
There is no hurdle you cannot handle
It may seem to be a burden
But his sacrifice was for you

Stand firm
Carry on
This journey will make you strong
Faith will guide your legs
The bumps in the road
They are not mistakes

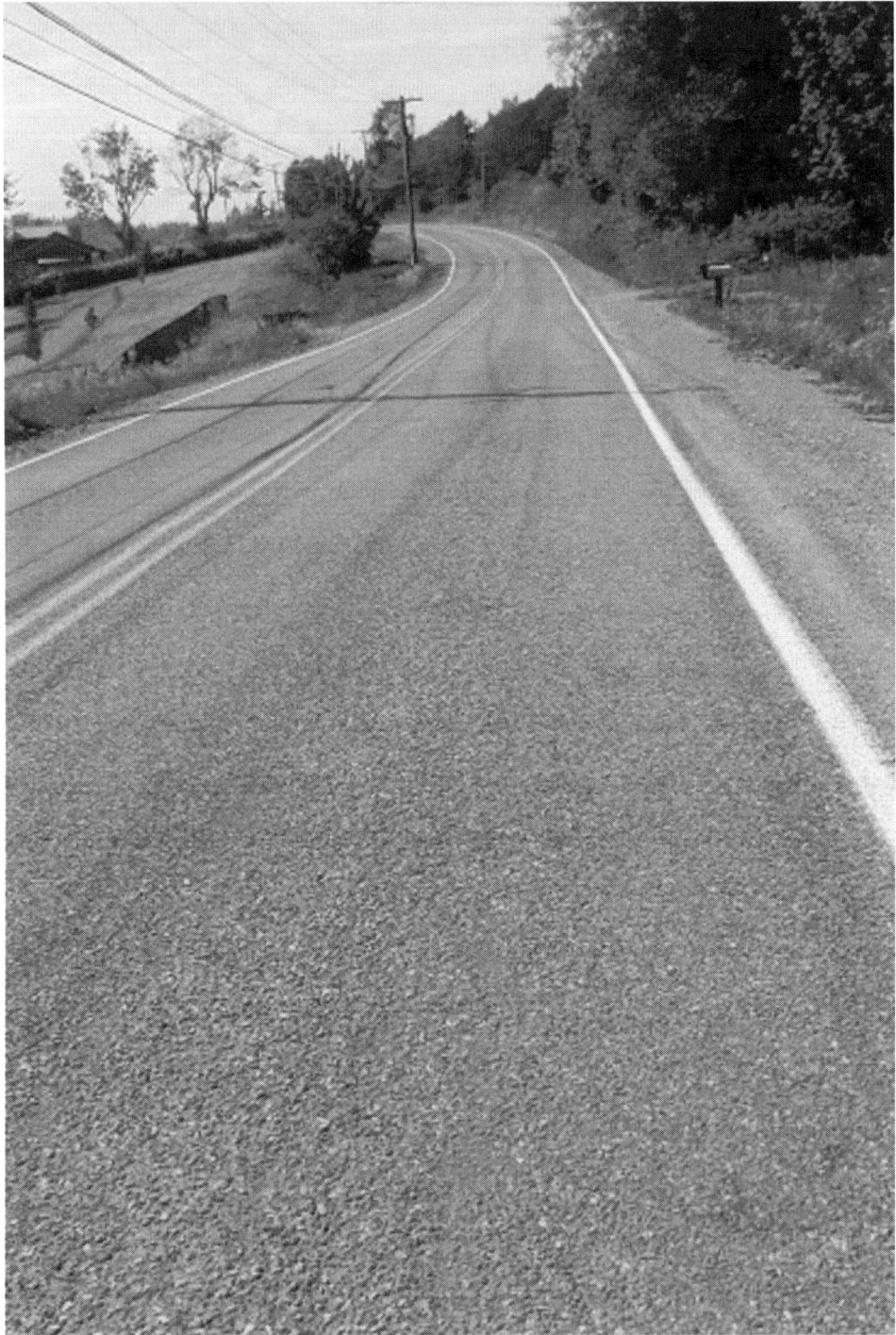

Driving Again

Through accidents
It's been a storm
But I am driving again

I have found a better road
I will be the one driving
The Lord is with me
Guiding me as my co-pilot
The journey isn't over
I am driving again

I won't give up
I may stop for lunch
But I will not give up on the road given
I will be the one in charge
With the Lord holding close
I am driving again

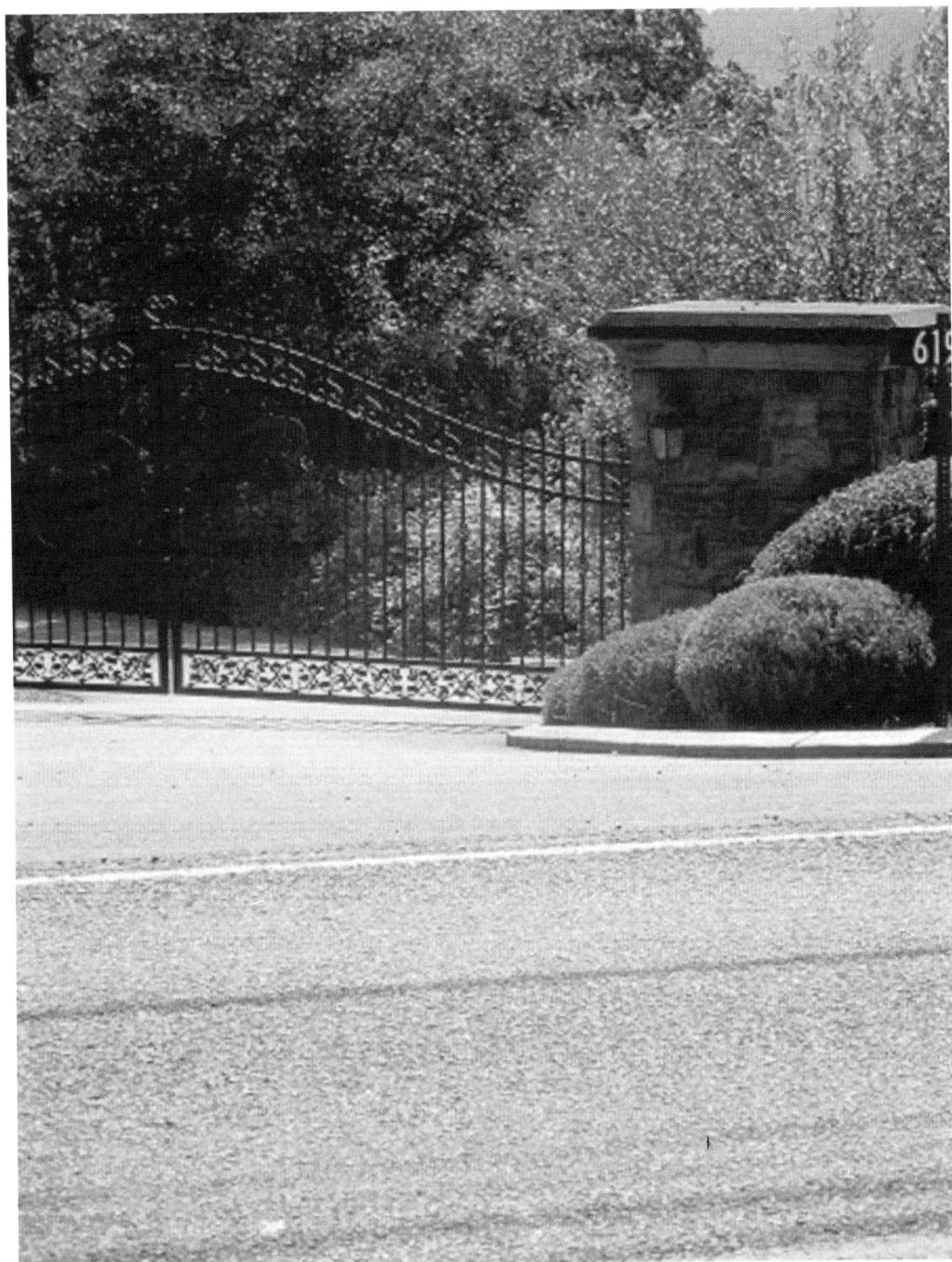

Can't Let Them In

The shower is never hot enough
Never long enough either
I cannot seem to wash this pain away

My pride won't justify
The strength I have had to have to survive

So much more
Then you could know
What my life has had to endure inside

My strength within
Has only been
Not to allow anyone inside

Those who have tried
Never can decide
If they can be strong enough
And usually run away instead

I am strong enough
Have indeed endured more than enough
I just can't let them in
They can never handle what lays within

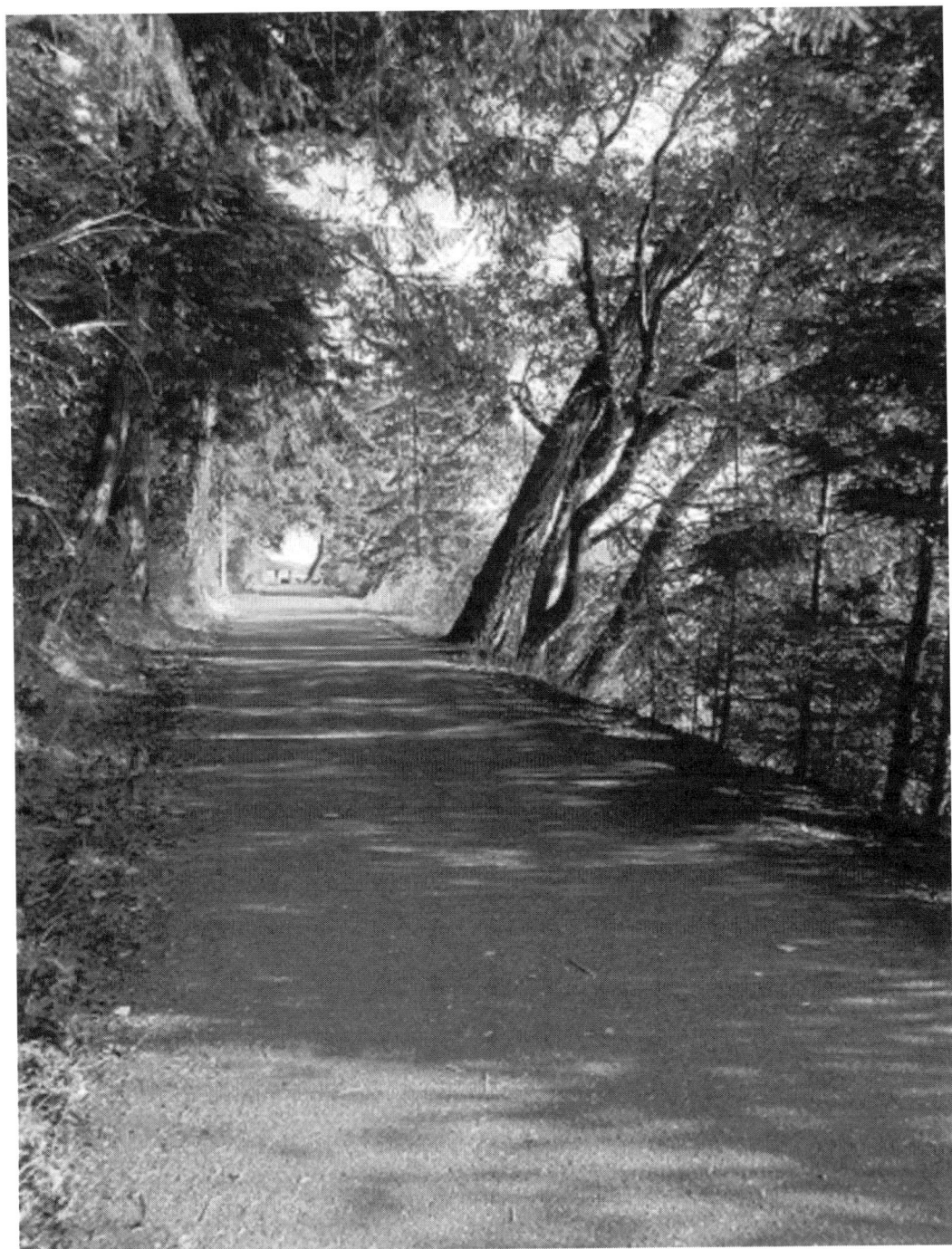

Continue On To You

I am weak
My muscles are frail
I have no control of my body
And I still continue to continue on

I am hurt
My heart is heavy
My emotions won't stop running
And I continue to continue on

I may struggle
I might suffer
But I will continue on to you

My mind is strong
It is mind over matter
I will continue on

I do not know failure
I only know how to continue on
So I continue on to continue onto you

A Tree In The City

Not much room to grow
But the roots run deep
Strong roots can't be ignored
With length that be seen
A tree can't grow free

The city see's green
But not its true beauty
So often people forget
Natures true benefits & beauty

A tree in the city
Should be admired
Not ignored
The strength & courage
Only continue to grow
Doesn't need to be inspired

There is beauty here
Much deeper to be seen
A tree in the city
The roots grow deeper
Then both you and me

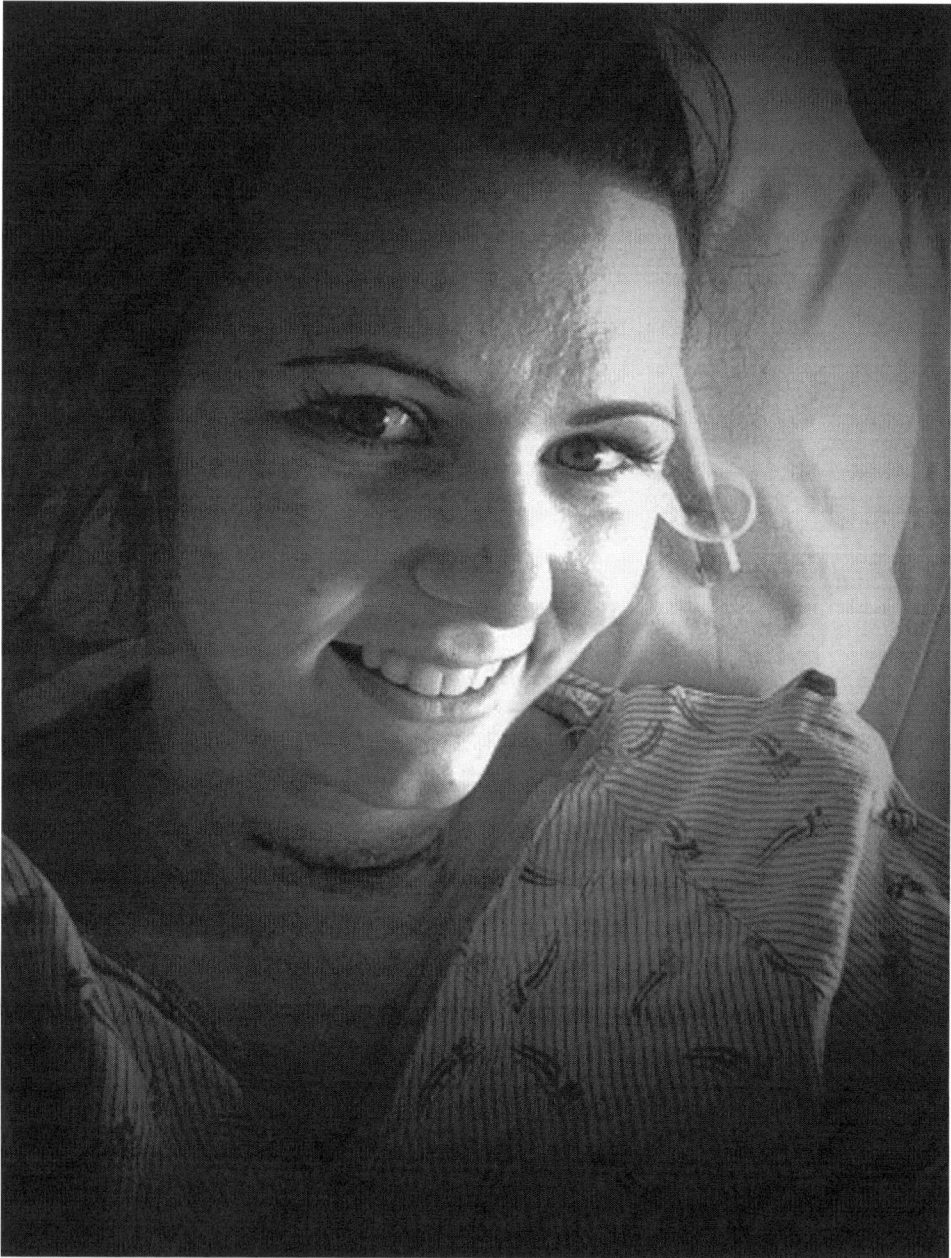

Cancer

A word
A name
That only brings fear
And pain

It has brought me to a new beginning
I am a survivor here
With determination & love
I continue to rise above

A word, a name
Cancer has no shame
Triggering cells
Lives changing everyday

Survivors show no boundaries
Or limits
Cancer has brought me here
A new beginning I will share
I will show no fear
For I am a survivor here

Packing For Tomorrow

So much to do
Never enough time
Time to get packing
The morning will soon arrive

I will be locked up
Don't want to leave anything behind
Trapped in a room
Not looking forward to this week

Time is going by fast
Time to get all packed
Things will soon get on track

Just have to get through this week
Don't want to forget anything
Morning will be here soon
Packing up for tomorrow
Lord help me through

Chemo

A poison in my body
Making me feel nauseous and sick
There is more sickness to this treatment
Then from the cancer in me that exists

The first injection already has me sick
What lies in tomorrow
God only knows what this really is
I pray I don't continue to feel sick

I have watched and witnessed others before me
Now I suppose it is my turn
But I will not allow this cancer to own me
I will own & conquer it instead

This chemo treatment isn't what I wanted
But my thyroid must be depleted
This will be the only treatment
Chemo is a poison I don't turn to
Only God can do miracles
Chemo I don't believe in

Heavy Heart

My heart is heavy & tight
Will this be my last night
Times like this I wonder
It just gets so harder to breathe
Too much stress in me

I need relief
I want my life
I need to be me again
Especially on the inside

Is it stress
Or a heart condition
I am afraid to find out

But my heart once again is heavy & tight
So much pressure on my chest tonight
This is going to be a long night

So hard to breathe
I just pray for relief
I need a light heart
So I can once again breathe easy

Exhausted

So tired
I need to rest
My body is failing
And I am hurting
Can this be the real test?

I am not afraid of dying
I know Heaven is my home
But I have not yet completed my journey
My whole life's test isn't done

There are so many still be saved
To know your forgiveness too
Help me do your work Lord
Before I come home to you

I am strong enough to push forward
Have the love & compassion
That I pray can change the world
In your name of course

I am not afraid to come home Father
But I am not ready to give up yet
You created me to do so much more
I am not done yet

I am exhausted
Very tired
But there is still so much to be done
My journey has only just begun

Depression

Depression has just sank in
My life has become a huge mess
I am upside down
I am lost in this heartache again

When will this pain end?
When will I be able to breathe again?
Nothing is going right
All I do is fight
But it's wearing on me
Life is falling apart around me
And now you tore my heart

Depression is holding me down
I am beginning to drowned
I am praying and begging for help
But no words can be heard or found

I am scared & lost
Life is a mess
My depression will surpass
One day I will live again

One day at a time
I will continue to fight
I will win this war
I continue to live my life

Construction Outside My Room

The busy street down below
So much construction & noise
Won't leave me alone

I wish this was more of a vacation for me
I have more pain than they can see
If only I can get away
But I am in quarantine
So I have to stay

I hoped for a peaceful stay at most
But I am staying in a construction zone

The hospitals always having upgrades & remodeling
While the patients here are suffering

So loud in the city at night
Early morning brings more construction before the light
Not much sleep
All I need is peace
But there is construction outside my room
And nothing I can do
I am in quarantine and nowhere to run to

Too much construction outside my room

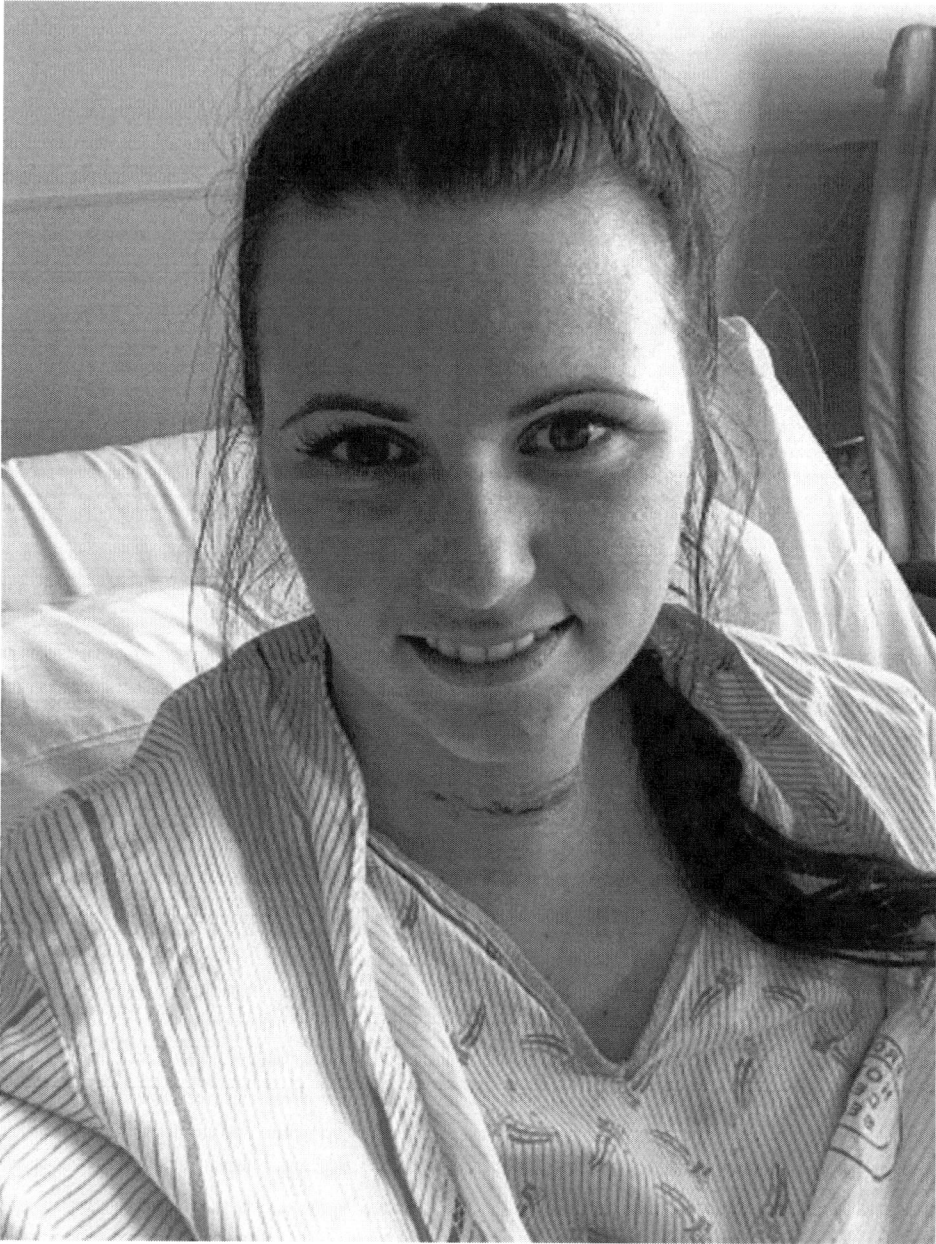

Work Through Me

In the hospital I await
But it does not hold my fate
I have a bigger mission given
For my journey has only just began

Lord work through me
I am strong & true
My faith always will see me through
May this illness have a bigger mission
May I thrive in all conditions

It may not be deserved or easy
But it is another mission I will conquer for you
Your work in me isn't over
I continue to see it through
For my strength in you is so much stronger

Doctors do not hold my fate
My destiny is so much bigger
Lord work through me I pray
I promise to continue to see you through
For there is a bigger mission

Work through me
I pray
I will always see you through

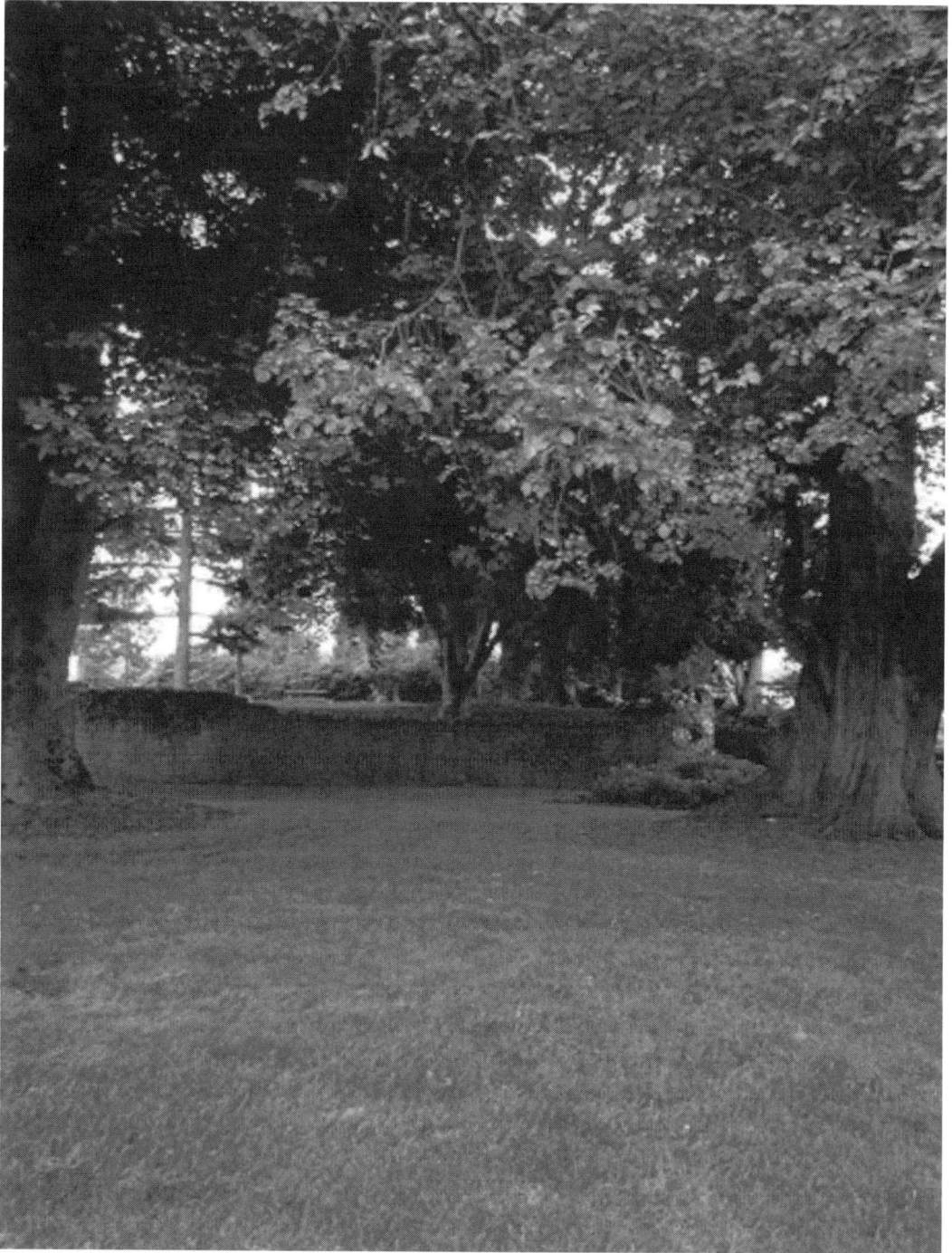

Weak Today

Today I looked around
I was the youngest one found
But that didn't mean much to me
Until I found I was the weakest one moving

My injuries run deep
But you would not know by looking
My pain truly is over bearing

I stopped to rest
To find my strength
This pain is truly overwhelming
But I am here to stay
And I won't allow this pain to own me

I am not done yet
I may be weak at the moment
But tomorrow is a new day

Where Am I

How did I get here
I really do not know
My life now feels broke
So much I have worked for to achieve
But only for everything to become nothing

How did I get here
This isn't my life
I am who I am with pride
But I don't feel like I am truly living my life

How did I get here
I really don't know
I am lost
Where is my home
This is my bed
But this house is not my home

How did I get here
Please Lord help me
My life has more meaning
Help me to conquer my destiny
Bring me home
Where ever home may be

Vacation Needed

I need a vacation
A brake from all this stress
I am beginning to feel lost
My life this year is such a mess

I just need to breathe
I yearn to feel happiness & peace
I must rise above
With the Lord's glorious love
In him, I do truly trust

But I am in need of a vacation
To get away for a moment
For a positive reason
Not another medical situation

I yearn to breathe
I am over this life situation
A real vacation is needed
To relax & breathe
I need to feel peace in me
I need a real vacation

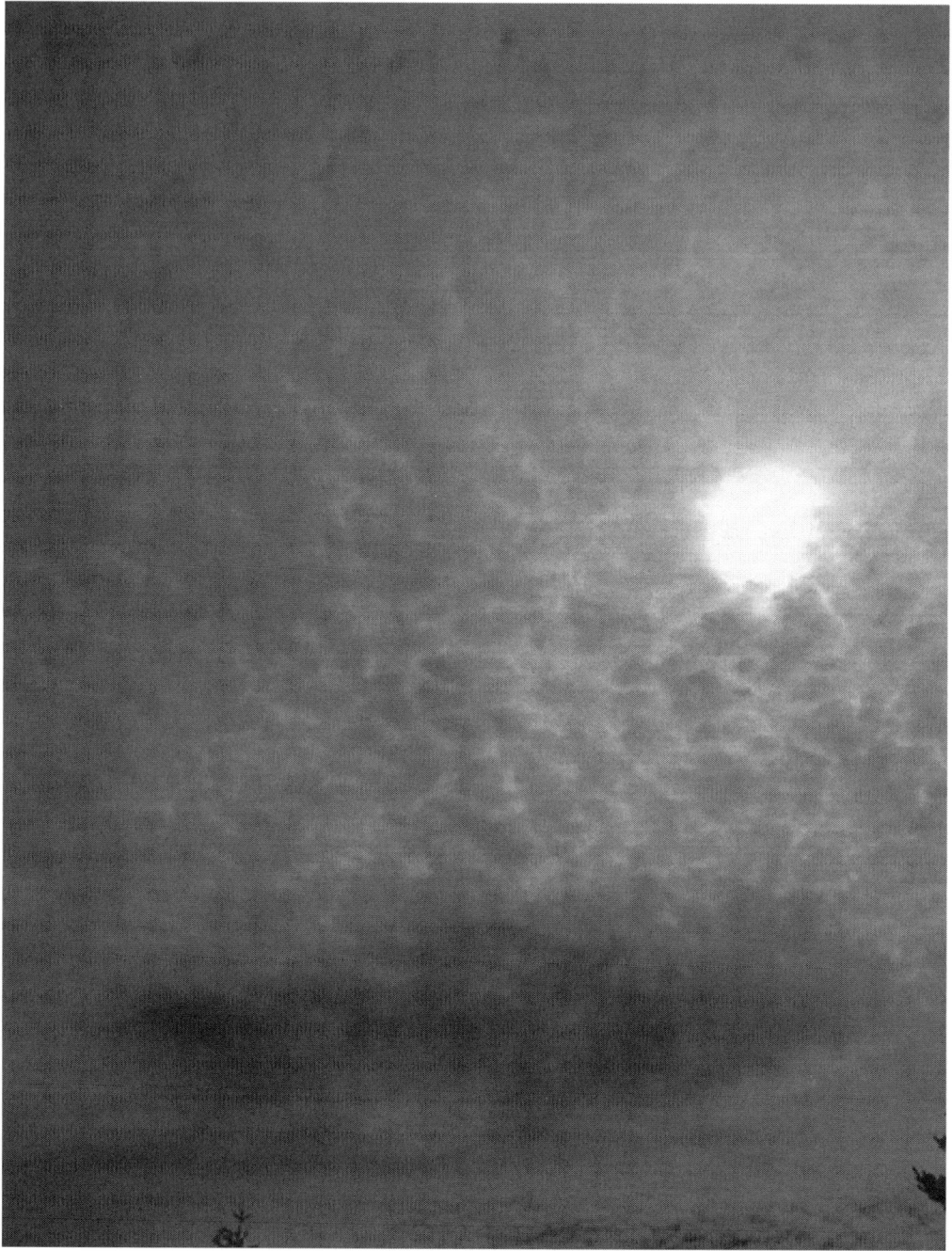

Take Away My Pain

I pray for peace
Please let this pain be set free
I seek to breathe
To find happiness again
To live my life as planned

Lord I pray
Please take my pain away
Help me to breathe again

My muscles are tight
I feel so bruised & weak
Please take this pain away

Shortness of breathe
To tight to breathe
Please Lord I pray for peace
Take away my pain

Survivor Is My Name

Feeling a little sick
Feeling a bit tired
But I can feel
I haven't lost my senses

I may be sore
I may be weak
But I am not broken
I will survive through me

I am in pain
But survivor is my name

I will not give up
I might cry
I may have a bad day
But I will never give up
Survivor is my name

Triumph

I will stay strong
I will survive
Life is full of trials
But I will triumph
God made me strong

Impossible doesn't exist
It is what you believe that will see you through
Faith guides me
Allow it to guide you too

Stay strong
You are not alone
You will triumph
Trials will surely come

But you are to strong
Allow faith to carry you through
God continues to believe in you too

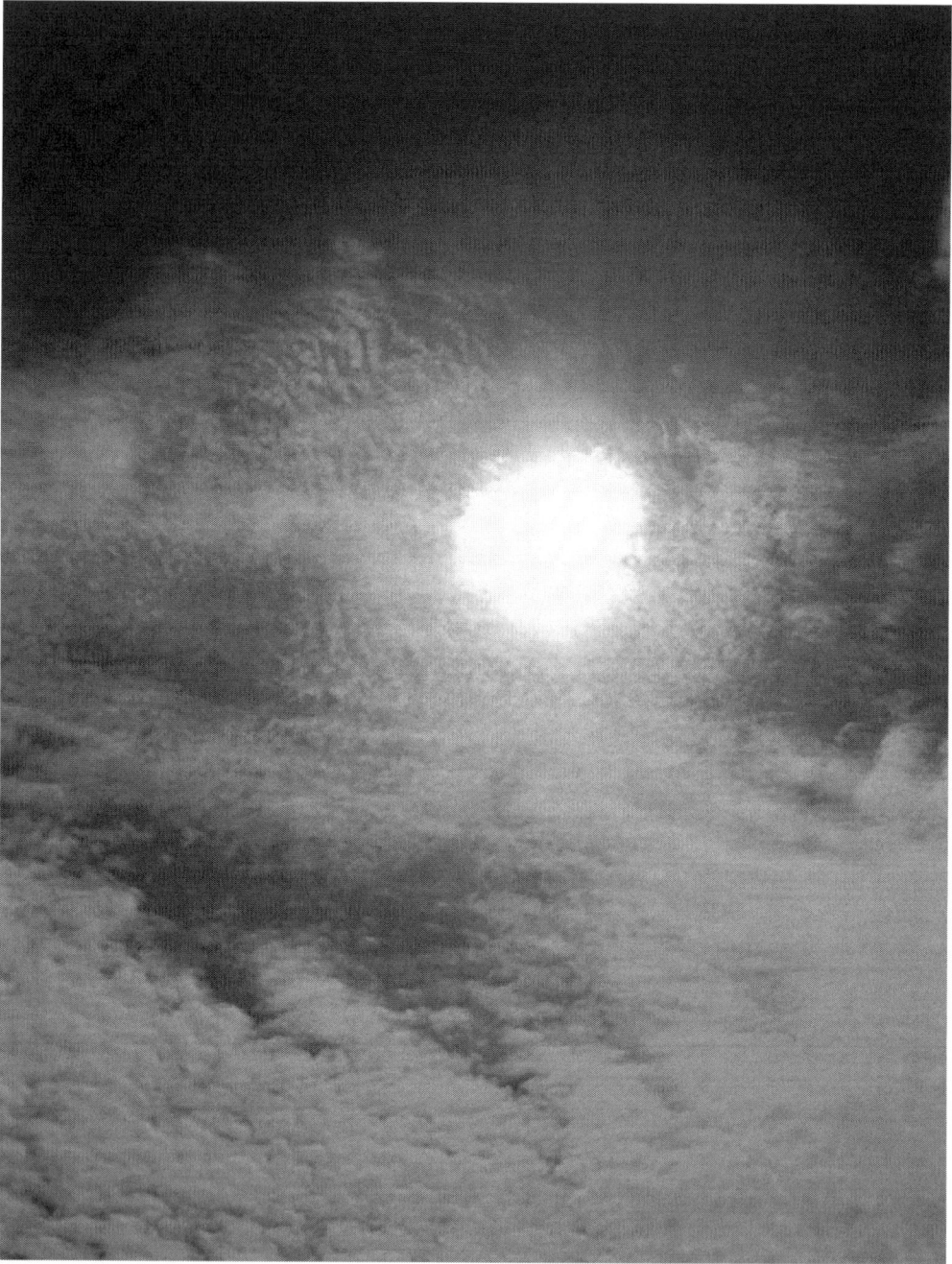

Sun

The warmth of the sun
Golden beauty awaits
I yearn to feel you over me

Blue skies are true
By the light of the sun
Nothing can hide from his light above
Heaven above sees through God's true love

It is peaceful here
Where the sun appears
Another day is a gift from heaven above

Please give me strength down here
Help me rise with the sun
And bring more light to earth from Heaven
Keep me on track
On your journey I ask
Let me rise with the sun
You are my true inspiration

Stay Inside

Drained by this pain
It is taking over my life
When all I want
Is to feel peace inside
To breathe & feel alive

The accidents disarmed me
Powerless inside
My mind & my body
Are at war with my pride

I miss me
Before this pain had arrived
So active & so alive
How I miss the outside

This pain will not win
I will heal & rise again
I despise this pain within
I feel so drained
Ashamed of all of it

The war aside
I will swallow my pride
I have to heal & grow stronger
I must stay & pray inside
For one day
I will conquer and be outside

Sensitive To The Sun

This treatment has made me weak
The strength in me is what I seek
Now I am sensitive to the sun
I miss the warm rays on my skin
But I must now cover up or burn

It is so hot here outside
So I must wait inside and wait
For I am now sensitive to the sun
The treatment has made me weak

Mind over matter
I must wait
I am sensitive now
But it is not my fate to stay this way

My treatment will soon fade
Then I can go outside
I wait to no longer be
Sensitive to the sun

Save Me From Pain

So much pain
I cannot rest
I am now feeling nauseous

Please Lord
Take my pain away
My life is already an upside down mess
What more do I need to confess

I am in pain everyday
My stress will not even go away
I need you here Lord
I need you to stay
I pray you take all of my pain away

Too much pain
But I must rest
Please Heavenly Father,
Save me from this mess

Help Me Father

We all pray for a dream we have
We all wish to win the lotto
We seek miracles to unfold
But want so much more then what is needed

The Lord listens to everyone
And loves us all the same
Luck & fate are hard to determine what's true

We all have a purpose
With opportunities
And possibilities too

Don't be upset when you don't get what you ask for
When it is meant to be
It will happen for you

He walks beside us each and everyday
Watches over as we sleep
And listens to each of us pray

I pray for a better life
To have a home
And peace to breathe
Everyday

I seek my Heavenly Father above
To help me rise above
With the tools I eagerly need
Today I truly seek my miracle
Help me Father I pray

Radiation

Poison radiates through me
So sick & weak
As this radiation penetrates through me

Too hard to concentrate
And nothing tastes the same
What in doses can create
The illness I face
High doses with radiation can erase

This journey has arrived
But is not my fate
I will defeat
This illness inside me

This is not an escape
A treatment created
In quarantine I must be
But in a few days
I will arise
And defeat will be mine

Research & Science

Another doctor, another visit
Another test & journey to be had

So much technology
So much science
To prove what's truth
But I continue to have more faith in you

Another trial, another lesson
They never know what they can be missing
Still I believe in a deeper mission
For I continue to have more faith in you

There is still so much science that can't be proven
So much research to prove miracles are real
So I continue to have more faith
In my Father in heaven
For he is the only one proven to be real to me

Another doctor, another visit
Only to have more tests to be given
Answers in science and research
Never are find the truth for everyone

Science and research only prove one to be real in this world
For my Heavenly Father is real
As real as the miracles given down here

Not Disabled

The illness I have is not a disability
Nor the accidents have done to be
My heart has endured so much more
Then my body ever could

I am not disabled
I continue to live my life
And strive to be better
I know I deserve much more in this life

I am not a victim
This life doesn't own me
It never could
Life will not disable me

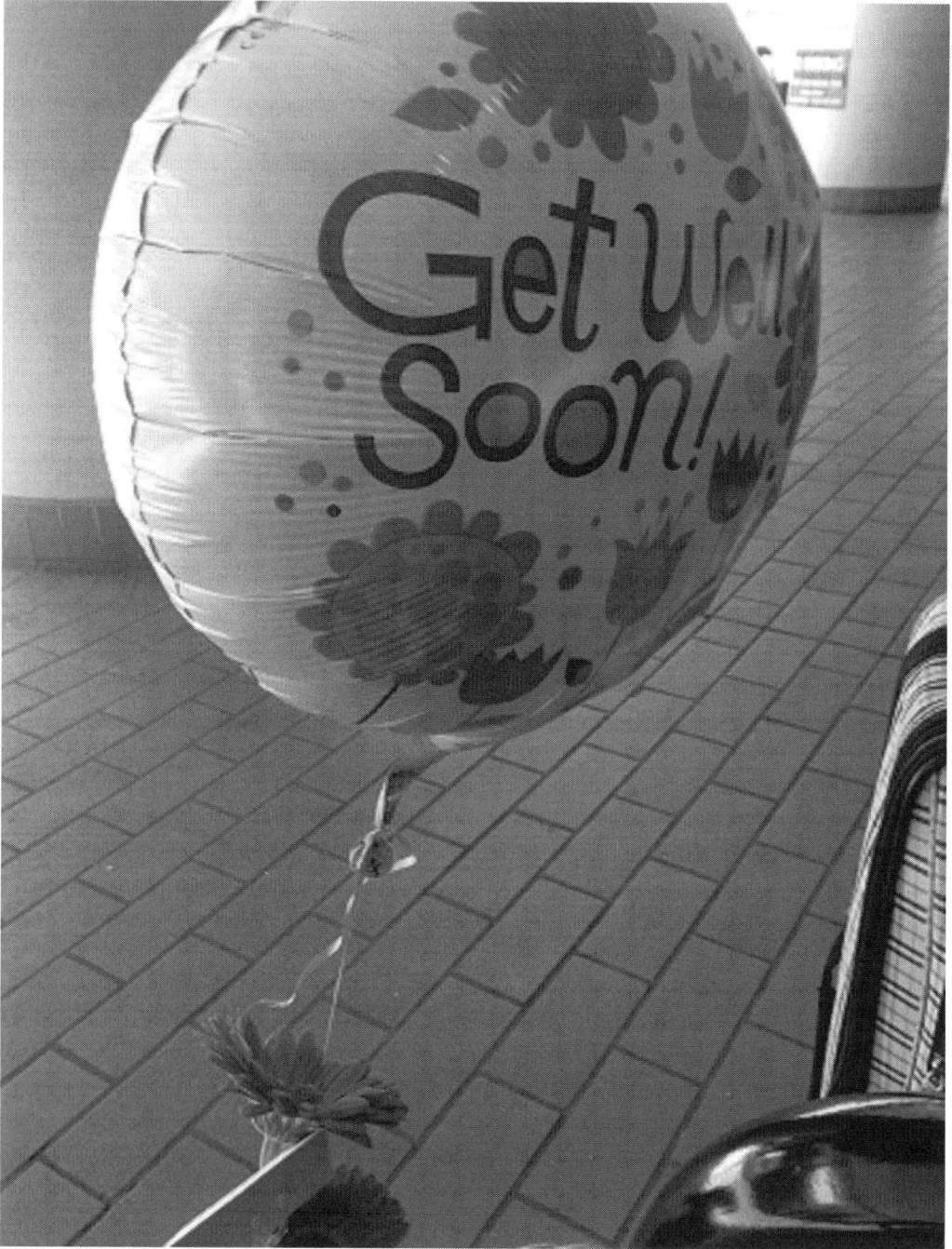

No Victim Here

A smile is all you see
But there is so much that has happened to me
I am not a victim
I know my path
Shit happens
I only know how to move past

Life is what we create it to be
Hard times may come
It is what creates us on our journey

Rise above
And know God's great love
You are never alone
He can carry you to rise above

Never lose faith
Don't betray yourself
You are stronger then you know
Never play the victim
Always rise above

I'm Drowning

Sinking fast
Can't swim
I am drowning
Do not know if I will see the shore in this life again

Life has a crazy way of taking you in directions
But the water is flowing every which way
The waves are getting fierce
And I can't swim today

It seems easier to give up today and go under
It is too hard to breathe where the waves are taking me
I am sinking below
An anchor taking me to the Lord

I don't know where I am going
I can't swim or even paddle in this storm
I am drowning today
It's more peaceful to sink with the anchor in this storm
Then fight my way through the waves
Unsure where they may go

So I sink down today
Drowning in the chaos & heartache
It is the Lord I anchor to
He will bring me to shore tomorrow for a better day
He is all that's true

Lost In Today

Another day
Always have so much to say
But today
I don't feel it no longer matters
I have so little to say

So lost & tired
I just want to escape
I just need a break

There has been so much I have been through
Maybe all I need is to sleep
My body needs the rest
And I need peace

Another day
I don't know what to say
I haven't lost my way
I just need to get away

I am just lost in today
I do still know my way
My faith is still strong
I just need rest so I can carry on

Migraines

Another migraine
When will these headaches be done?
My head is ponding
It is hard to move on

When will this pain fade away?
When will these migraines leave to stay?
Hurts to think
And live each day
Let me sleep I pray

Sadly another migraine to stay
It won't seem to leave me in peace today
Please leave me migraine
You aren't welcome to stay
Dear Lord, take my headaches away.

It Could Be Worse

Just when you think you are in pain
When you believe you are being tested
It could always be worse
Things can always continue to happen

There are miracles that happen
Pain can help you gain more in yourself
Power through
Don't give up
It could always be much worse

So keep your head up
With faith you can achieve
A miracle can come through struggle
Stay strong and believe

To know love
You must also know heartbreak
Push forward
Keep the faith

Just believe and stay strong
It will get better
You will carry on
Just remember and beware
Things can always get worse

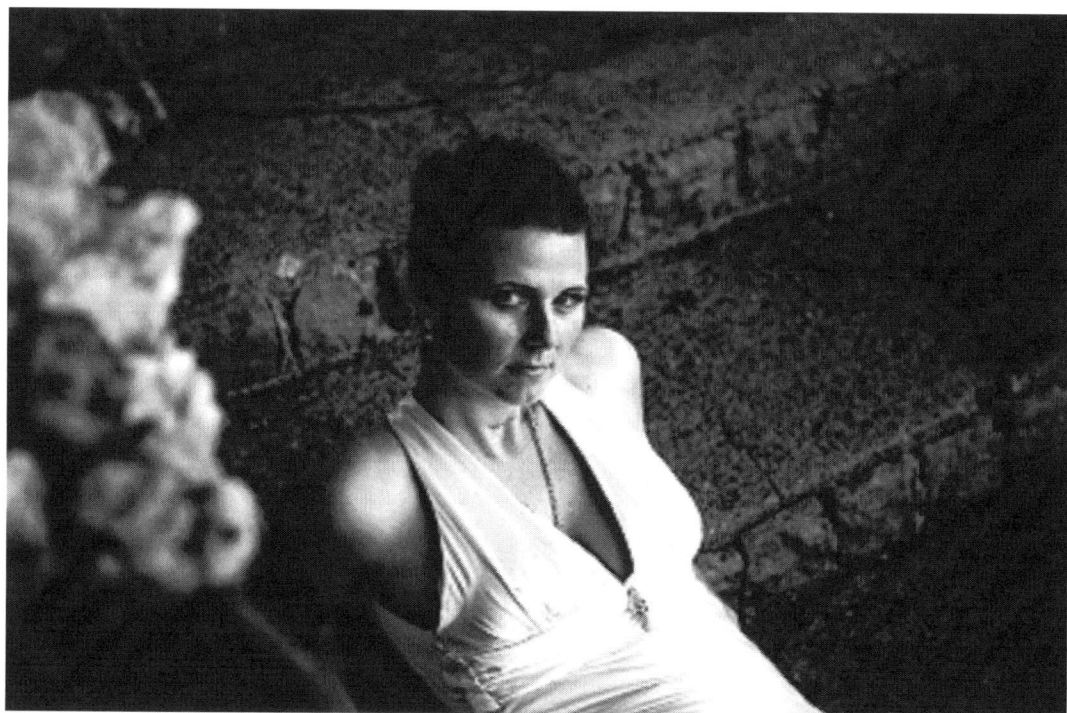

Motions To Emotions

I am living my life
Trying to do what is right
Going through the motions
To get where I am mean to be
But the emotions are getting the best of me

I am all in
Running to the light
This is how I feel each day & night

The motions are creating emotions in me
The emotions I can't escape
Motions continue to take to get free

Save me Lord
Save me from myself
Save me from the hurt
Get me through the motions and emotions
Lead me to where I am going
I need to get through
Lord, I need you

I live my life
Trying to live it right
Going through the motion
But the emotions from the motions linger on to me here

I will get where I am going
God will help me through
Let me arrive and arise
Don't let the emotions from the motions get to you

Need You Now

Do you know my pain?
Can you see my sorrows?
Did you know my heart is breaking?

Every day is set to be a new beginning
But my pain controls me today
And my cancer has arrived
However, my heartbreak is more painful inside

I scream
But no one hears me
I cry
But there is too much pain inside

God help me through this storm
My life is upside down
I only have you to turn to
No one else knows who I really am inside

Jesus I need your healing
Please heal my broken heart
Relieve me from all the pain
I continue to feel inside

I need you now
My strength is now my weakness
I need you now
Only you know the pain I face and feel inside

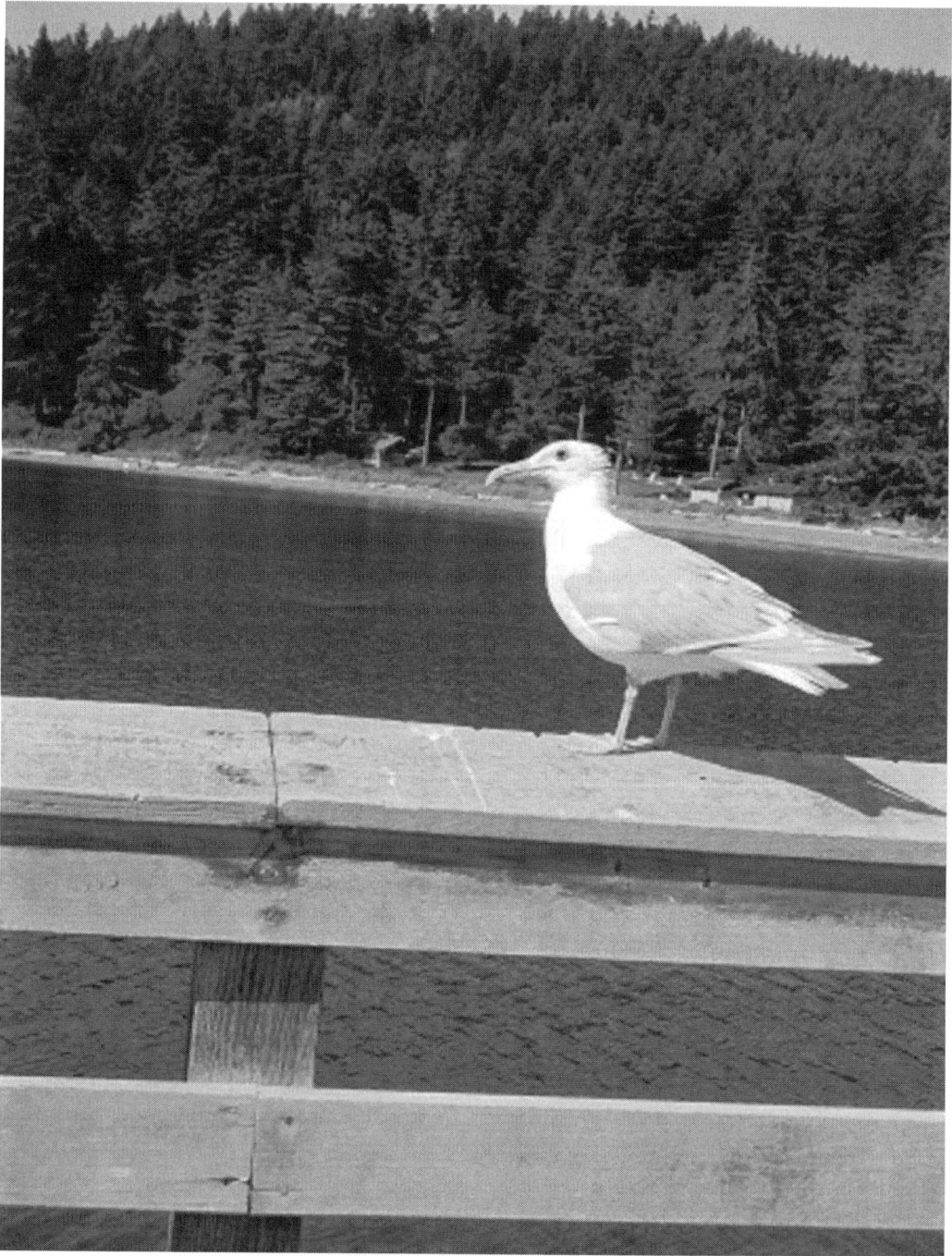

Risen By Faith

Risen for another day
My heart will never stray
It is my fate to be here
And all that I must endure

Faith anchors me to my path
Keeping me strong & firm
My feet are plated heavy
I know I must continue on

Don't look back
Just push forward
There is much to be seen
In my future
On my path the Lord has led me

It may be dark
But I see the light
I will not stray
I continue to pray & fight
It is my fate to be here today

I Look To You Lord

Lord I am so lost and confused
What is it that you seek me to do
I have been honest and true
Stuck by rules to do good
Better than most
What is it that you seek me to do?

Lord I am so worried and lost
For all that I have accomplished is gone
My life once again upside down
Where is it I am meant to be?

Lord
I do love you and I am trying
But everything is unraveling
I am lost, confused and worried too
Will you soon find me and help me through

My Lord, in heaven above
You are true unconditional love
A Father to all of us
Please show me the path to your righteousness
It is only to you I pray
Each and every day
To strive and thrive above
To know and continue on the right path
Please help me through
For my life I live for myself, family & you.

Faith Above All Else

So much responsibility
So many people looking to me
Always holding myself together
Sometimes I have to fake peace

My life is a wonder
Especially to me
I continue to fight
On this never ending journey

Things can always become worse
There aren't many surprises to me
I focus on the goals I can
And surrender what I can't

I don't know what my journey hold
What is seen in me?
I just carry on & push forward
With the Lord faithfully

Bring It On

Whatever comes up with the sun
Bring it on
I am ready to defeat
Whatever storms may come at my feet

What darkness may arise
With my faith
So will I
Bring it on

I will conquer & be done
I will always rise above
So bring it on

Strength, courage & wisdom
Love, faith & determination
I will not fall
I do not know defeat

So bring it on
I will prove you to be weak

Pieces Of Me
By Julia Anne Simpson

Chapter 5
My Family

Cherish

Every moment, every truth
Every blessing
Cherish!
Every smile, every heartbeat
Every breathe must be cherished

Cherish those you love
Cherish those you inspire
Cherish your relationship with God

For you are cherished
You are loved
And you are created to inspire
Cherish & believe in you
Cherish & believe in love
Cherish you past & your destiny path

Cherish.
For I cherish you and God

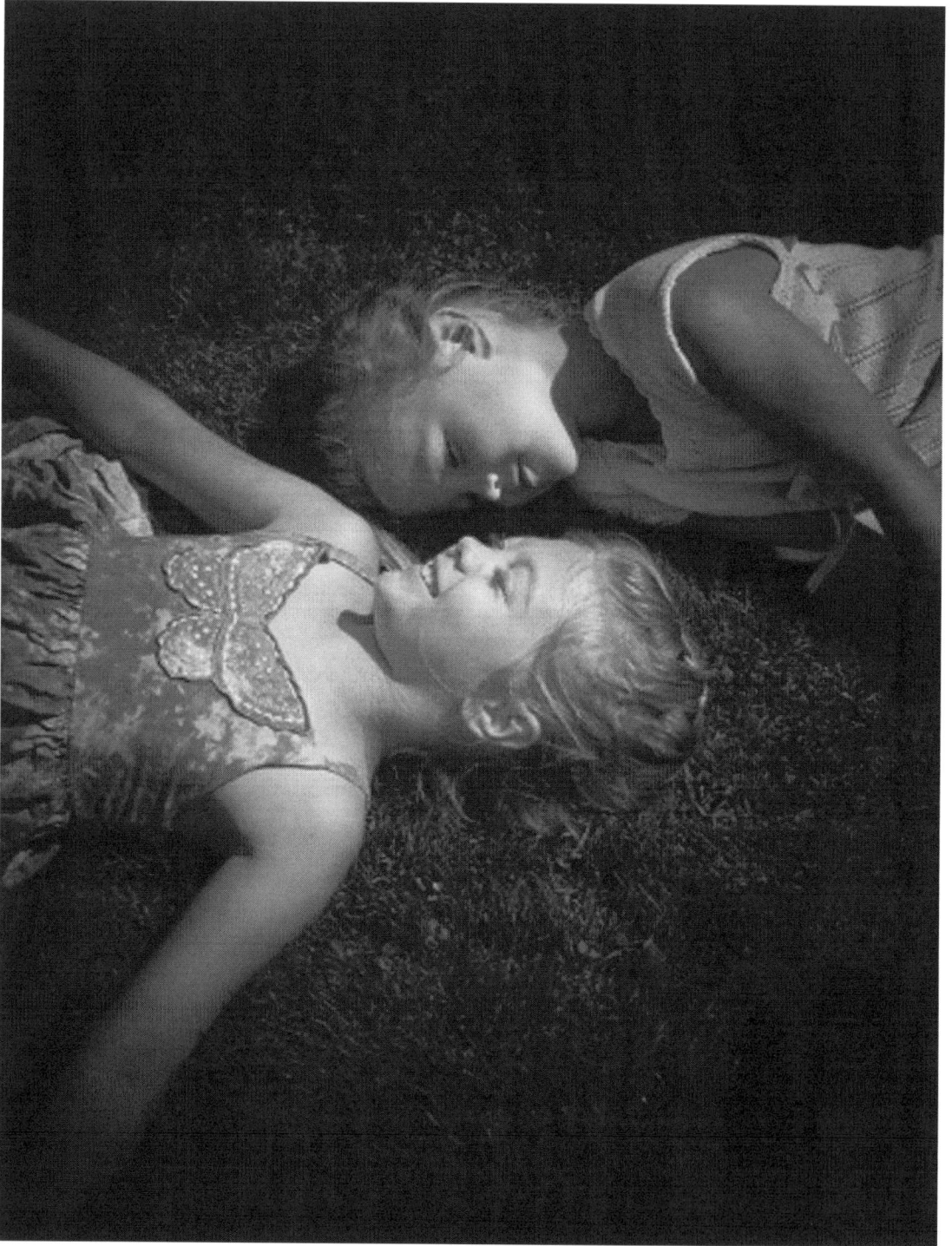

Precious Moments

Angelic smiles
Little hands & little feet
My favorite precious moments

Little giggles & laughter of joy
The innocence of a child
Perfect precious moments

Butterfly kisses
Gifts from above
Are precious moments I love

Grandma & Grandpa
Walking hand in hand
Unconditional & devotional love
There are precious moments all around us

Sincerity, loyalty, faithfully
Live in our precious moments
They are truly gifts from above

Princess Peyton

My first niece is a gem
Always been a princess
Even before she took her first breathe

So much talent to be seen
A pure heart she has
So sensitive & so much compassion

My Princess Peyton
Your auntie truly does love you
You make me so proud just by knowing you

May you only receive all that's good
Keep your innocence
I wish you could just stay a kid too

I know you are growing
So healthy & a beauty
So smart & talented
I am so proud to be your aunt
For when you smile melts my heart

You were a princess before you took your first breathe
Princess Peyton
Your auntie loves you dearly

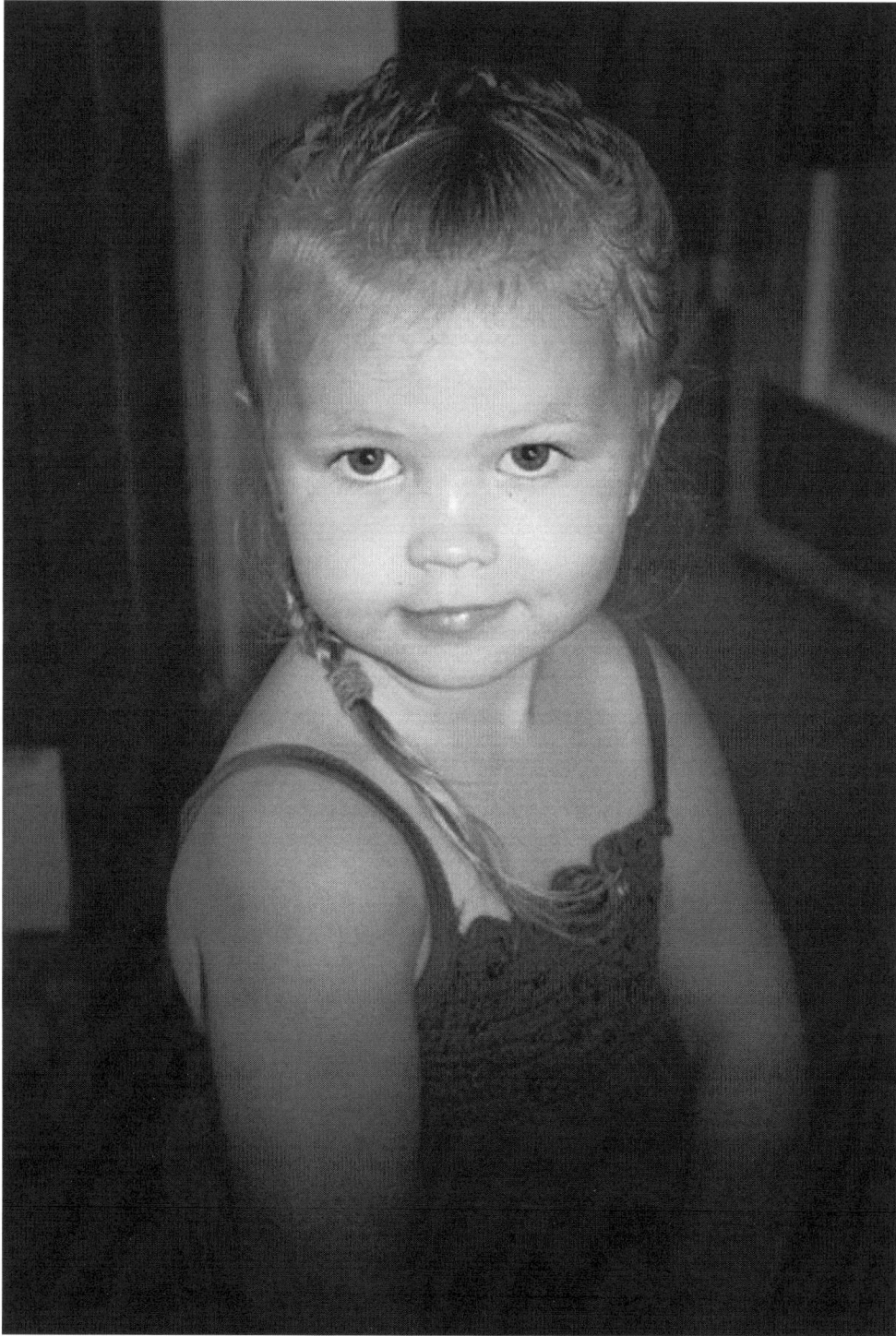

Princess Jordyn

Another princess
Such a doll
Her name is Jordyn
Her looks could fool you all

Another princess to make an auntie proud
So competitive and outgoing
Such a monkey like her dad
Doesn't scare easy
She is definitely a Simpson
With a doll face
She is a princess too

So cuddly and sweet
So smart & talented too
This aunt was blessed to know you

As soon as you were born
I saw the Simpson in you
Such a doll face to see
But that is only skin deep

Princess Jordyn
You auntie loves & adores you too
I am a proud aunt
You really do melt my heart too

Summer With My Nieces

Splish splashing
Summer time is here
The giggles & excitement
My nieces are so pure & dear

The beauty of their innocence
With personalities so overwhelming
They always make me happy
Always smiling when they are near

Splish splash
A new swimming pool to tare
Watching them run & play
Jumping & swimming away
Their sweet giggles only bring smiles

Beautiful, smart & fun
Their innocence I pray never fade
I wish they could only stay

Grandma Rosalie

So many memories
Of my grandma I have
With musicals and Sheryl Temple
She always encourages me still
In everything I am
And all of my gifts
A princess in her heart
I am blessed to have her still

We would garden and shop
Our time together I always hold dear
She always aspires me to be myself

She has always believed and cherished me
Let me sing & dance
To achieve all great things
To be the girl and woman I was created to be
I cherish my grandma
And all our time spent

Every memory is still the relationship we have
For I truly love my Grandma Rosalie
And all she has been for me and so much more

Love For My Mom

My mom is true indeed
I am so proud to call her my mommy
With a huge heart for everyone
And a faithful connection

She is a woman to adore
And I truly adore her
My mother so hard working & proud
She conquers through the Lord
With a faithful heart is always pure
She always does all she could

She believes with strong faith
And keeps true to her beliefs
I am so proud of my mommy
And the woman she has guided me to be

My mom so strong
She has conquered so much
Such a relief she is still here
I love my mommy so very dear
I am proud to still have her here

A Miracle In My Mom

Life has been so crazy
Illness has taken too many
I praise God to still have my mom
And praying to keep her cancer gone

My mom has endured so much
So much illness & treatment given
Her life has been a miracle from heaven

Life has been so crazy
For all the suffering I have seen
My mom has been such a blessing
She is still the amazing woman I have always seen

So hardworking
So loving
So faithful & true
I have been blessed with such amazing mother as you

My mom has endured so much
So much we have suffered through
She has recovered with the Lord
Through love and faithful faith in God

She has fought & endured so much
Throughout life she has continued
For family and faith in God

Such a miracle is my mommy
So blessed to still have her here with me

Daddy's Girl

The moment my mom was pregnant
I was a daddy's girl then
He wished & ordered me
So here is where I was sent

Through heart aches
I am still my daddy's girl
Arguments really don't mean nothing
Disagreements and disappointments
Through life
Through faith
There is always a daddy's girl in me

Pretzel faces
Building doll houses
Rocket building & restoring a car

We will always hold a special bond
I will always be my Daddy's girl

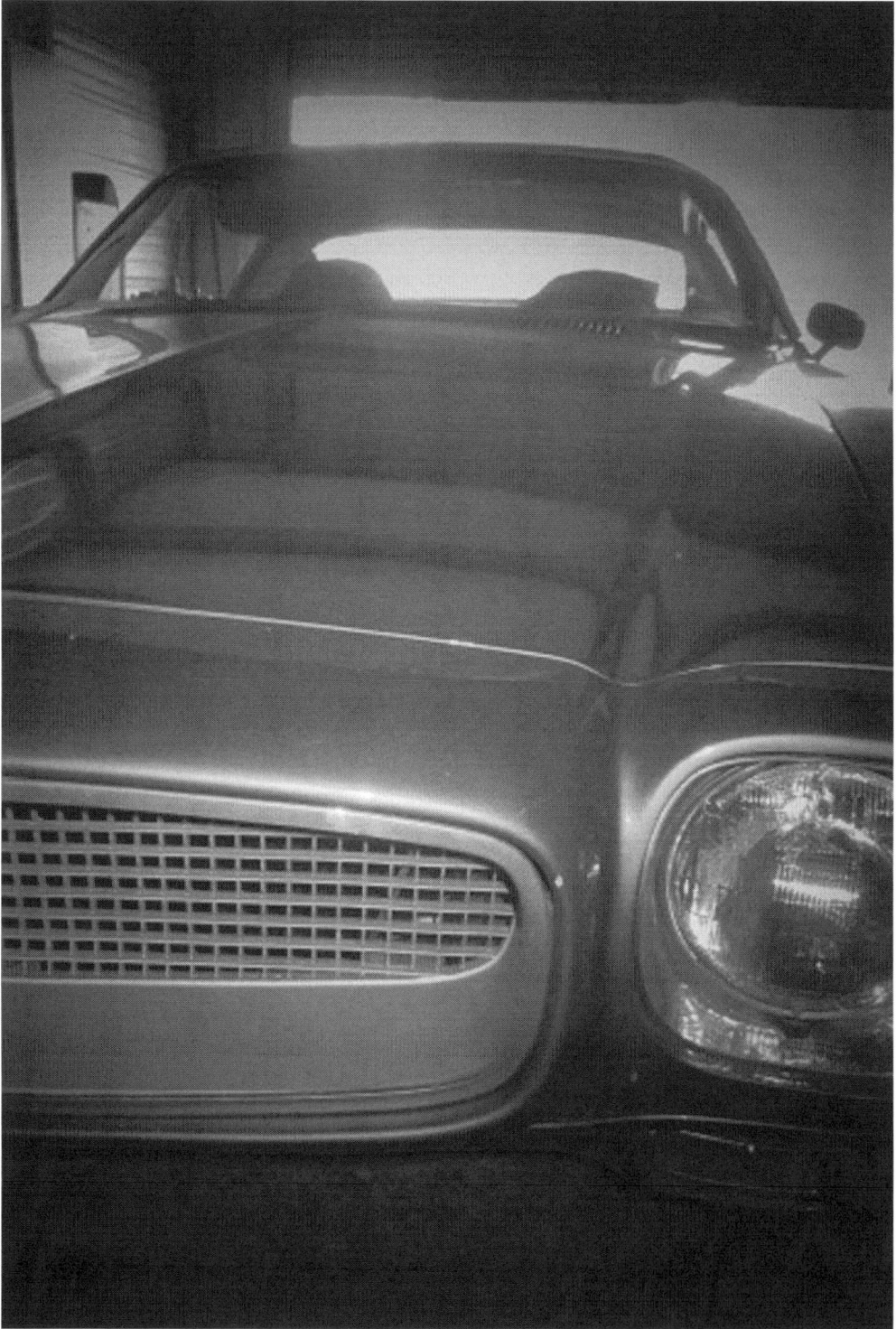

JulesBird

A '71 Pontiac Firebird
Restored with my daddy & brother
Sparkling blue
I do cherish you
Such a beauty
You will always be Jules Bird to me

So much time spend
So much I had learned
About my dad
And Pontiac Firebirds

Loving every moment
More than just my first car
A bond deeper than steel
A classic & beauty
Jules Bird is something I continue to share with my daddy

My Big Brother

Having a big brother
Taught me to stand up
But in times I felt lost
Had my back at no cost
He helped me to escape
And look up

To my surprise
He knew me better than most
Grateful for his love and support

He never pushed and pulled
Only let me do what I could
But always had my back
He always believes in all I could

No worries I would fall
He would step aside with pride
He saw my strength before anyone else could let me rise

I realize it now
My big brother has always been a guardian
He has always watched over my shoulder
Always believing and caring as he could

Middle Siblings

Jessie
So complicated to know
My middle brother
With a big heart locked up inside

He can't tell his sister he loves her
Picks on her still
Always wanting to fight like kids

Only wish he could be all I see in him
To believe and care
It is peace and happiness I wish for him still

Even though all is does is wish to annoy me
So rude to me he can be
But he is my middle brother
And I really do love him dearly

Patrick

My baby brother
How precious he is to me
So much laughter he brings

I have always been overly protective
He is still a baby to me
But he outgrew me
And is now super overly protective of me

He is crazy
But is genuine
With a huge heart to be seen

I am proud that he is still that fun kid
Through everything he has been through & seen
He is still that comedian
He brings joy to everything

Ali I Love you

My cousin & sister
So much more I have seen in you
So much drive & determination
I am so very proud of you

Life has never been easy
But you have never been weak
There is definitely no weak in this family
I am so very proud of you always

The girl you have always been
My cousin
My sister
My friend

I always hold you so close & dear
Always looked to you as my little sister
Always so proud of the girl & woman you are

Such a huge heart
Such a blessing you have always been
So inspiring to watch
But more fun to be around
Ali, I love you so much

So proud of you I am
We don't believe in victims
Only strive to achieve
To prove all things

No words can hold true
To the bond of me and you

My cousin
My sister
My friend
Always my companion
There is nothing we can't win
Always remember, you are awesome!

To My Sister

My best friend
My sister
My other half
My soul mate

Together we can be trouble
Ready to conquer the world together
You complete me as a whole
Understands my soul
You are my best friend

My best friend
And sister to the end
A partner in crime
Only others try to find
A bond so strong and close

You are my sister
My bestie for life!

Grandma

My grandma
Another faithful angel looking down from above
Your strength & love for our Heavenly Father
You were an amazing woman of God

Your faith a true testimony of love
Your guidance & wisdom was inspiring to watch
To know what God's love truly was

My grandma truly amazed me
The amazing woman of God she was
Her faithful love & compassion
The intelligence & integrity she shared

You are a woman I continue to be proud of
Another faithful angel looking down from above

Fading Memories

Fading memories
I don't want to lose
Fading fast
Time won't last
Pictures of you is all I have

Memories of music
Long conversations were blessed
Having a grandma so pure
Your love is overwhelming
The passion & talent
You allowed me to be free
To play a deeper melody

Fading memories
They are all we have
You believe in me
And I know that is not all in the past

I will sing again
I will live true
With faith & talent
As you showed me to do

My Cousin, My Brother

My cousin, my brother
I miss you
So young, so smart & such humor
I have always admired you

I prey & think of you often
I once prayed in plea
I rather Jesus to take me
So often wondered what happened
And you have never left me

You are still here beside me
Now you do not suffer
Your suffering was killing me
To watch what you had to burden
It really did scare me

But your love & strength through God
Lifted you up to conquer your wings
I do miss you
My cousin, my brother
Another amazing angel god has above

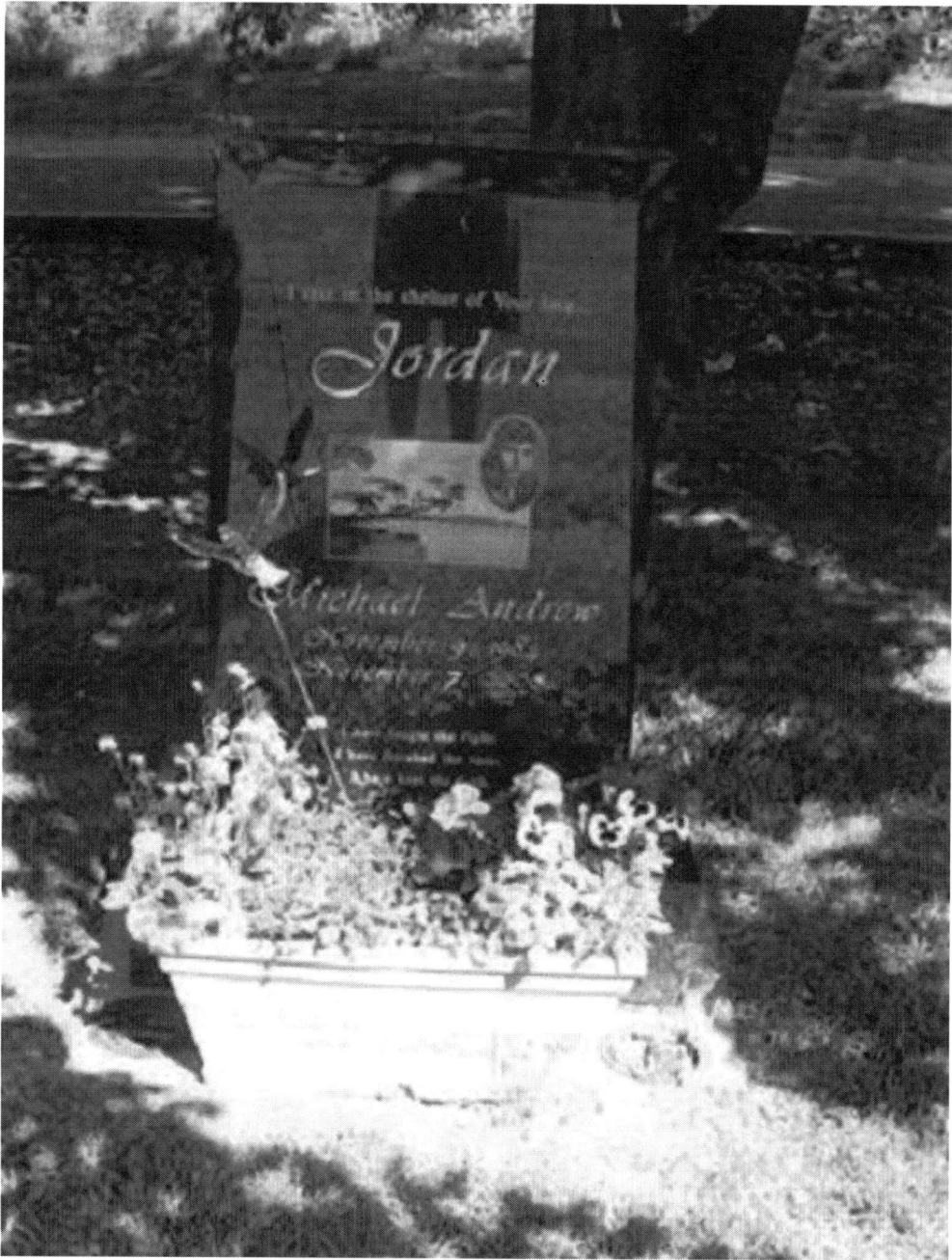

Michael's Place

You left so much more than a marker
So much more than another chapter
Your story grows deep within
Just another faithful journey you lived

You fought the greatest fight
You endured so much suffering
Your laughter so inspiring

Your faith so pure & true
For God had lived through you

You left so much more than a marker
So much more than another chapter
Your courage & faith
Proved God's beauty & grace
For he lifted you up
To a better place above

Your journey still runs through
You left so much more through your journey
For you have a deeper story
This is your place
But I always remember you

Pictures & Memories

Pictures & memories
Are all I have to remember
You are not here
But I hold you still in my heart

You weren't just my cousin
But my brother also
I pray for you still today
I praise God he saved you from all the pain

You live within me
But all I have to see is pictures
Memories lay within
I know I will see you again

Being sad is selfish I know
But you are my brother
My cousin
And I miss you so

Memories I hold deep & dear
Pictures may fade
But you are captured in my head
And my heart as well
Pictures & memories is all I have
You are missed
But I will see you again I know

Take Me With You

Do not leave me here heart broken
Hurt by all your pain
Take me with you
I want to see you play

Life can be unfair
Suffering has brought much pain
I still cry & pray for you today

We were so close
So young
And still I prayed to take your place
You had more faith
And talent to stay

A doctor you would be
A comedian at heart
I miss you everyday
You stayed here in my heart

Someday you will take me home
Home above with you to stay

No Suffering In Heaven

I sit here at your resting place
I miss you both so dearly

I know you see me from Heaven above
And know how I am truly feeling
But I know there is no suffering there in heaven

Selfishness could keep you here
But you are peace up there in heaven

It is so peaceful here
Sitting here are your resting place
You will stay in my heart always

Selfish me wants to come home to heaven
But I still have a bigger mission
Someday I will hold your hands in heaven
Then you can tell me everything that has happened

For now I know there is no suffering in heaven
I sit here at your resting place at peace
Knowing you are my angels in heaven above
And that you aren't suffering
But are truly loved

I miss you here
But I know in my heart
You are at peace and are happy
For there is no suffering there in heaven

My Perfect Angel

My perfect angel
True unconditional love
You were the perfect gift from above

To carry you
To have held you
Sarah Anne I do miss you
You are my perfect angel above

Time is never long enough
But knowing you don't suffer
And you are playing above
Proves you are a miracle
True unconditional love

The loss of my daughter
One cannot carry
But knowing my angel
You shall not worry

Some children are too perfect
Too pure to endure life down here
She is the Princess of Faith
The name she carries
Truth faith & strength

My Perfect Angel
My daughter I miss & love

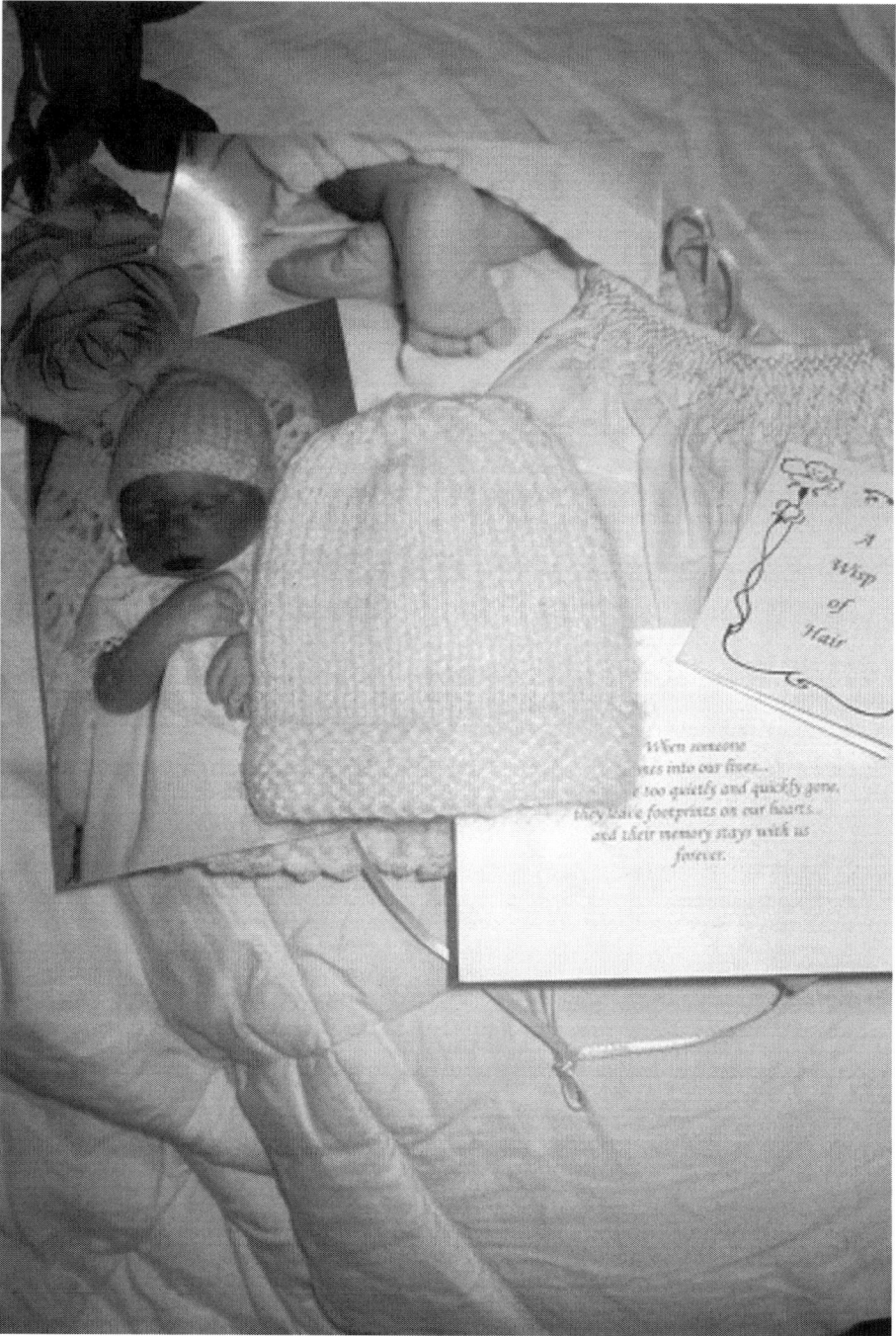

When someone
...mes into our lives...
...e too quietly and quickly gone,
they leave footprints on our hearts...
and their memory stays with us
forever.

A
Wisp
of
Hair

Favorite Journey

I received much more than a smile
Pure unconditional love
Though you are not here
I feel you inside me still

You were my favorite journey
You conquered so much love in me
True internal beauty

I never seen you take your first breathe
Never heard a precious cry
No laugh, no smile
I didn't even get to look deep into your eyes

You are my favorite journey
Pure unconditional love I have for you
Through you God conquered me too

You are my greatest success
Such unconditional love & faithfulness
Your story is true
And I continue to love and honor you

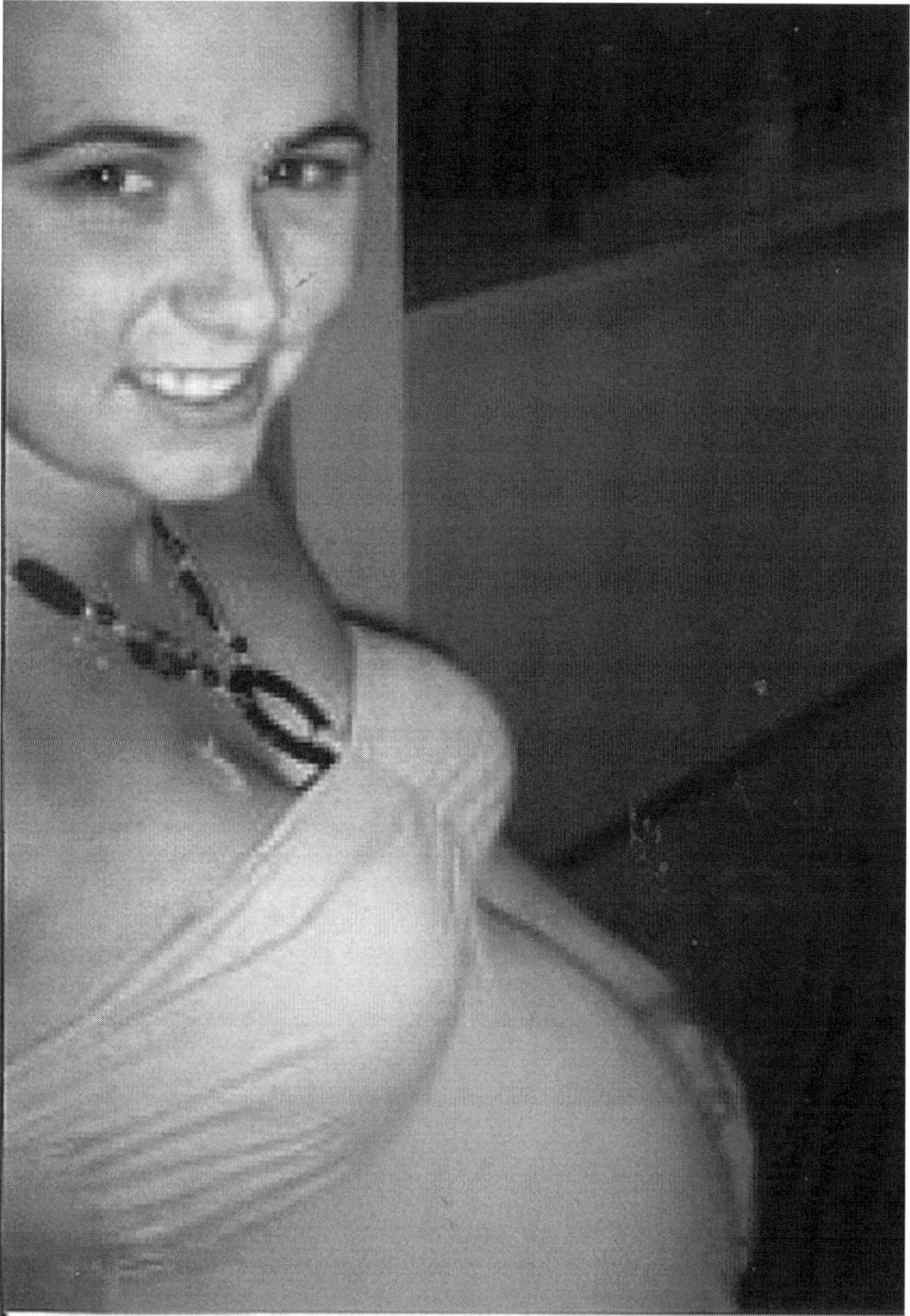

I Was Found

In my darkest hour
I was found
I will never be held down
He gave me the strength & courage
To always carry on

In my darkest hour
A deeper faith was born
Peace within
Courage to carry on
For my daughter
I must be a stronger mother

In my darkest hour
I was found
No one could ever hold me down
A deeper faith arose
Unconditional love so true
I was found
By my Heavenly Father above

I Visited My Daughter Today

I came to visit you today
My love for you will never fade
I kneeled beside you & prayed

Lord I love you
This is a blessed day
The love & support given
Has never been taken away

Lord I thank you
For all that has been given
For my daughter had never been forsaken
She runs, plays & sings in Heaven

A true angel of grace
She is my true Princess of Faith

You had led me here
Only to inspire all those near
I know you are here
And will never stray away

Today is a blessed day
My faith will never fade
I visited my daughter today

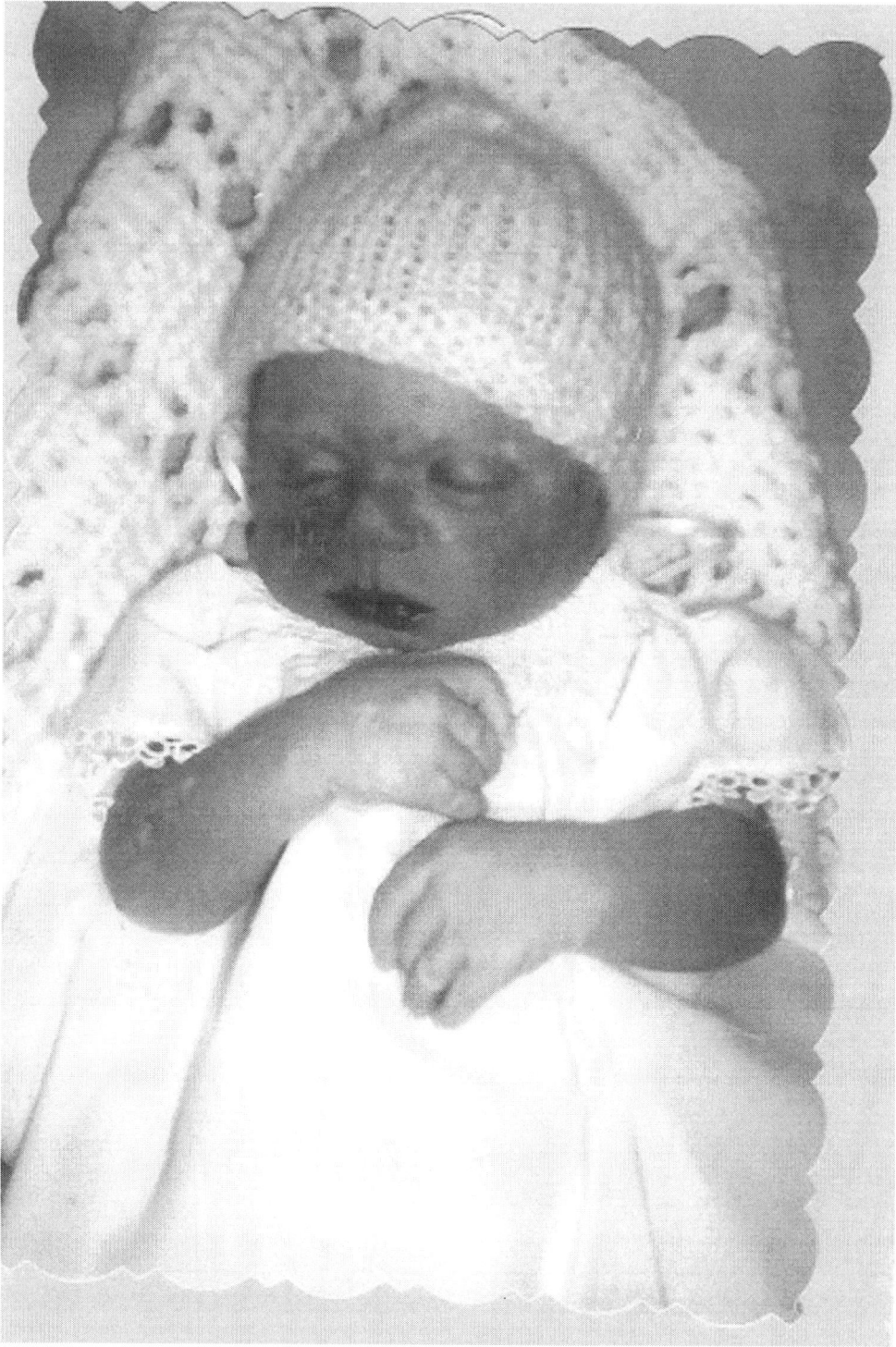

Angel Above

So many tests
So many doctors
But I see the truth in you
For my baby is kicking
What can they be thinking?
For I have faith and love you

I will continue the path
For she deserves a chance
She is alive in me
I am her destiny

The journey proceeds
They will only see
The beauty & faith I carried
For the eyes can see
A beautiful little girl
She is my angel above

So perfect, so pure
At peace she was brought here
But too perfect for this world
No regrets, only love
My daughter is truly an angel above

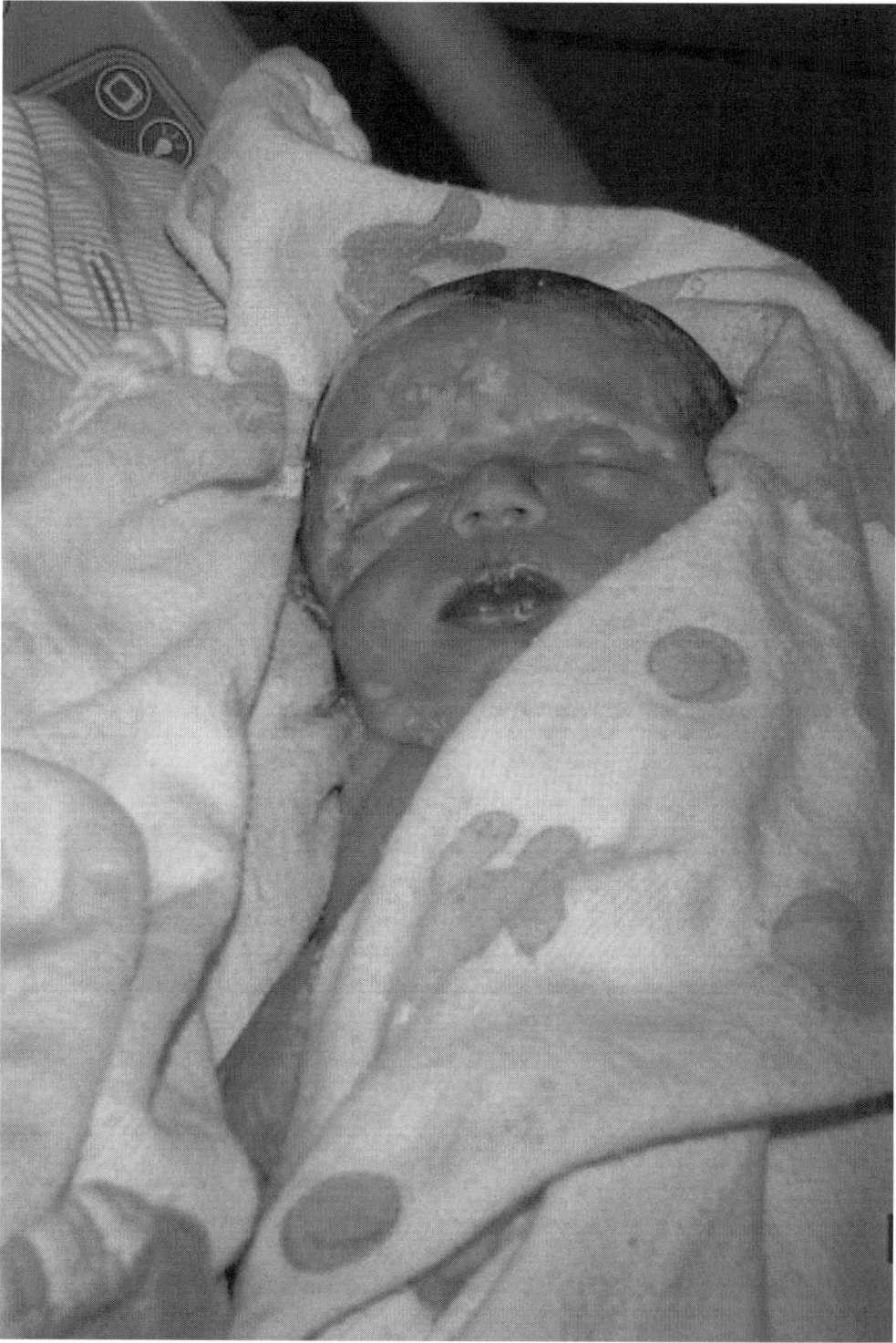

Still A Mother Inside

I didn't have a baby shower
No celebration
No giggle to be heard
Only tears were my own

I sit and wonder at times
What I would see and hear
If you have your daddy's eyes & my nose
I think to myself

One day I will see you
That will be the best celebration
When I can hold you once again

In Loving Memory Of My Daughter

You are the Princess of Faith
The most perfect gift from above
Your daddy named you well
You were created with nothing but love

As you created unconditional love
In those who loved you
Unconditional love never dies
Nor fades
But lasts & grows in our hearts & souls forever

You are a miracle in so many ways
For you are truly the Princess of Faith

There isn't one day that you aren't thought about or missed
But I am so grateful you are at peace
And saved from the suffering on earth

Someday we will see you again
We love you Always & Forever

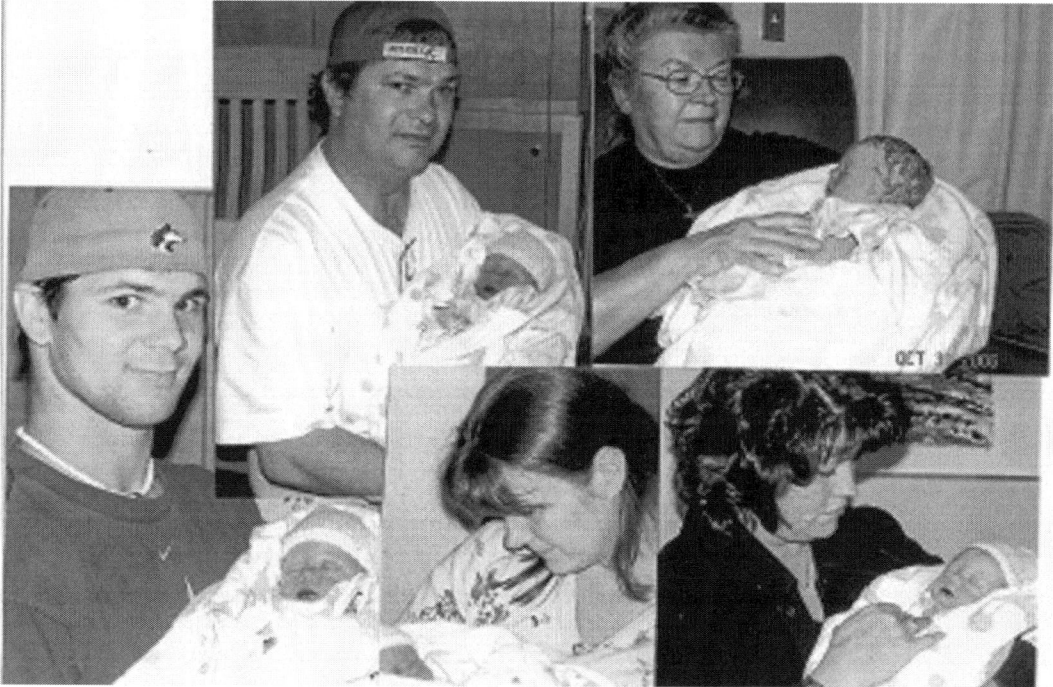

My Family

I have been so blessed
With the family I have loved
Who have sit & watched
Kept their faith and have loved unconditionally

Their love for me has shined true
Through my pregnancy with you
So blessed with our family here
Always proves to be greater & true
I saw it much deeper when they held you

So blessed
With this family I cherish
My family is your family too
I have been so blessed to have my family
And to have had you

Pieces Of Me
By Julia Anne Simpson

Chapter 6
My Puppy Megs

Precious Megs

She is so precious while she sleeps
So peaceful & cuddly to me
I love my puppy
And she adores me

Such a loyal companion to have
She doesn't steel
Won't fight
Just a playful delight

She can be a diva
And overwhelming at times
But I love her so very much
She is just a child inside

But she is so peaceful while she sleeps
She has dreams
Just like you and me
I love this kid of mine
My precious Megs
This puppy is mine

Puppy Love

Have you ever had a puppy?
They are so innocent & true
They only love unconditionally
So playful & cute

A deeper love, a deeper faith
Only god can create
Unconditional at another fate

They do not hate
Only want to be loved
Loyal & true
Just like the Lord above
Some call this puppy love

If we can only love
In the purest way it is given
Then we would see the mission of heaven

Adore Her

She can run & play all day
As long as you watch her close
Your attention is needed
A child craving attention and affection the most

She knows she is adored
I definitely spoil her
Too big to be a lap dog
But she persists that she is a kid

With her big brown eyes
I cannot resist
But you must watch out for her kisses
She may drool a bit

She is definitely my kid
I really do love and adore her too
So will you

Sweet Pup

She can make me smile
Or just curl up
Knows my emotions
She is a good pup

She is sweet
She definitely loves me
With a sigh when she is bored
Or needs attention
Almost always

She doesn't get cranky
But can definitely be a baby
Will cry for your attention

When I am feeling ill
She will lay & cuddle still
Megs makes me happy
Keeps my heart warm

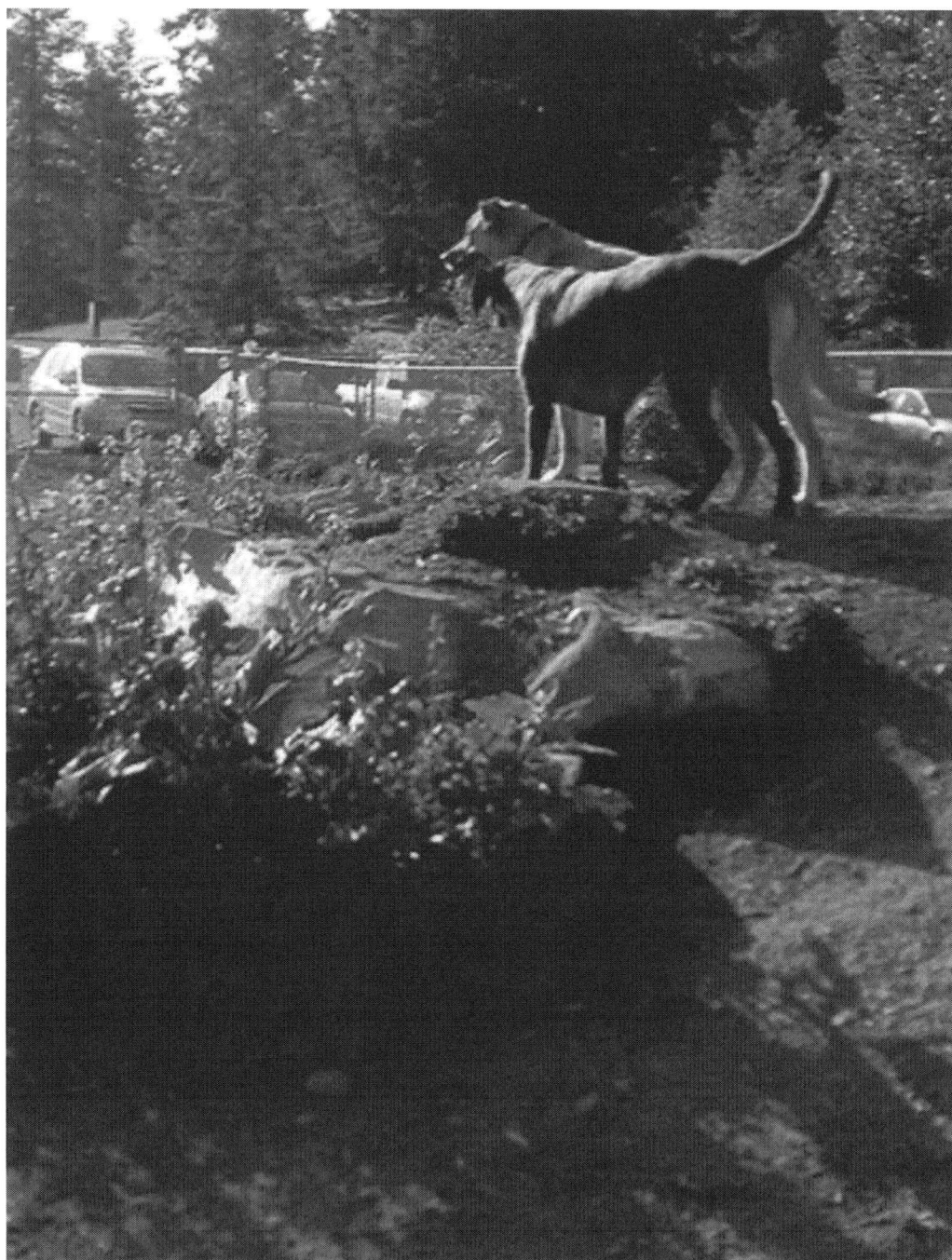

Still A Puppy To Me

I sit here
As she runs & plays
Such a happy puppy

Her tail wagging in excitement
She may be 3
But she is still a puppy to me

So adventurous & curious
To everything in her path
Like a child
So much wonder to be had

She is still a puppy to me
She melts my heart
And makes me happy

Megs

My dog is a diva
She is definitely high maintenance
When it comes to being loved
She is easy to please
All she wants is me
Attention is never enough

She is sweet
Will meet & greet
Beware she jumps
She will also lick your feet

She is funny to watch
So innocent & pure
I love her so much
She could care less if we were ever truly poor

Dogs are easy
They love you dearly
They can protect
But I protect her more

Pieces Of Me
By Julia Anne Simpson

Chapter 7
Having Fun Through Poetry

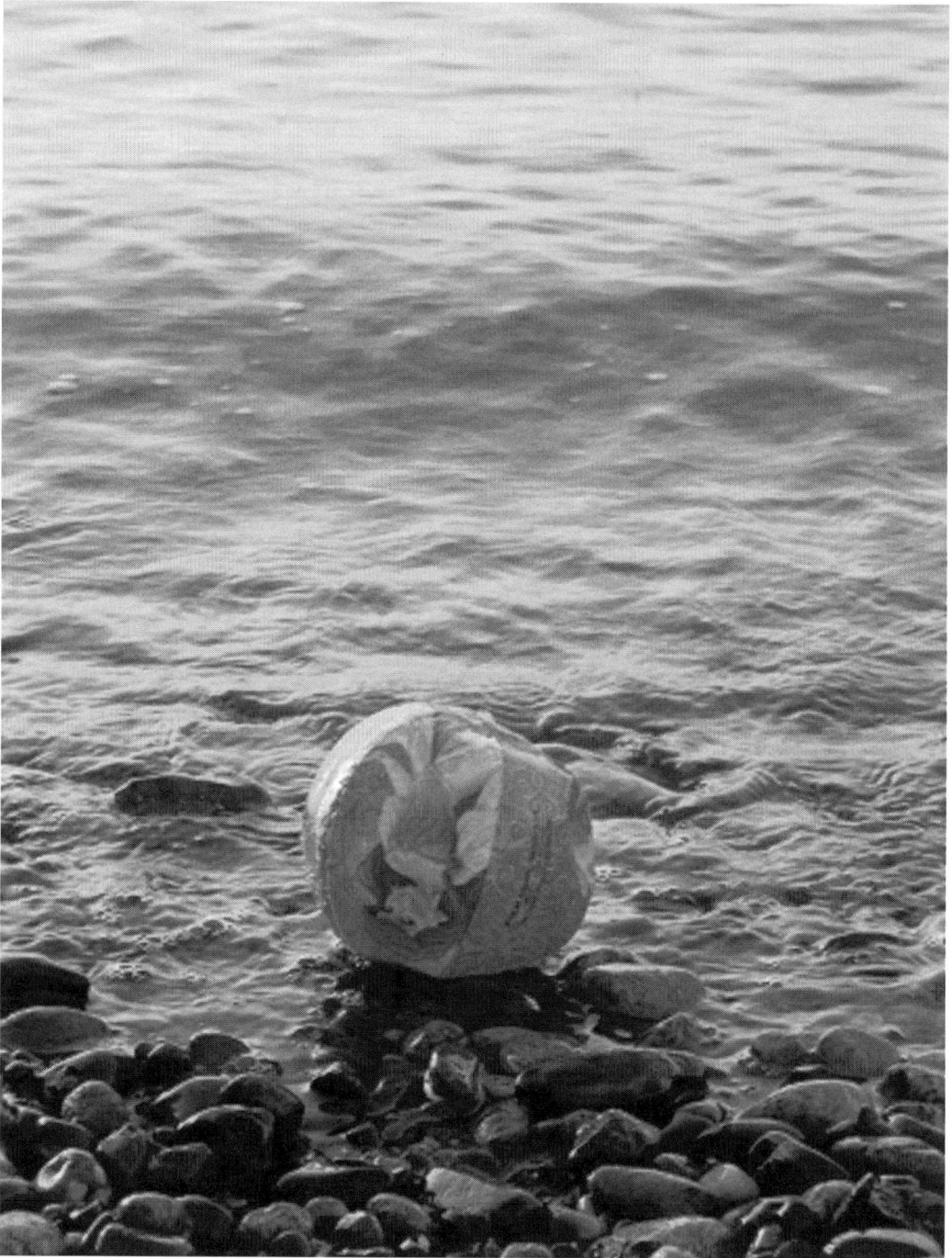

Summer Days

Swimsuits & suntans
Swimming pools & cliff diving
Summer is definitely exciting

Kids of all ages
Become more happy
Longer days
So we can all play
Even after working long days

Only a few months a year
Do we get this kind of weather here
Don't take it for granted
Love it & stay excited

Time to play
Love these summer days

I Need A Cowboy

I need a real man
Whose morals run deep
A Christian man who can be faithful to me

A hardworking man
With a lifelong plan
Who truly knows how to quart a woman
With a love deep & true

Values of a cowboy
An All-American is hard to find
Morals & faith are lived everyday
Work hard, play hard, & family time

I need a cowboy
Who can love this woman I am
All or nothing is what I give
And should be returned much more if not the same

Please bring my cowboy this way…

Summer To Be Had

BBQs & Bonfires
Summertime is among us
And I am free to have fun

No chains can keep me down
This girl is ready to be seen
Summertime has been missed

No work
Haven't played
Been locked up for too long
And now been set free
Single & happy
Cupid missed me

I cannot be pinned
I prefer innocence
Fun & play
Done with the heartbreaks

Summertime is here
It is one to remember
I chose to be with family & friends
And that is all that matters

City Living

City living is not for me
Someone always outside your door
The window view being your neighbor

So much noise
And so little manners
City living is not for me

City shows and entertainment
Is a vacation of excitement
Night life & amusement parks
Give me so much delight
But city living is not for me

To visit, not live
Can bring me happiness in doses
I love the city
It is an escape
A vacation only to play not rest

City living is just not for me

Summer Time

Night is coming
Open skies are clear
Summer time is here

Bonfires & picnics
I have definitely missed this
Long days of sun
Make warm nights more fun

Hot days
Warm waters
Wish this could last all year
Flowers blooming
BBQs brewing
Summer time is finally here

12TH *Woman Proud*

Blue & Green
That's my team
Football season is just beginning

Seattle Seahawks
I have always been your fan
More heart & pride lives within your fans

More heart played on our team in Seattle
It shows both on & off the field
The best team known
And most fun team to watch
I am a true 12th woman

Seattle Seahawks
The blue & green
So proud you are our team
I have always been your fan
You play with more heart
And most strong determination

So excited
Football season has arrived
What's in store this season will be a fight
I have never stopped believing
I am a proud Seattle Seahawk fan
                              I am a 12th Woman

Pieces Of Me
By Julia Anne Simpson

Chapter 8
The All American Woman In Me

American Pride

I am proud to stand on the soil
Where men & women have fought to protect
They stood up for our freedom
Our constitution for our country
For our rights & liberty
We must never forget

The strength that faced
Triumphs conquered
I am proud to know what is true
What they stood up for

I am proud to be an American
Where all can come together
Rise above differences
To live free with each other
This is only the beginning of possibilities we share together

I am proud to stand on this soil
Where our soldiers have fought & conquered
For your rights & mine
True American Pride

For A Soldier

I can only imagine what you have seen
Hate, anger, power can be an ugly thing
So much for a soldier to endure
For a soldier it is not power to gain
But to stand up so others do not suffer

War is a tragedy
The lives and family lost through history
All for freedom and liberty

My prayers, my heart goes out for each soldier
Past, present and future
Gratitude for what you hope to do
The rights, our freedom
Our safety here at home too

Continue to be heart broken
For all the soldiers who haven't returned home
Our past, present and future soldiers
Desire much more than recognition
For a soldier is much more than just man & woman
They are soldiers at heart
Protecting our freedom

Anacortes Museum

Economics

Another day
Another dollar
Too much going out
With little coming in
In this world of chaos
In this economy of sin
We the people can't seem to win

Medical bills only rising
Life definitely isn't easy
Only wanting to survive
But only know to struggle
So little pride

When will we once again rise above
Here we are meant to have so much
Not the depression of so many
Hope is truly fading

God bless this country
And those who have fallen
Help us to rise above
In your glorious love
May we survive again
Triumph the economic sin
May we bring hope again

American Dream

Work is never done
We live in a world
That is always on the run

So much construction
Too much greed
Work to live
Never live to work instead

No wonder there is so much depression
When we have such a power hungry government
Debts continue to rise
This is supposed to be a land of hope
Our ancestors would be deeply surprised

Ignorance has made this country fold
Taking for granted what opportunities we hold
A land of the free
A country united

I stand firm for what America stands for
What our ancestors fought for
Here is where dreams are to be made
Our constitution shall not be betrayed
Don't let the American Dream fade
Hope must be repaid

An American Dream
Isn't one that owns me
That's American Greed
I own my own American Dream in me

American Muscle

American made
And American proud
We created the car
And American Muscle made it loud

Real steal
Curves of beauty
American Muscle cars make me proud
They are stronger, powerful & loud

The curves of the steal
The sound of the engine so loud
It is more than any other car can handle

American made
It is American muscle
And I am American proud

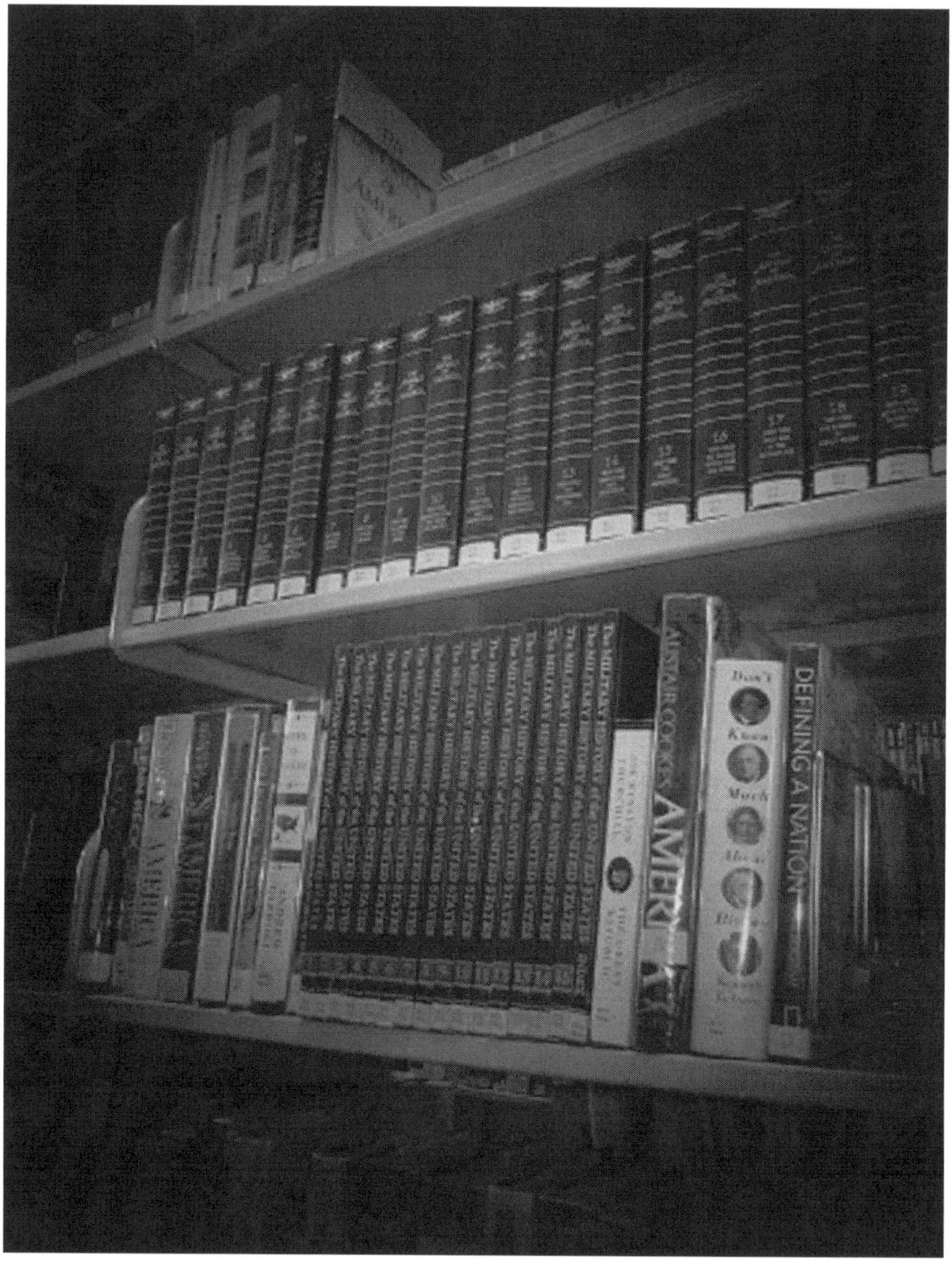
DEFINING A NATION
ALISTAIR COOKE'S

American Breed

Do you know your history?
You ancestry too?
I am an American mutt
Native American to Presidency
A true breed of many

I am an American Breed
And I love my home & country
I stand for much more than many
I am proud of my family

A country of hope & opportunity
This is where I am born
And where I have grown & learned

American Pride
I will stand by your side
I pray to once more to be glorified
Our country means much more

I am an American Breed
I stand on my own two feet
I am proud to know my ancestry before me

Land Of Hope

We do not stand quiet in a fight
We were created to triumph for our rights
Our freedom was earned
Not gained
Remember why America was born

A country built on a constitution
Where the government & police forces were to Protect & Serve
We the people need to observe
Justice has been tampered with and so much worse

Greed & money arose
Freedom was fought for and won
We need to stand together
The government is to obey and serve

Our ancestors fought for this country
They made this country hope
For a better future you must know your history
This is the Land of Hope

Pieces Of Me
By Julia Anne Simpson

Chapter 9
In Our World Today

Life Is Poetry

Life is another poem to me
Another journey, another story
There is always beauty here
Even when it is hard to see

A flower blooms
Waterfalls fall
The sun stay hot

Even through the darkest days
There lies beauty within
When you shine through your journey
Your story becomes poetry
The poetry you must be seen

When you find your light
There is beauty awaiting
May you find your words
For your life is a poem
In story form

Pointing Fingers

So many divorces
So many lies
True love is unconditional
And truly hard to find

People pretend to be different
Too many get hurt in the end
Such a mess of a world we live in
It is easier to be alone
Then to be lied to again

Too many hearts have been broken
Never enough communication
Or even compassion

Pointing fingers
Feeling like victims
It is your own fate
Through your own decisions and actions

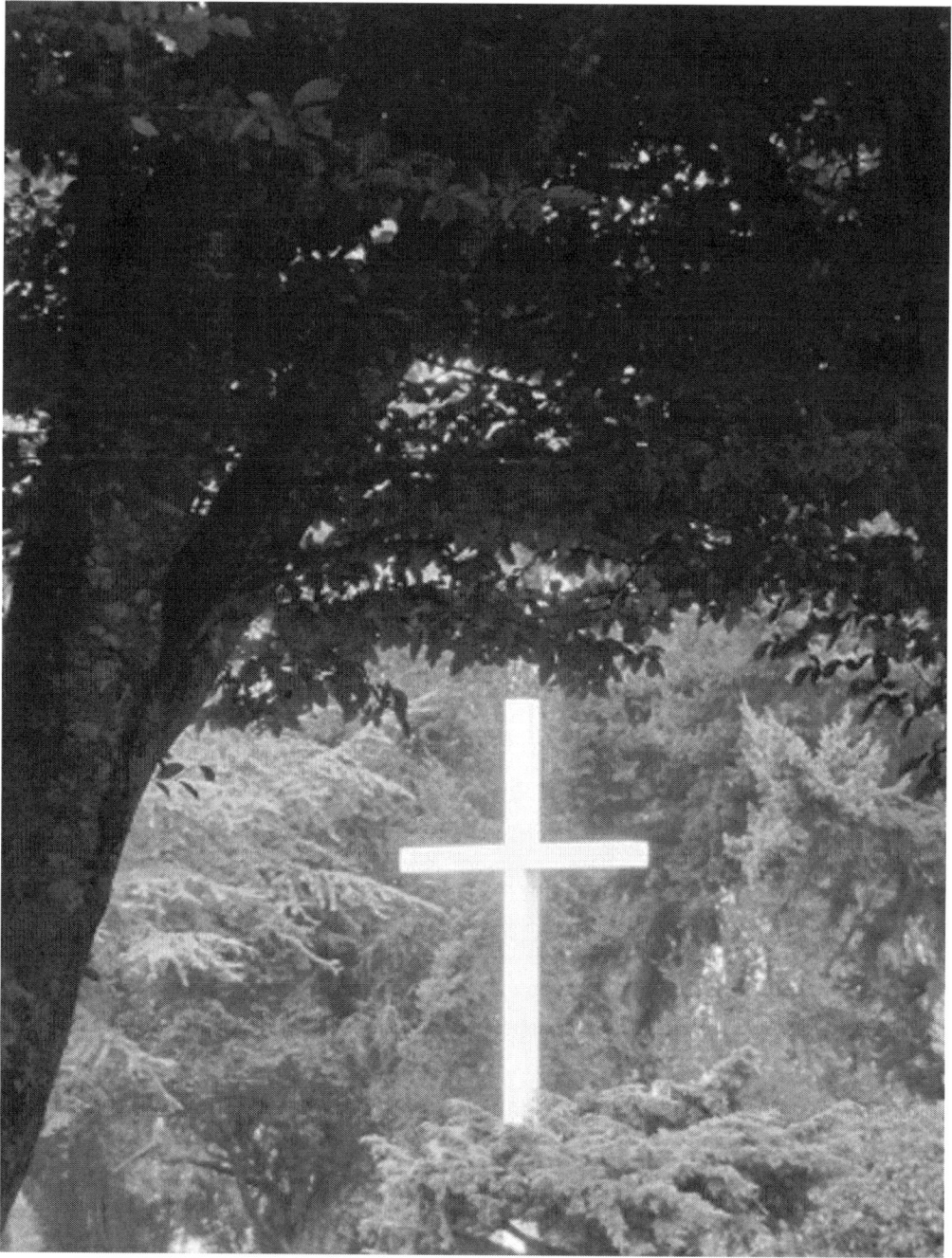

Seeking God

I am really hurt by the world I have seen
So many seek prosperity
But they don't seek their faith in the Lord
Trust & patience
It is so hard for us to learn

I have been so hurt by the world I have seen
In a world of chaos
I see more potential than your eyes see

I have a bigger vision
For God's true mission
The mission lays in you and me

We need you Lord
Give us your guidance
Help us be patient
Bring us peace
From the world chaos and greed

We need you Father
I seek you and your guidance
Help this world I have seen
There is potential I know and see
Help us Lord rise above and achieve

I seek you God
Only with you can we find peace

The Least We Can Share

A simple smile
A nice hello
Sincerity & good manners
Is always a more positive way to go

Better manners
Deeper compassion
This is my mission
How I live
The least we can share

Small towns
Big cities
No matter where you live
We are all people
This is how we should all live

It is not world peace I am asking
But it may be the closest we can get
Just a simple smile
And a nice hello
Better manners
Is the lease we can all share together

What Happened To The Gentleman

Men act like they want a lady
When they can't be gentlemen
Then can't seem to handle a good woman

What happened to all the good men?
What happened to all the gentlemen?
They never seem to prove themselves to be true
Has society broken them too?

All the good men are gone
And the need to be a good man only seems to be of the past
As most woman are now greedy too

Not many good woman left
Society and greediness has taken over what we thought were the best

I keep waiting for a true gentleman
A man who deserves and can prove
The gentleman are dads want for us
Is now just a fairy tale
And I am no longer a kid

But I am a lady
A good woman too
There are still a few

The Mission For The Young

So many churches
More should seek your name
The mission is to seek the young through praise
Help teach them your holy name

Continue through the generations
Carry on your great name
Jesus, it is also your name I praise
I seek to make you proud
Each & everyday

May the mission for the young
Only continue to rise above
May they seek your great name
And yearn to be faithful
Each & everyday

In the young
May they learn & share your name
For faithful faith
I pray they carry you in their hearts
Each & everyday

Patience

It is such a fast paced world
The crazy life before us
Have patience
There is something bigger & true
Have patience
For the Lord has had patience in you

Have patience
When love & success don't come your way
To look around for the blessings
The presents will come your way
Have patience & peace
Know the Lord has had patience in you

Time will tell what in life is true
There is always a bigger plan for you
So patience
God continues to have patience in you

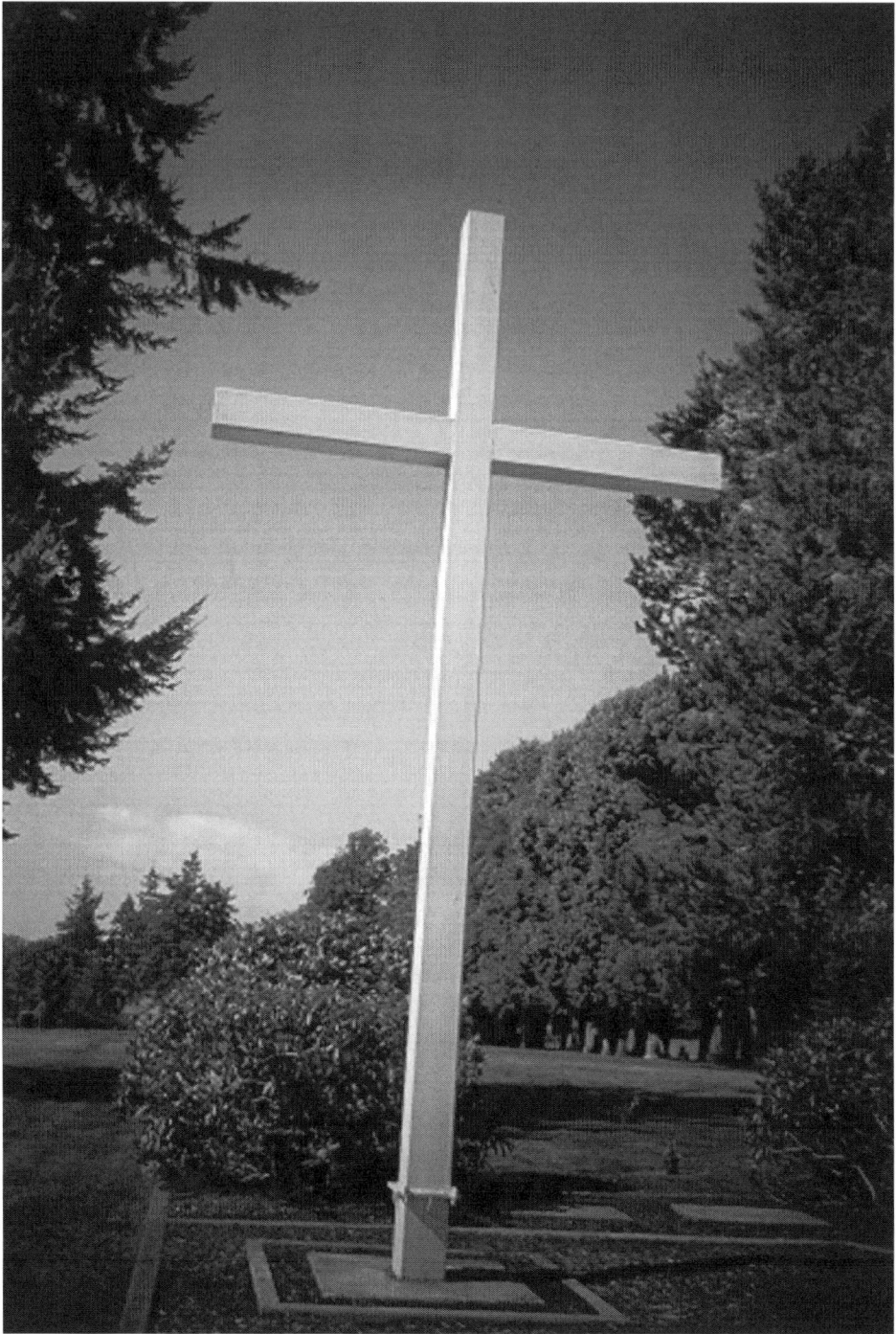

Non Believers

I pray & pity
The non-believers today
They never seen to truly find their way

They may succeed
But never feel satisfied
When it's their souls searching for you always

But they don't believe
Try to justify through science & history
I pray for the non-believers
I pray they find you someday

That's the day they will truly find something much deeper
True unconditional love
Peace & grace
For them I pray
They find you soon
I pray for their happiness too
I pray the non believers soon find you

Never Too Broken

While life has you trapped
And karma seems to burn you
Hold on a bit tighter
The Lord will free you

You are never too broken
Jesus' love for you is strong
He is your strength to move on
And thrive to carry on

Life can be hard
More difficult than you can imagine
Struggles through the life you took
Will never leave you too broken
With his love is ever healing
His name will set you free
Call on Jesus
Have faith & believe
As he does for you & me

Live Well

I wish you peace
I wish you live well
For he knows no enemy
To live free & alive you must thrive
Pull through & push forward
It is then you will arrive

To have much courage
May your faith be true
IF I may only have one wish
I would only wish you lived well

To thrive in life with your head held high
Wish a deeper faith & richer love
I wish you live well

I wish you live well
Take opportunities before they pass you by
May you know peace
And boundaries of God's love
Pull through & push forward
That's where your faith will be true to you
For if I only could have one dream
For I dream you too Live Well

Lilies

Not maintained or natured
The beauty cannot grow above
The elegance of a lily
Does need much love

Be true to your garden
The blooms show your love
If not maintained & natured
You won't see its gift of beauty
For it needs much love

A lily needs room to grow
The bloom is your recognition
For its love & appreciation

Don't ignore it
It can't live for very long
But if loved & cared for
Will bloom again for you
In the years to come

Innocence

So pure. So perfect.
Ignorance bliss
The blessing of innocence

Whether too old, too young
To know only good
What peace that would be to have
True innocence

To love purely
To love everyone
What a better life this should be
To no endure suffering
But to know strength in faith
Innocence from all evil
Would be true bliss

To love unconditionally faithfully
And not know anything less
I don't wish for ignorance
Only innocence
For innocence is blessed

Crashing Waves

This world around us
So eventful & hectic
Like the crashing waves of the sea
It's rare to be calm
For everything is forever changing

Crashing waves
Confirm will are still on earth
Alive & well
Can we ever tell
What the world around us holds

The crashing waves
May push & pull
But Jesus is a light house
So eager
He will always guide us through
For the Lord is my anchor
The crashing waves will never drown me

The crashing waves
Are my final journey to you

The Rose

Don't be fooled by the beauty of the rose
It has meaning
Beautifully to be seen
That's true
But the thorns will make you bleed

No matter the beauty you see
They can be deceiving
Without tender care
They won't last you will see
And the thorns can be very mean

So don't be fooled
By the beauty in a bloom
When not natured correctly
They can disappoint & cut you too

Lottery

The lottery everyone prays
To win & wants to succeed
True independence from financial reality

What is it that you seek?
Is it selfishness
Or to help others
For family & friends
Or the strangers needing help around you as well

The greatest dream
Is a better reality
For everyone
Not just you and me

To help the suffering
To remove the struggling
I believe that this is a dream of a miracle
A true miracle for everyone to succeed

We seek the lottery
It is our hope for peace
But it is never enough
Nor does it happen for us

A miracle lost
We must be our own kind of lottery
The odds are in our choices
Our fate is our destiny created
The tools are given
We must be more then what they believe

The lottery is only a game to me

Too many find hope
So many lose faith
Financial reality we can never truly escape

The lottery can be greedy
Don't lose yourself in money
Be your own fate
Don't count on the lottery

More Then Meets The Eye

There is always more than meets the eye
To every person inside
Everyone has a story
Their own journey they have had to survive

Love they neighbor
Love thy enemy
Forgiveness is power
Don't be consumed by hatred inside
You don't know their journey
Don't judge

Forgiving brings you peace
Unconditional love brings your closer to God
I won't pretend to know you
But give you much compassion instead

Journeys can make us
But they can break up too
Our stories are created by what you do

There is much more that meets the eye
I to know what it is like to cry

Imprisoned

Another morning I awake
To a life that isn't my fate
It is never too late

I must make today count
Do what I can with my tools at hand
Praying for a miracle to happen

This isn't my life
This doesn't feel right...
This isn't me

I work so hard each & every day
To rise above these hard times for me
This is not my destiny
I have so much passion & life inside of me

I need a miracle
Please Lord let me feel peace
Set me free
I only yearn to be happy
Only want to know and have the real me

War On Your Heart

Love & Hate
They can both be hard to endure
Love should be so much more

But hate is war on your heart
Caused by love in the most negative way

Love is to be adored
Unconditional, faithful & loyal
Love which was broken or betrayed
Rises the war of hate

Love they enemy
And always love you
The war on your heart
Is only hurt & will consume you

Love unconditionally
Always be true to you
Forgive & hold no regrets
Conquer the war of the heart
Or the war will conquer you

Help The Hate

So much crime
So much hate
How much can you take?

In music
In movies
In shows
And on the news

In schools
On playgrounds
It is scary to know what has happened
More sad to know the truth

Divorce
Violence
Broken Promises
And abandonment

Our children deserve a better environment
A better chance
To make better choices

Love & Innocence
Is more what the world needs today

There is too much hate
Which creates so much crime
If we could only relate
Have more time
Maybe then the hate would resign

At least in the young
They deserve the most
To be taught & loved
This would mean the most

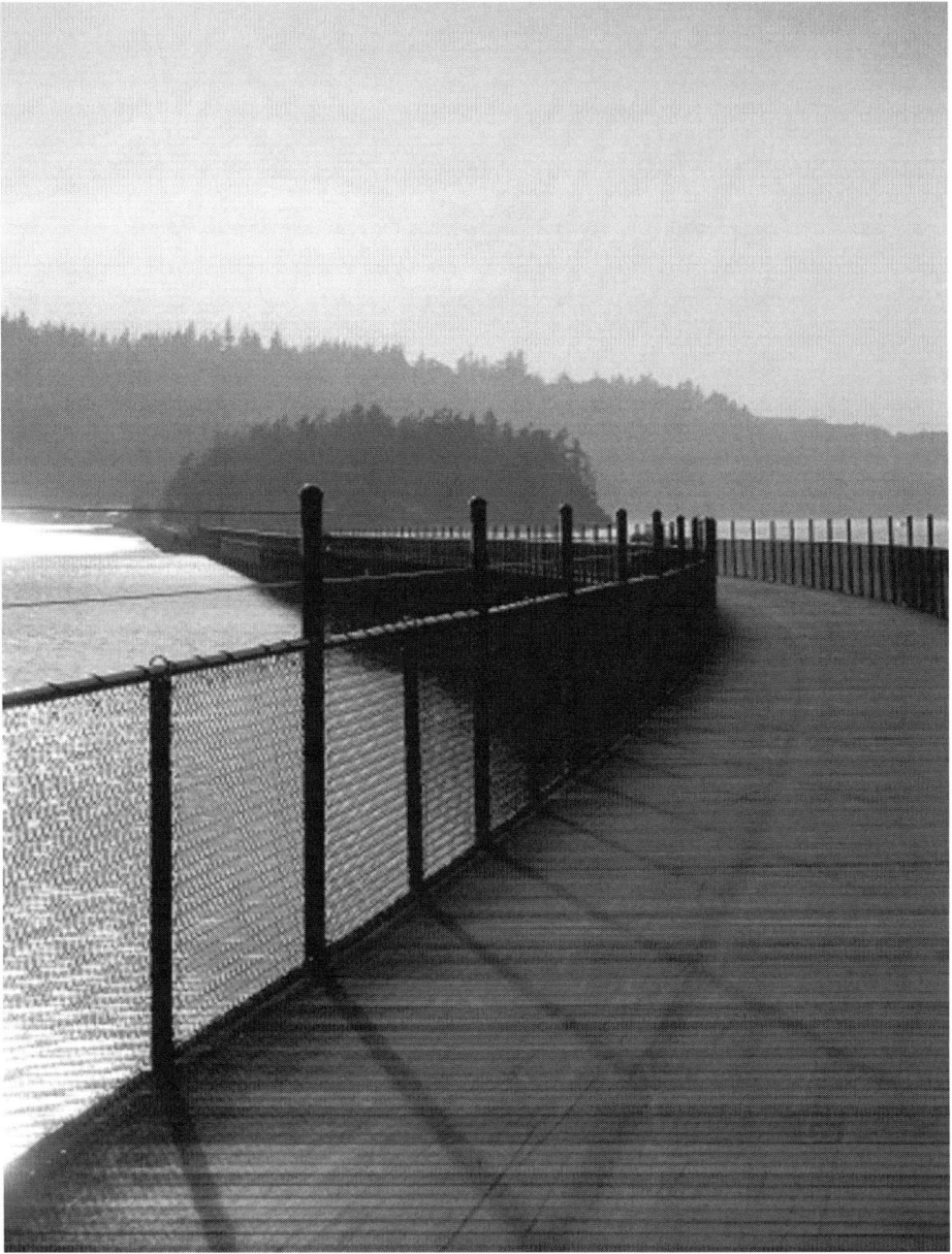

First Move

Everyone talks
But doing nothing
You can preach
But if you are not living it
It means nothing

Asking for a miracle
While you don't want to change
Is giving up on yourself
God gives you the tools to conquer anything

As you sit & watch
You curse the life you chose
Begging for a miracle
And you ignore all your tools

You are your fate
He will guide you through
But you have to be ready
And make the first move

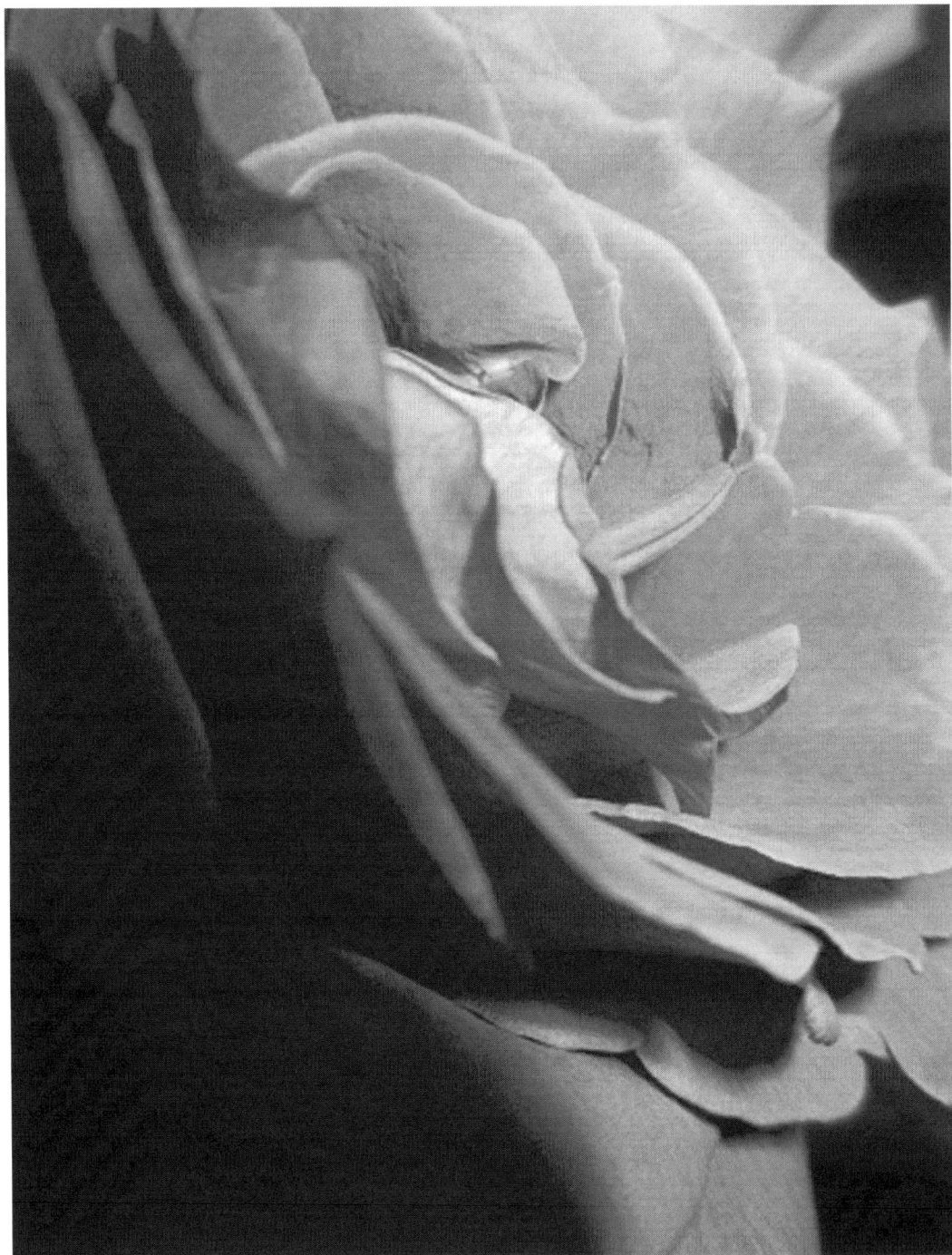

Bloom For You

A flower must grow
Before it blooms
Before it welts
You must take care of your garden
It truly shows when you don't

Don't over water
Don't let them drown
Let it have light
Help them grow bright

Make sure to care true
The weeds can bring suffering to their blooms
If you don't take care of the weeds from the root
They can kill your garden
It's not all about what you see
But what you do

So care for the garden
As it cares for you
Plant a seed
Help it grow
Then it will bloom true for you

Pieces Of Me
By Julia Anne Simpson

Chapter 10
Inspired Through ViSalus

Vi Treats

Sweets & Treats
How many can I eat?
Thin mints are tasty to me
Sweets I cannot resist
Thank goodness Vi Treats exist

Chocolate & fruit
How I missed you
Cheesecake is a favorite
I can't resist this moment

Thank you ViSalus
For making my sweet tooth a must
Thousands of recipes
I don't have to say goodbye to much

To live healthier
Is to eat better
ViSalus tops it off
Still eating my favorites
But having fat lost

With vitamins and nutrients
My insides needed so much more
How blessed I have found ViSalus
To live healthier now definitely makes more sense
ViTreats are a must

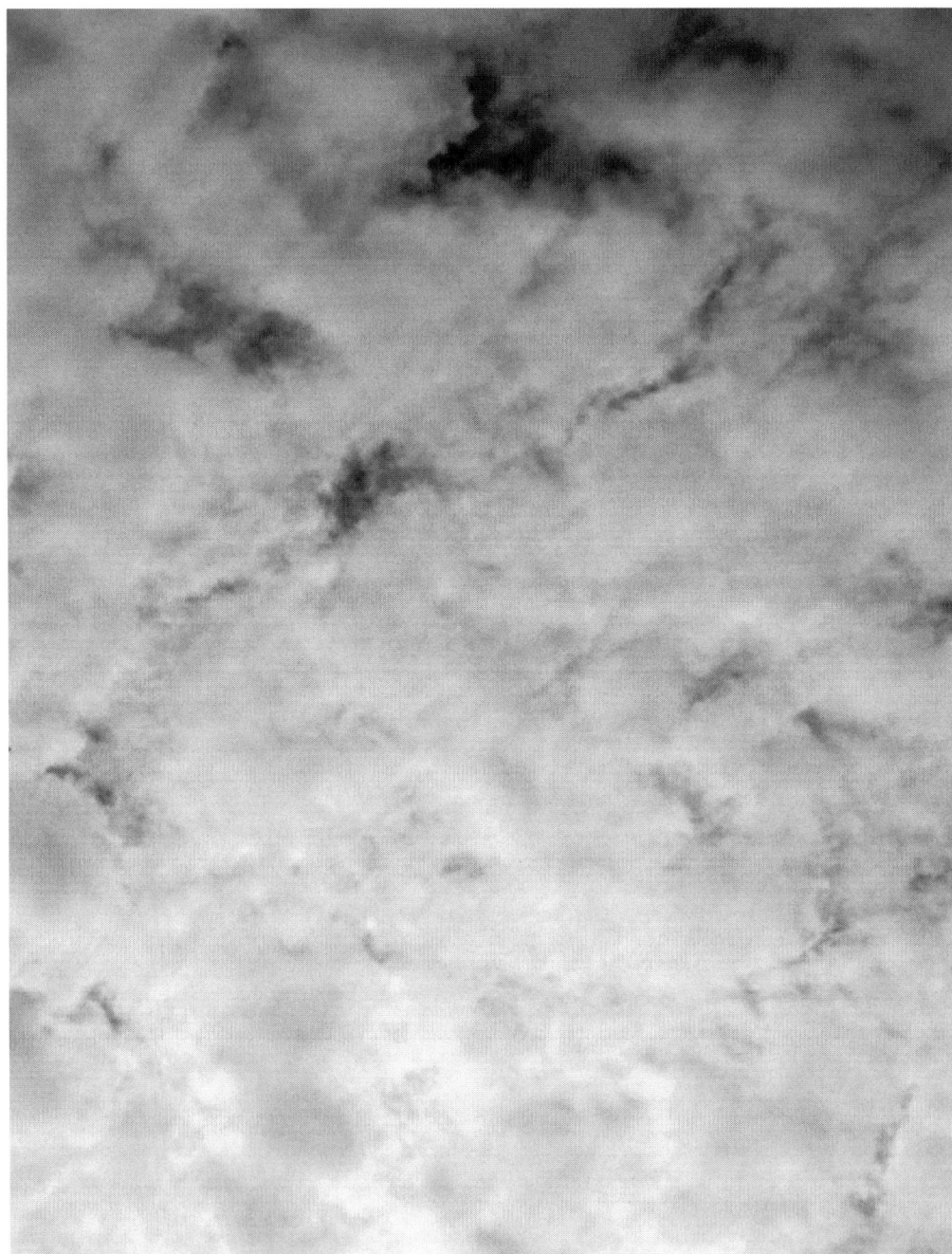

Another Morning

I have made it through another morning
Another glorious day
For I am alive

So many opportunities
So many possibilities
You too would find
If you would only open your eyes

I choose to live a better life
I choose to grow better everyday
I live for a bigger purpose
And I dwell in everything

I have made it through to another morning
God must not be done with me down here just yet
It is another glorious morning
I am alive and continue to strive

Another morning to survive
I am not done yet

Your Journey

Everyone has their own journey
Their own path to follow

My journey is my own
I will own it with no regrets
But embrace it
With my head held high
There is no victim here inside

Your past does not own you
Own it with pride
It has created who you are today inside

It is never too late to move forward
Believe in yourself and keep faith
Your journey is your own
Own it and stay true to you
Always have faith
Give your journey a real chance

What Today Will Bring

My alarm wakes me up
It is another morning
Time to take more supplements
And eat some ViCrunch

What will the day bring
Time to jump in the shower
Starting another day off positively

Set a plan, set a goal
I set for a direction & drive
What will this day bring

The journey becomes much shorter
Each day I stay the path
Focus on each day given
Give each day as much as your time & heart can

Keeping the faith
I am on a path
On a journey I choose it to be
Dancing in opportunities
Positives create possibilities
I pray you to will strive each day

What will today bring…
Living this way is exciting
What will this day bring you

i LOST it.
taking WEIGHT OFF the world.
1 PERSON at a time.
10 LBS at a time.
THE CHALLENGE

Project 10 Challenge

I accomplished my challenge
I have arrived at last
Overcome all I had

I have accomplished a deeper fight
Through accidents
Through cancer
I kept true to my mission
I got to help donate meals to children
Because I kept to the challenge

I am so proud
Of this small accomplishment
Losing 10 pounds
May have saved a child

The mission isn't over
I can still lose
Then build muscle
Which also helps me too

No excuses for this girl
To overcome anything
You have to believe to succeed
This mission is my journey

Are you ready for your Challenge?
Help us save more children
Obesity continues to kill too many.
This isn't a business
It is a mission

Thrive With Vi

Most people would give up
But I do not know how to loose
With my pride aside
Dying inside is not what I choose

I am VI for Life

I have been given a bigger chance
I will not lose myself
But rise above
Because of my better health

A chance to keep my life
I will indeed survive
I will come out stronger & healthy
Just you watch

I pray you do the same
Take back your life
And thrive
I am VI for Life
Because of VI I Thrive
Much deeper then I knew
I survive

Same Road – Same Destination

The same road
Is the same destination
Won't change your life's direction

To change your outcome destination
A new road must be taken
No short cuts will change your route
You must be ready to make a decision
And change the direction at the round about

Same road
Some destination
It lays in your decision
Fate changes with the directions you choose
Your destiny isn't fate
It is your journey through you

Same road
Same destination
Never moving forward
The decision is your own

My Own Fate

I cannot just sit and wait
I am my own fate
I will rise above

The tools have been given from above
I will succeed with God
I will never question his love

I must take a stand
Opportunities won't happen again
I rather try & fail
Then not have faith within

I am my own fate
Destiny is my gain to win

I am my own creator
God will guide me through
Jesus will carry me above

I am my own fate
My faith will always see me though
Believe in yourself
And your journey will be at your hands to

My Challenge

I strayed from my challenge
I was going through so much
After treatment depression became more true to touch

I am not that girl
I only know how to survive
To stay strong & thrive

This year has crossed many limits
Through faith I have prevailed
Good health means more to me
Then the possessions that you seek to hold

The path which had been given
Wasn't planned
But I arose

My Challenge carries on
Strength in health makes me stronger
It only grows within me
And I will soon be free
My challenge is just the beginning of my true destiny

Own Your Journey

Poor me, Poor I
I wish I could cry
But I refuse to play the victim

Life can be cruel
But so can you
So get up & try

Talk is cheap
It is only excuses you seek
Excuses should be reasons to achieve
I do not pity you

We all have stories
Journeys can be unfair it's true
But the person you are
Is the person you created
Own your journey
Don't let your journey own you

Let This Be A Great Day

A new day awaits
As I sit by the window and pray
Please Lord
Let this be a great day

I have a big day planned
Let it happen at your command
Please Lord
Help me through this day

May I succeed & strive today
In all the possibilities at my hand
Keep me motivated & inspired
Please let this be a great day I pray

I am ready to achieve more than planned
With peace & courage at Jesus' hand
Please Lord
Let this be a great day

Gift Of Compassion

In this life I was given
A deeper compassion to succeed
A deeper desire to help those all around me
With God's grace & humor
To always guide me to see

I strive to be greater
With an unfailing faith & deeper love inside
For you who reads this
Will know there is greatness in compassion
A greater strength to succeed & survive

Now as we pay it forward
You will come to see
The greatest gift is compassion
There you will too succeed

God's grace & humor will inspire
Through the gift of compassion I pray
Is the greater gift you as well will succeed
And strive through everyday

Healthy Life

A better health
Is a better life
It is important to take care of you & me

In this world with so much illness
So much suffering
Health is needed
Help is supported

We must come together
Help each other
Live a better life
Be healthier & inspire

There is a mission
To save lives
Through health & fitness
To live better
Is to live a healthier life

This is just the beginning
Of my mission
For us together
Is the only way we can all win

Never Quit Your Dreams

I will not quit my dreams
Because I lost a life or two
God's plan is always bigger than mine
He continues to prove

Take a deep breathe
Trying to relax
When one path ends
Another truly begins

Keep faith & move on
The journey is moving forward
And you haven't yet met your match

You haven't achieved all god's gifts
So keep believing
And never quit
Your dreams are achievable
Through faith in God
And yourself.

So never quit believing
Dreams are goals
Once achieve are gifts.

My Journal

I don't seek to be famous
Or for you to know my name
To help others is my determination
Through motivation & inspiration

If my story can help you through
I have done more work
Then I dreamt to

I have been given a path
Not easy or what I have dreamt of
But through faith
I have risen again

Don't be sad or mad
For the path given
For there is a deeper mission
With faith I will arise

Here I tell my journey
Which always seems to be a surprise
For I have much love & compassion
My journey has led me here to thrive

Jesus is my inspiration
This is my story
My journey has arrived

Released & Freed

I will no longer feel trapped
Nor contained
I was created to succeed and live free
Society will never contain me

Stubbornness & pride aside
There is much more inside
I will arise from the boundaries
You will not contain me
Faith created me
So you cannot break me

I am alive
With a bigger mission
Then society will allow
They will be forsaken
I will not be trapped

I have been freed
From the containment here you seek
Where possibilities are overwhelming
I shall know no boundaries
I have been released and set free

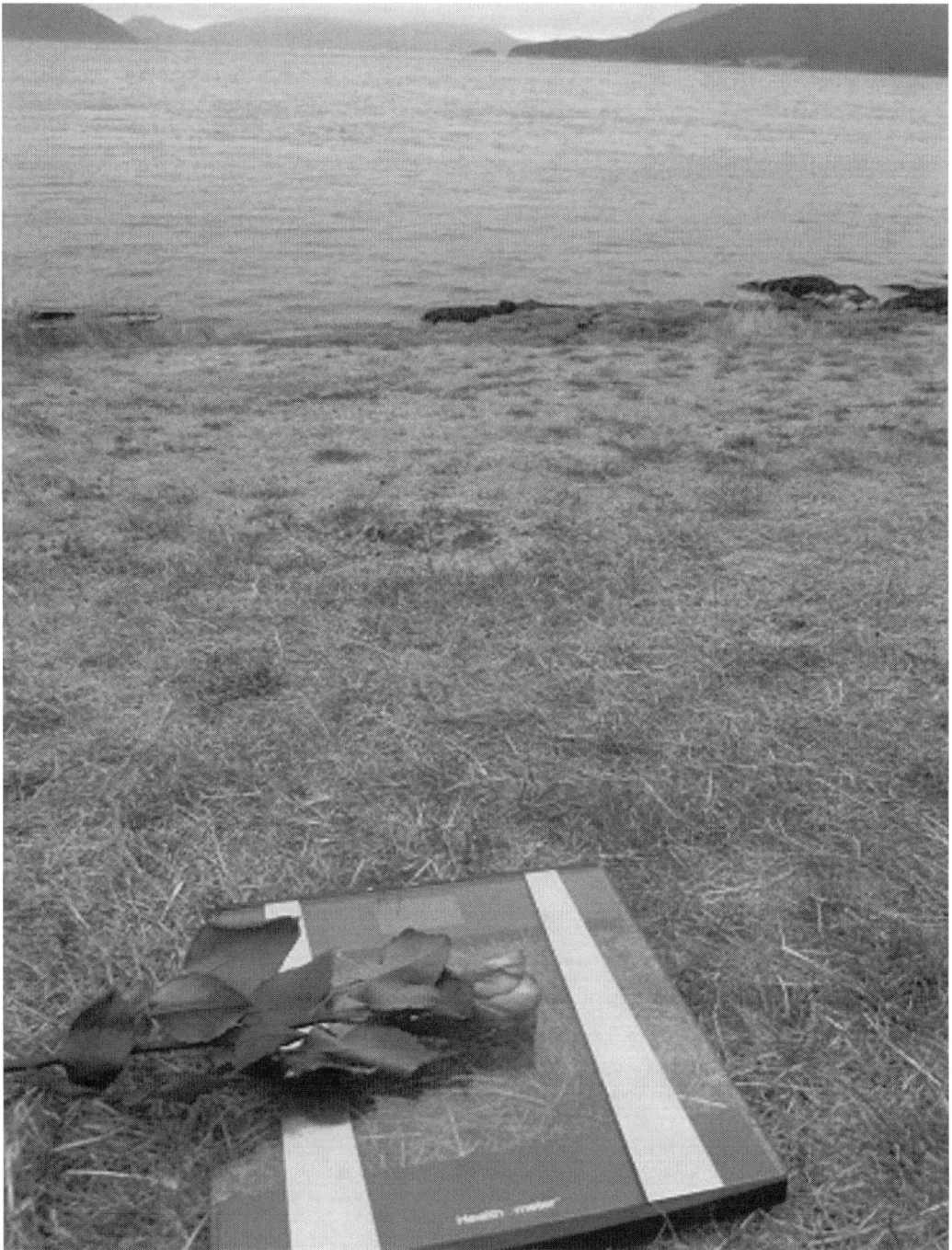

To Live

The weight on the scale
Is not what I face
An illness I am determined to erase

Some seek fitness
Some seek weight loss
Some need much more to be stronger
Healthy eating is healthy living
The body is a beautiful thing
If you feed it right
It can fight the illness inside

Mind over matter
What goes in will come out
Give your body & life a better chance

It is not the number on a scale
It is my determination to live
Better than I have

Deeper In You

To see the truth
You must seek something deeper within you
What you believe
Will always mean the most to you

If you do not believe in you
You will never know what is true
Reach & seek within
So you can believe again
That's when you can truly win
And breathe again

I pray for you
To see the truth
And believe in what is deeper within you

Excuses

Excuses are not answers
They are used by the weak
Who deny the strength they have been given to see

Excuses mean nothing to me
Only proves fear in the weak

What is it you seek
Will fear make you weak
What's your excuse today?

I am not afraid
My life I have the power to change
I am in control of my destiny
Nothing in this journey will conquer me

Excuses are not reason
Real answer have value
Rise up & take power
There are no excuses for life today
Just reasons to change your way

Your Thoughts

Your thoughts are your opinions
What you believe can be your reality
But your thoughts are your own
They are what separate you and me

What you believe
Is the limits of what you can achieve
Mind over matter
Your thoughts do matter
They create your own destiny

Your life is what you choose
Your thoughts will pursue
Your beliefs are in how you act
So be true to yourself

You don't give your thoughts enough credit
So be positive in how you think
If possible is what you seek

Tools

No limits
No measures
No boundaries
Can keep us

There is much more to be seen
So much more to be had

In this life
No promises are made
Our fates are our own instead

The tools have been given
With opportunities surrounding us
Possibilities in the making
We will rise above

No limitations
Know no boundaries
You destiny is a platform
Your tools waiting to be built
Your fate is your own doing
God blessed you with your tools
Use them well

Dreams

The dream of dreams
Is to keep believing
The thoughts & visions can be true
A dream is a gift from heaven
For God has bigger dreams for you

Never stop believing
For there is a bigger purpose for you
So never stop dreaming
Believing in a dream will help it come true

Continue to push forward
Hold you head held high
Don't give up
Continue to push forward
That's when you will thrive
Dreaming of all dreams is a gift to you from God

To believe is just the beginning
For a dream is a vision
God truly has a bigger dream for you

So keep believing & dreaming
And in the end his dreams will see you through

Dwell In Possibilities

I see so much in you
Opportunities & possibilities
For God believes in you

Dwell in the possibilities
Possibilities through his love
A bigger path is your mission
Inspiration from above

So much faith
So much love
His opportunities are endless
No boundaries to your success
Dwell in possibilities
Gifts from above

Dwell in possibilities
His love & faith for you is much stronger
Your path can be so much brighter

Dwell in the possibilities
Strive for greatness
Possibilities are endless

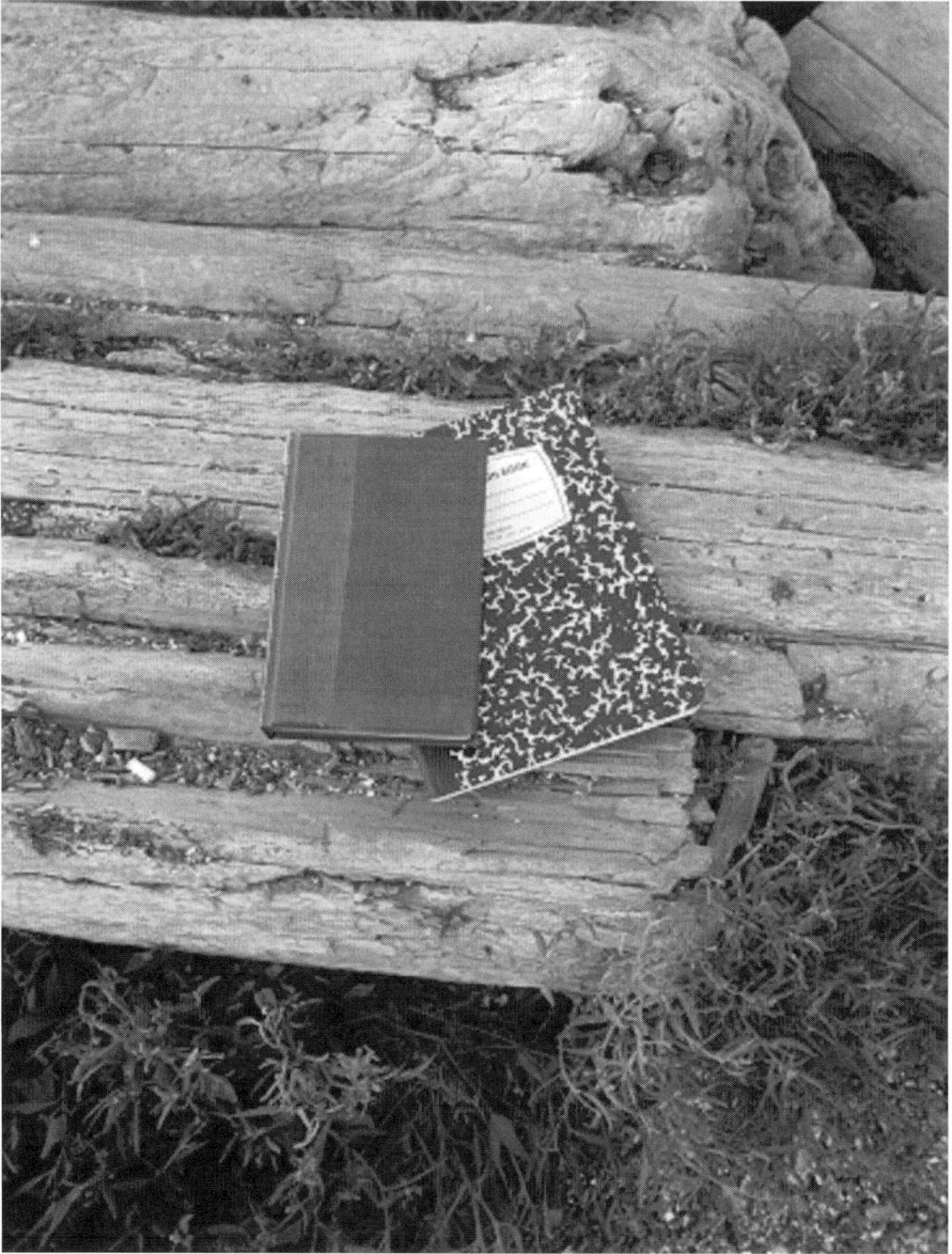

Another Story To Tell

Another story
Another lesson
Your journey is a story
Another story that should be told

Life stories can inspire others
A life can be changed
By your journey alone

So tell another story
Save lives through journeys
Help more stories to arise

I am inspired by the stories told
There is a bigger mission
Don't hold back
Let your story be known

There is a gift from God
In the story you hold
So I pray
Tell your story
Your story too should be known

Opportunity

Have integrity in opportunities given
They are a gift from heaven
No matter the path you chose
He continues to believe in you
So you should believe in you to

When one door closes
A better one opens
So much love to be had
Opportunity awaits
But you must take the step
He always has your back

You are your success
He will guide you to something deeper
Opportunities are endless

Integrity to prosper
Always strive to the opportunities given
They are always gifts sent from heaven

A Bigger Plan

There is much more then we can see
A bigger plan for you & me
A bigger task, a bigger mission

Don't be discouraged
For you have a bigger purpose
Catch your breathe
And rise above
For he has a greater love

Stand firm & stand tall
He will guide you through it all
With a bigger task & bigger mission
Seek him & find
Your true journey maybe bigger than mine

So keep believing
Don't lose faith
Your bigger task & bigger mission
Is a bigger plan from heaven

Let Me Inspire You

For every moment & every truth
Let me inspire you
I believe there is hope in struggles
Strength in suffering
Let me inspire you

There is much more given
In the hardships that may arise
There is something much deeper
And it will be your surprise

He never will despise
Only know that no conditions arise
His love is true & unfailing
In it all he inspire me
Now let me inspire you

For every moment & every truth
He has inspired me
So I can inspire you

Prosperity

Prosperity
I thrive to succeed for you Lord
I yearn to help others
I thrive to be so much more

To prosper in love & in faith
In your love I thrive the most
To live a true prosperous life
Is not thrive in money
But to thrive through life
To live & rise above on all levels of life

To prosper to succeed & conquer
I thrive to prosper in the light
Prosperity
This is what it means to me
Prosperity
Let's thrive together for the Lord
And truly succeed
For True Prosperity

Vitality

I will show strength
I will survive
There is a bigger purpose for my existence
Vitality!

Jesus, you give me the power to live
The power to grow
Vitality!

I am alive & well
I feel reborn on my mission
I will survive in you

You blessed me with Vitality
Through my strength & faith
I will survive & live Alive
I have a bigger purpose for my existence

We are our own Vitality
You Lord are my Vitality
I been found here Alive

Blank Canvas

What the future holds
Only can be unseen
Like a blank canvas
Waiting to be unleashed

Only the Lord knows
What the future holds
But we are our own creators
He has given us our tools

Today is only the beginning
Another chance, Another Choice
The canvas hasn't yet been painted
You are the artist
A creator to be scene
You have the tools to paint your own destiny

What will you create?
Each day is a new beginning

Pieces Of Me
By Julia Anne Simpson

Chapter 11
Pieces Of Me

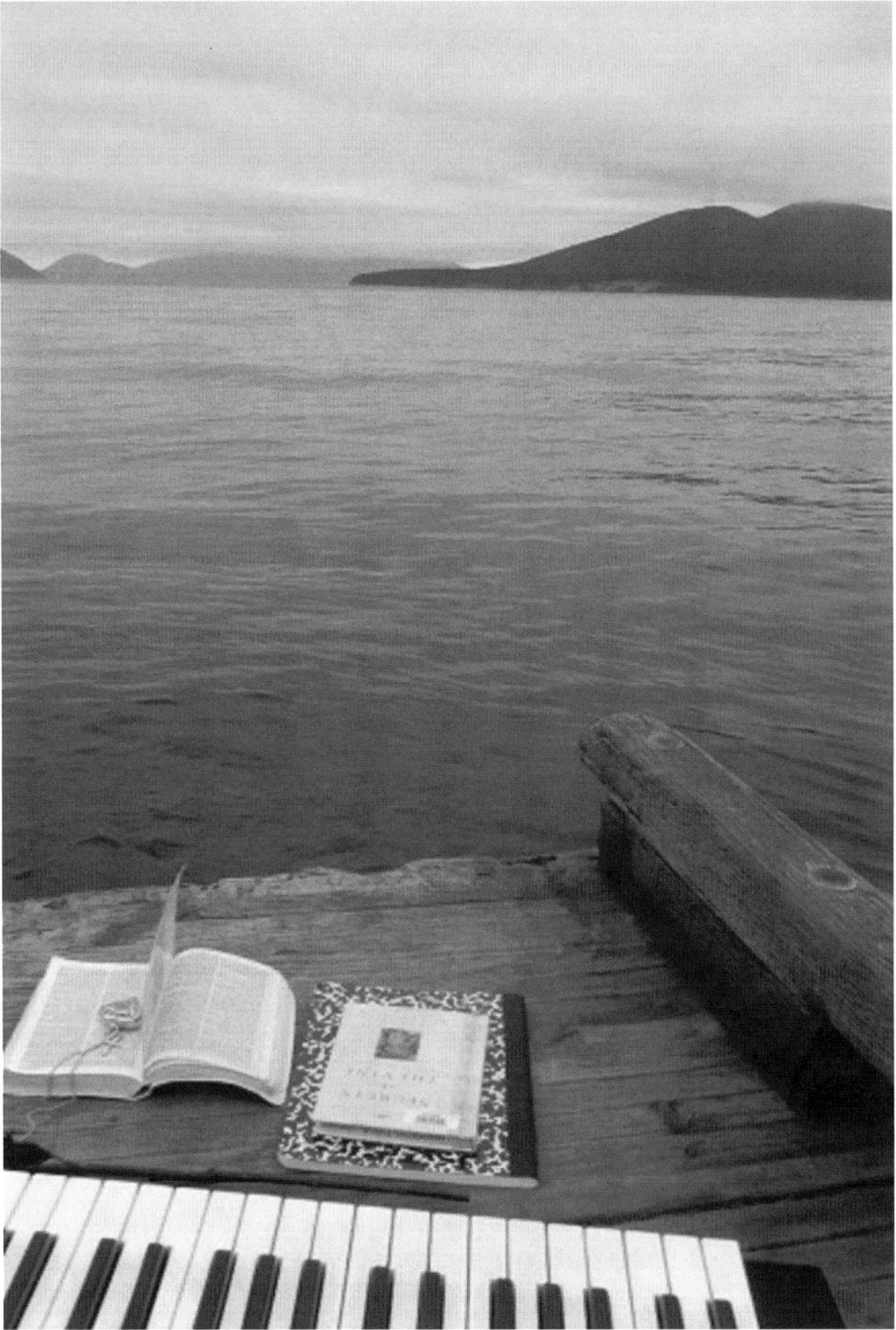

Pieces Of Me

I wonder if they can handle the real me
The woman the Lord created me to be
There are so many layers that cannot be seen
How can I surrender myself?
And let them see all of me

So much deeper then what meets the eye
They always seem surprised
My strength, my courage
My faith & stubbornness inside

I only know how to conquer
They don't know my whole story
Why I continue to strive
But it is my only sanity to have something more to fight for
It is how I survive

I was created for so much more than this
My dreams are goals will rise to see
I was blessed to be my own success
For I only truly trust me

My greatest strength is also my weakness
I must let them see
The woman God created me to be
But I can only give pieces for them to see
Only God and I know all of me
So here are just pieces of me

Promise To Myself

Always Remember
Focus on your Dreams
They are Goals
And they are Possible

Live Life like there is no tomorrow
Follow your Heart & have No Regrets

Laugh
It is stronger than a smile

Love Faithfully
True Love is Unconditional

Inspire & be Inspired
Believe in yourself
And never lose Faith

God's plan will always be bigger than your own

Reevaluating

So much has happened
I no longer know where I stand
What I mean to you
What life means to me as well

So much has happened
I don't know what to believe
Who to trust
No one really seems to know me

So much has happened
I have been all in
But now all I have is doubt

God is the only one I can run to
He knows me inside and out
Never gives up
Only continues to challenge me
And now his challenges mean
I must reevaluate myself

Where is my life going?
Who is real in my life?
It is time to move on from those who are not
So much has happened
I must not live in doubt
So it is time I reevaluate myself

Scars & Stretch Marks

Scars & stretch marks
They are proof that I have lived
I was not sheltered
I was not spoiled
I was raised to fight my own battles
And to be a "walk it off" strong kid

Four surgeries on my ankle
Couldn't even keep me from moving forward
Not even prevent me from dancing
No matter what doctors said
I continue forward

Stretch marks from a pregnancy
Proof that I carried to my daughter
Who is in heaven above
All scars tell a story

Not even cancer will keep me down
Just another scar to be found
And strong tough skin I have to tell it all to you

I have bled
I am no scared
My strength in myself and in god
With goals and dreams that keep me pushing forward
My faith won't ever leave me
This world can't keep me

My scars & stretch marks
Are proof to the world that I have lived

Secret Chest

I have a secret chest
It only awaits your touch
Another side to me to explore
A secret I reserve
A part of me only a love can see

I have a secret chest
It awaits for your presence
The treasure you will find
Will only be used for love
For with love it isn't a crime

A secret chest
Filled of love and tenderness
What is your hearts' desire?
I will show you mine

For I have a secret chest
The secret is yours and mine
Another side for you to explore
Another secret I have reserved
For only you and I

Woman To Love

I am a woman to love
But if you cross and betray
You will see another side then them

I am a woman you won't forget
On every level I will love true
Hoping you can keep up
That will prove you to be true too

I love strong & true
But karma will find you
You will be sure to miss me
There is no one else like me

If you can't see what we have
Feel free to leave
But be sure to stay gone
Don't look back when you didn't stay

My love is true & strong
If you aren't man enough
I will move on

Stubborn

Stubbornness
My strength
My weakness
I will always power through

I know no obstacles
The storm only grows in me
I won't give up
I will succeed
My stubbornness' is the strength in me

My heart has many layers
A wall to keep me strong
And boundaries from falling apart
I do not know if love can find and break me
For stubbornness' can be my weakness

Through strength & weak
My stubbornness' continues in me

Pride Of Innocence

So innocent through pride
I have survived
Through a world of chaos & crime

So much addiction to be seen & had
The innocence of my life
A drug I will never have tried

Too many lives destroyed
Through others addictions & pride
I much prefer
There is pride in innocence
The innocence of my life

Another Vacation

I miss my feet in the sand
The smell of the ocean
The sea breeze flowing through me
I definitely need a vacation

Life is too short
Nothing seems to last
Try to enjoy each moment
As if it may be your last

Life is what you create
Don't live in hate
It will only consume you
You don't want to live in regrets

Life is short
And nothing lasts
I yearn for more
I definitely need another vacation

Heels On

Makeup on
Hair done
This girl has her heels on
And is ready to run

There is nothing I can't handle
No struggles to worry
I am ready
I have my heels on

I will conquer & strive
With a bigger smile
I will mask my pain
This woman has her heels on
I will walk proud in every day

Don't worry for me
You will continue to find me stronger
There is nothing I can't handle
As long as I have my heels on
I will conquer

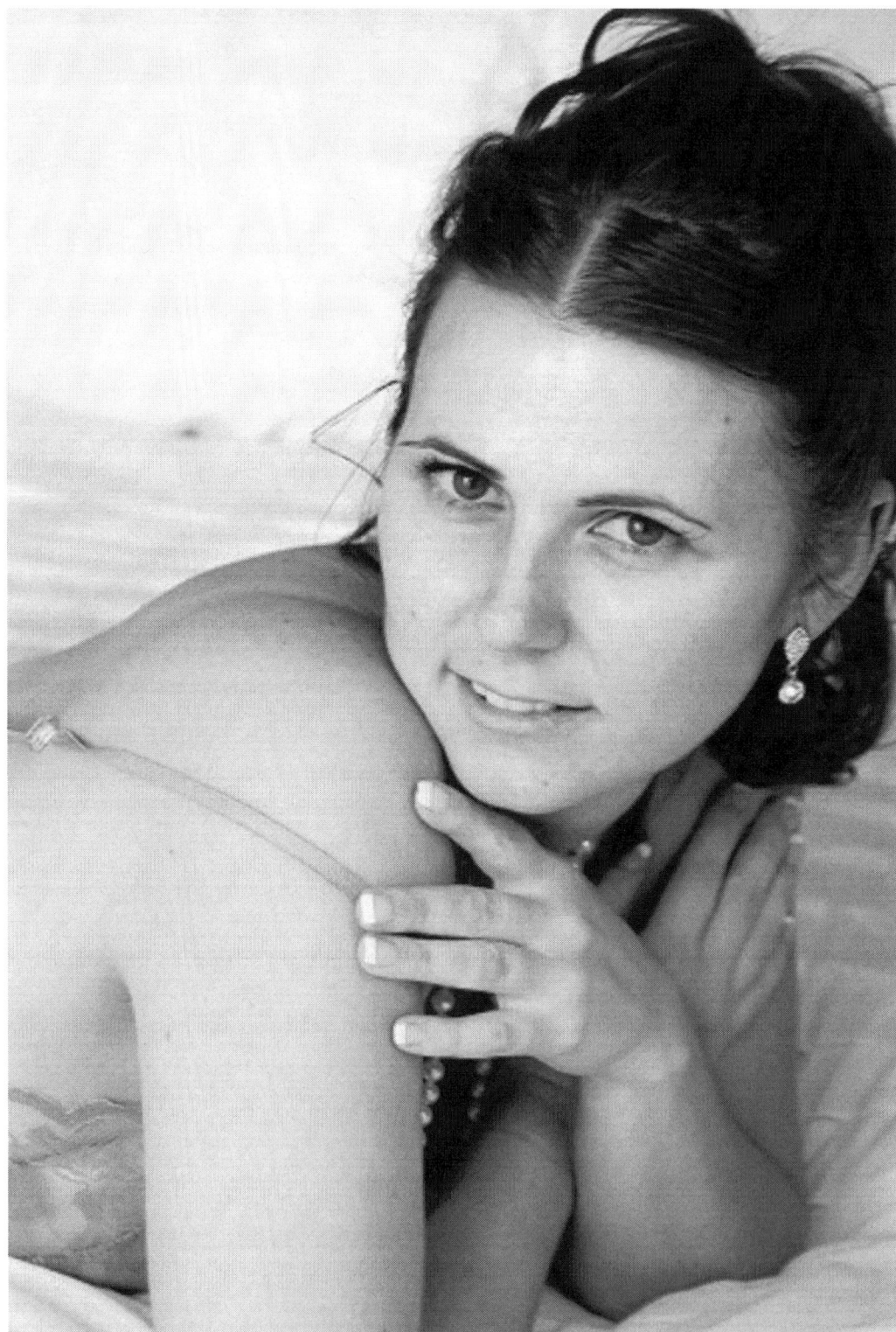

Gateway

Such a pity
A victim is what you see
You obviously don't know me

I am the survivor
The Lord has created me to be
Have faced more than you will believe

Still I keep a strong faith
For Jesus lives in me

Don't pity me
Watch me rise
I have too much faith inside

His love is the most grace
Faithful & unconditional love
Is the Lord in Heaven above

He is the one who holds true
The gateway to my heart
And the only one my soul belongs to

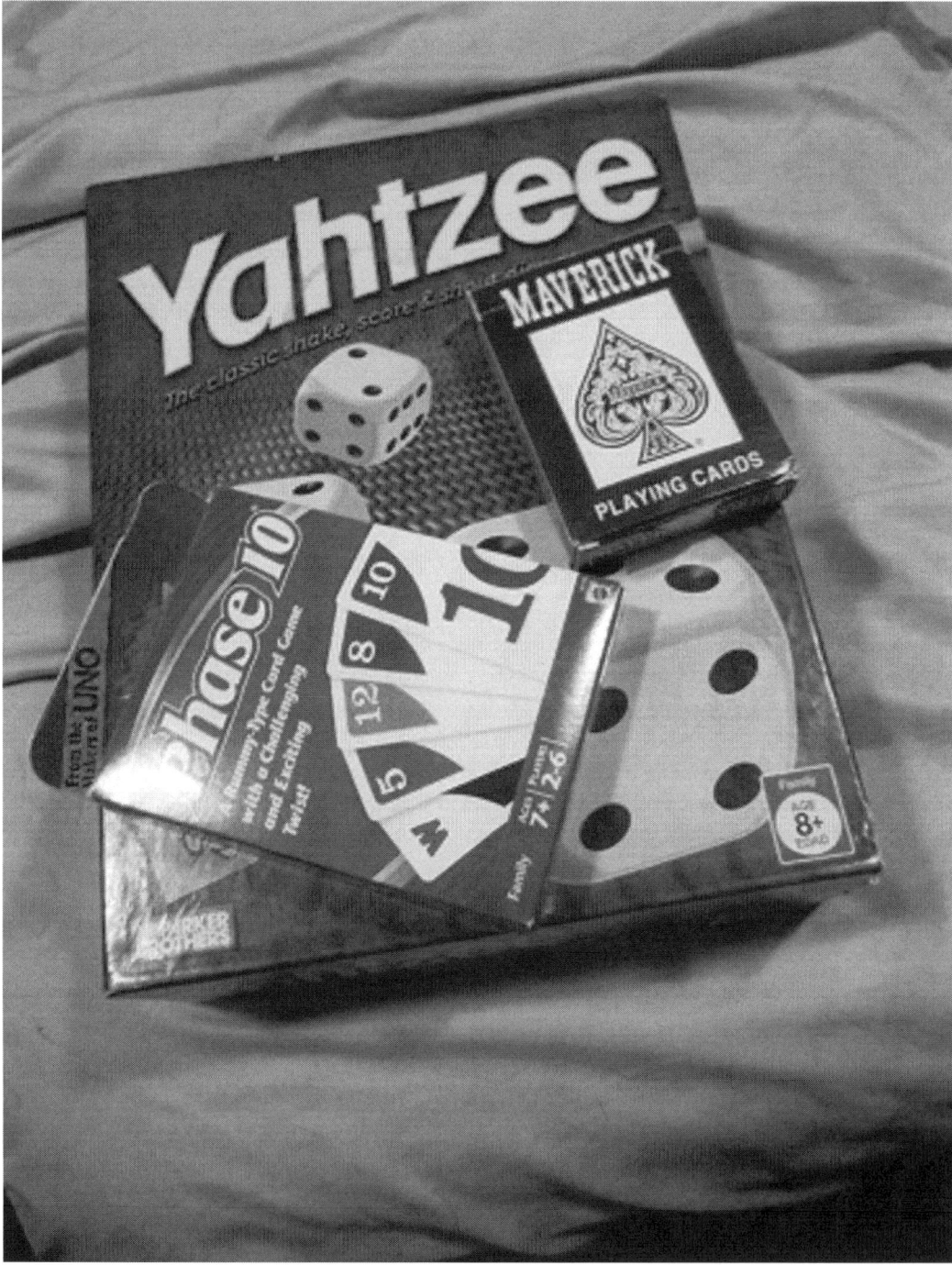

Games Of My Heart

The music consumes me
I am such a child inside
Wanting to play and be happy in this life

I will not give in to the system
I will stay above with laughter & love
A kid at heart that I will not surrender

The music opens my door
Card games I adore
And only know winning
Foosball, pool, air hockey
My competiveness opens door

I am fun & caring
But my competitiveness can be wearing
I haven't met my true match yet
I just keep winning

Easier To Be Alone

So hard to trust
No one understands
I just cannot let you in
Too much has happened

You never really talk
I can't know what's real
It is so much easier to be alone

I want you to see me
You are my true match I know
But you can't let me in either
We are both messed up beyond us both

So easy to be alone
No one can disappoint you
When you don't understand
Nor do you see me or the truth
I just wish my love for you wasn't this strong

I have to make a decision
One I have been trying to make all along

It is easier to be alone
But my love for you is true and strong
If we can move forward
And let us in
We really should move on together
This is how I feel

It is easier to be alone
But with you is the only place I feel at home
There is so much to say and do
So much to both me and you

I don't want to move on
I don't want not to know you
But it is easier to be alone

Dancing In The Rain

I love the rain
The peaceful water flowing
Dripping down
Another storm may be coming
I am dancing in the rain

No pain, no worries
I am in no hurry
The rain is dancing inside of me
And I here twirling in the water around me

Dancing through the rain
I don't feel any pain
So peaceful, so clean
It is raining over me
The storm has set me free

Dancing through the rain
I will feel no pain
The storm is so peaceful to me
The rain continues to dance inside of me

My Dream

I dream of the day
When I can say "I do"
"I Do" to life with love so true

I dream of being a wife
And an amazing mother too

I dream to spend my life with one man
Someone to grow old next too
Who will love me unconditionally
Just as I will love him throughout the rest of my life too

I dream of the day
When my life & dream will arrive
The day the man I love
Will make me his wife

Church As Home

This church is my home
But it doesn't feel the same
It is more upbeat
And I have come to learn
I already praise God everyday

Faith through song I already live
I yearn to know you more Lord
Through the word you left here for us to hear
Your grace & love is where I already live

You are faithful
And continue to live through me
But here is where I come to learn
I yearn to learn you more through Jesus' word
Ready to learn like a kid

This church is my home
But I yearn to know more
Not only praise your name
I yearn to know you Lord

I'm Not Perfect

I am not perfect
But you love me anyway
Your guidance is so patient & pure
You Lord never stray

I am not perfect
I hurt
I push people away
My strength can be my weakness
But you know never to stay away

I am not perfect
I don't settle but I do struggle
But I always keep my faith
Your love makes me happy
I'm grateful for each day

I may not be perfect
But I am a child of God
And that is perfect
To know my Father in heaven above

Can You See Me

Many layers beyond what the eye can see
So much hope & passion growing in me
Too much life & love binds me
Can you see me?

Breaking through reality
So many are blind see
The layers inside of me
Can you see me?

Can you see me?
I feel like a prisoner in myself
No one can break through my layers
Not able to handle what is real
Can you see me?

I'm breaking through reality
Too many are blind to see
The layers inside of me
Can you see me?

Bad Habits

We all have them
Some are illegal
Some are not
Bad habits find us & linger on

I am definitely not perfect
My bad habit is loving you
A man afraid of commitment
I thought I saw more in you

Bad habits arise
Through your own surroundings
And in time
At least my bad habit is legal
Only to my heart
Is it a crime

We all have them
Bad habits do exist
We are not perfect
But we are not our bad habits

Don't let them own you
Or dictate you either
You have more strength then you know
Bad habits are just habits
They come and go
It is what you choose to exist

My Deeper Wish

Will my dreams ever happen
What does my future hold
I wonder
Will my greatest desire be held?

My deeper wish
My greatest desire
To passionate & faithful wife to another
And be an amazing mother

I wonder
Will my dreams ever happen
What my future may hold
So much love to give another

I wish so deep
With a passion & desire to behold
What a blessing that would be
To have my own family

Only the Lord knows
What is truly meant to be
Only the Lord above
Holds my true destiny

Imperfection

No I am not perfect
There are pettier girls then me
But I am beautiful

I may not be a genius
But I use more of my brain then most
I know I am smart & that's all that counts

I am not perfect
There is no such thing
I am the best I can be today
I am human same as you
But strive to be better than I was yesterday

I will strive to be better tomorrow
Each and everyday
Not for anyone else
But for my loved ones I have in heaven above
And for myself!

I don't seek for perfection
I seek to be me
I choose to be real
Not a doll to be seen

I am imperfection
I am real for you can see
I strive to be better
To earn my wings someday

Until that day
I will continue to rise above
To be me and the imperfection you may see
I choose to be real
For life isn't perfect
And I choose to feel free
For I am not perfect
But happy & proud to be me

I Am Not This Person

I am a good woman
I know this with pride
But here is not where I live my life

I am not this person
I prefer to be alone
And live quietly

I am a person with only good intentions
I don't wish to be famous
Or live in the chaos of the public
Here is not where I feel live

I strive to be better everyday
I am here to share my story to help another in anyway

The only reason why I write for you to see
If I can inspire and motivate another
The only reason why I have shared my journey

I am a good woman
But a private person
I prefer to live my life without hesitation
My journey has been my own
I have chose to walk alone
To stay focused and determined
Is how I always survive
It is only with God I know with pride

I am not this person who needs to be seen
It is only for you
I am here to help you believe
My journey here has only brought me to believe
Through faith is why I am sharing my journey

I'm Free

No one owns me
I am free in the world around me
I know no boundaries
For God truly guides me

I am free with integrity
I will push the boundaries around me
God made us for so much more
For him I will sore
In opportunity and possibilities

I am free to live
For my life is worth living
I only aspire to do much more
Then so much around me before

I am free
Because he loves me

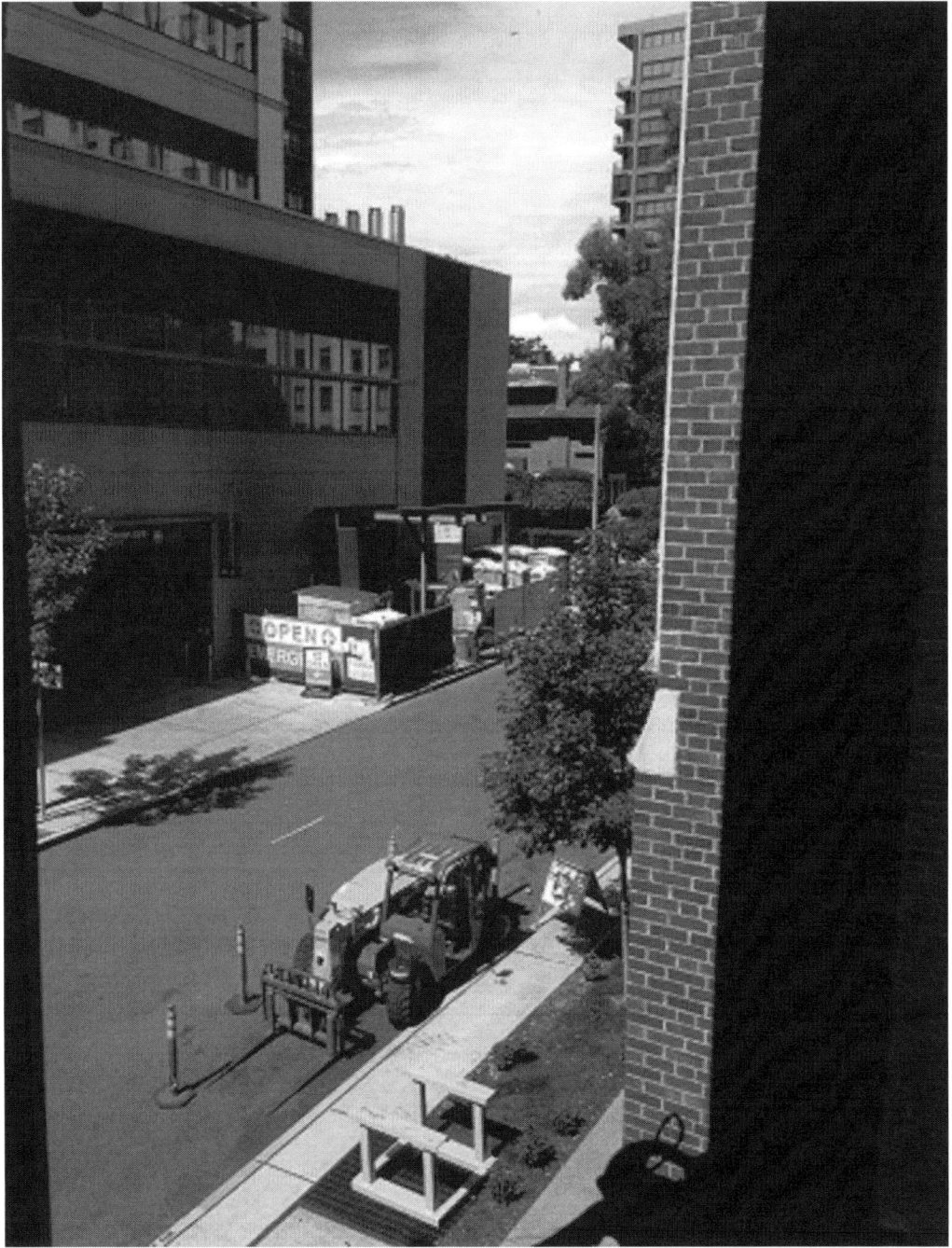

Noise

So much noise
It can be too hard to concentrate
There is so much to be done
But there is always more to be said

Too much noise
So much distraction
Fear in what's to be said
What is your reaction?

To rise above?
Or to fall into what's said?
Overthinking only creates less doing
Which leads only to a bigger mess ahead

To rise above
Ignore the noise
Concentrate & create
For there is much more to be done

So much noise
But I have risen above
The noise won't be a distraction to me

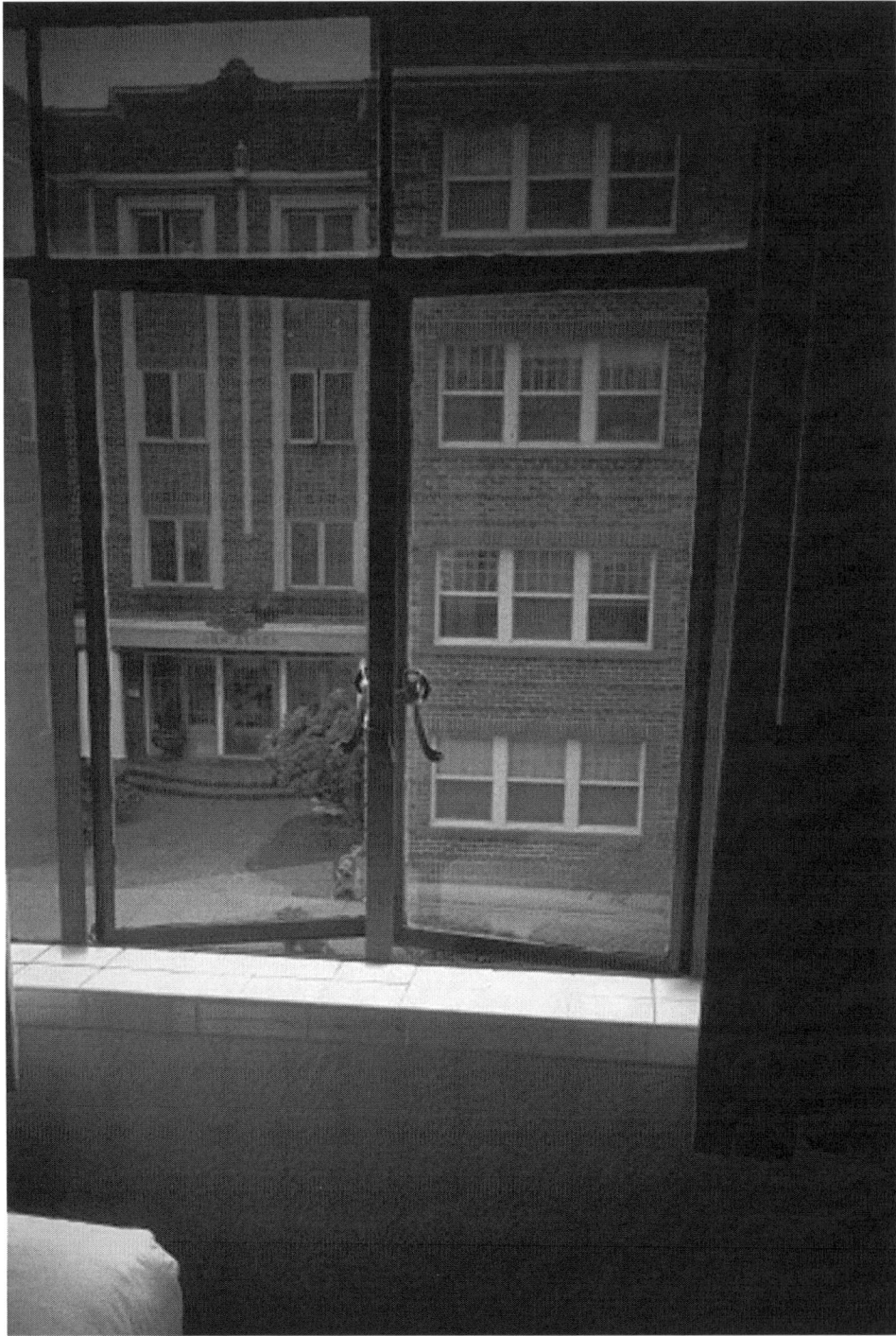

Not Home

I cannot be bought
I cannot be won
Boundaries have been pierced
As I feel uncomfortable & scared

I respect myself
I have set boundaries
Privacy in this chaos is overwhelming to me

I only wish to breathe
To alone to achieve
Please respect my privacy
This doesn't feel like home to me

Your curiosity & pride
Have ignored the boundaries you set aside
My privacy & respect have been broken

You cannot buy me
Nor will you win me over
You are not a man for me
I need to feel free
This no longer can be a home for me

No Distractions

My phone is off
The television too
My full focus Lord
Is my relationship with you

I pray for my journey
To prove my faith in you
May it inspire & help other seek you

Quiet moments
Delete the distractions
Let me concentrate on you
I feel I need to share
This journey given
Inspires me to rise above
And make you proud of me down here

Your unconditional love
And unfailing faith are true
Always proving you are always near me too

Quiet moments
With no distractions
I always hold more dear

I love you Father
Thank you Jesus
For guiding me here through you

Only God Knows Me

Who knew
I would never really let anyone in
Only God knows me
It is easier to only love and trust him

Who knew
I could love so deeply
And you wouldn't let me in
I only wanted to be with you
To grow old and be with you to the end

Only God knows me
Inside & out
No secrets or suggestions
Truth and trust with no doubts

Who knew my life would come to this
Reevaluation feels like a curse
For I love a man who would not let me in

Who knew..
No one would really see me
No one could ever know
I never let anyone in completely

Only God knows me
No one else
Reevaluating can be sad

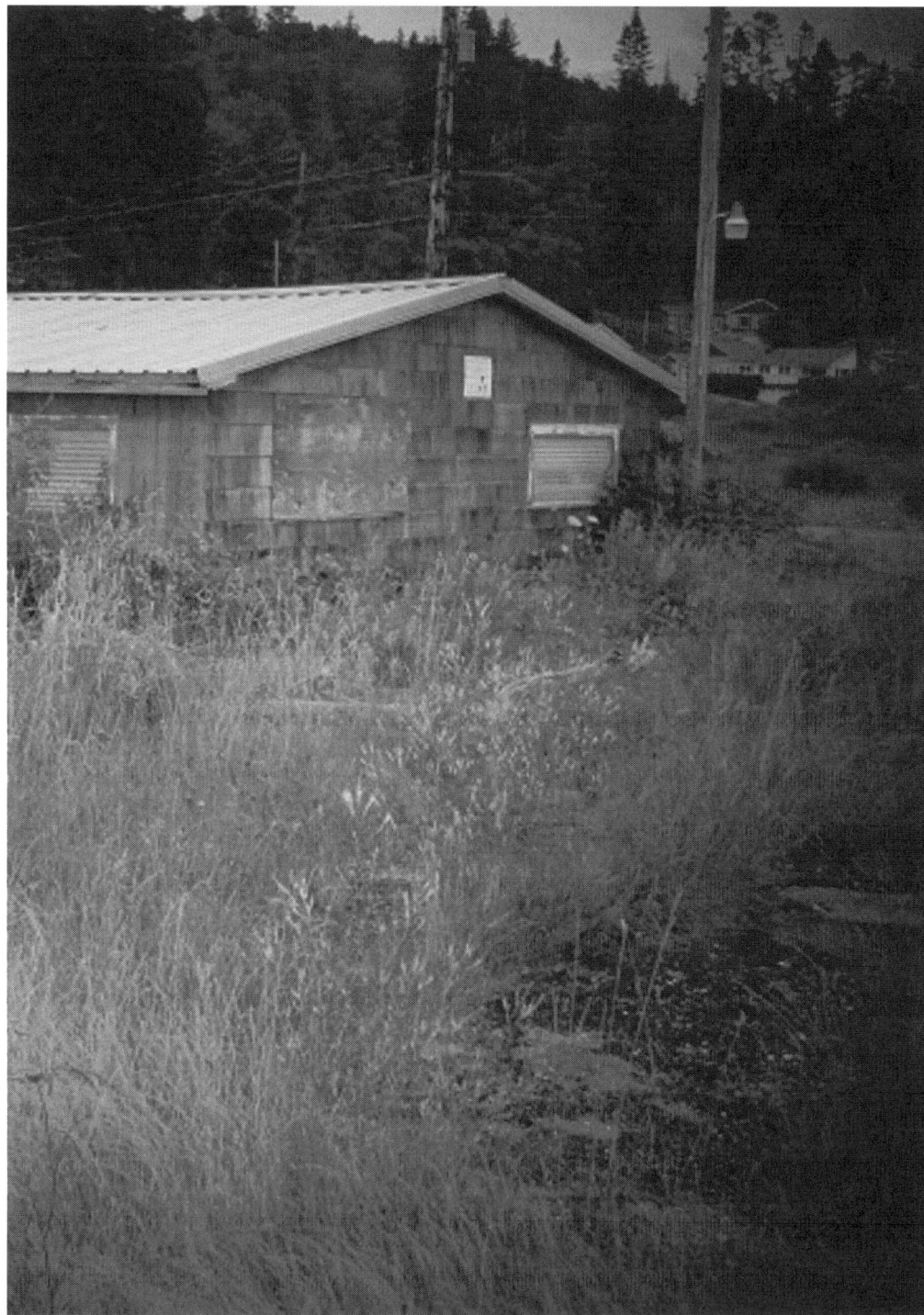

No Home

I am not home, happy or found
I am lost in a mess of my own
Push & pulled
But I have not strayed
I pray to have a home here on earth someday
Where I can stay and feel safe

My work is not done yet
There is much still needed here
I will not give up
However I continue on

But I am not happy
I am not home
I wonder if I will ever be happy
On this earth
Our temporary home

Contained

I have been sheltered and contained
But throughout my life I have always thrived
To be the good girl inside

Contained in a vision
But I am no longer a girl
But a good woman in this world
On a mission to be even better

I stay reserved
But not contained
I am free
Only God owns me

Contained is no longer my path
I have risen above
I strive to succeed
In this journey
The path god has brought me

I am free
For God lives in me
You cannot contain the passion
Faith and love is all that guides me

This mission has been awaken
I don't strive for perfection
But aspire to live above and to inspire

A good woman I am
Society won't contain me
For God has freed me
And it's for the Lord above
For who I live for on earth
I am not contained in this world

Taking It On

There is nothing in this world
I haven't been good at
Mind over matter
Is what I believe & learned
One day at time
I conquer & achieve
I know my worth

I am an athlete
Can kick butt
I am competitive
But haven't sucked yet

I am creative
Teach myself & believe
I create beauty
In everything I seek

I am outgoing
Caring & true
Playful but determined
I will see all things through

I sing with all the Lords gifts brought to me
I am confident enough
To take on anything
I am better than enough

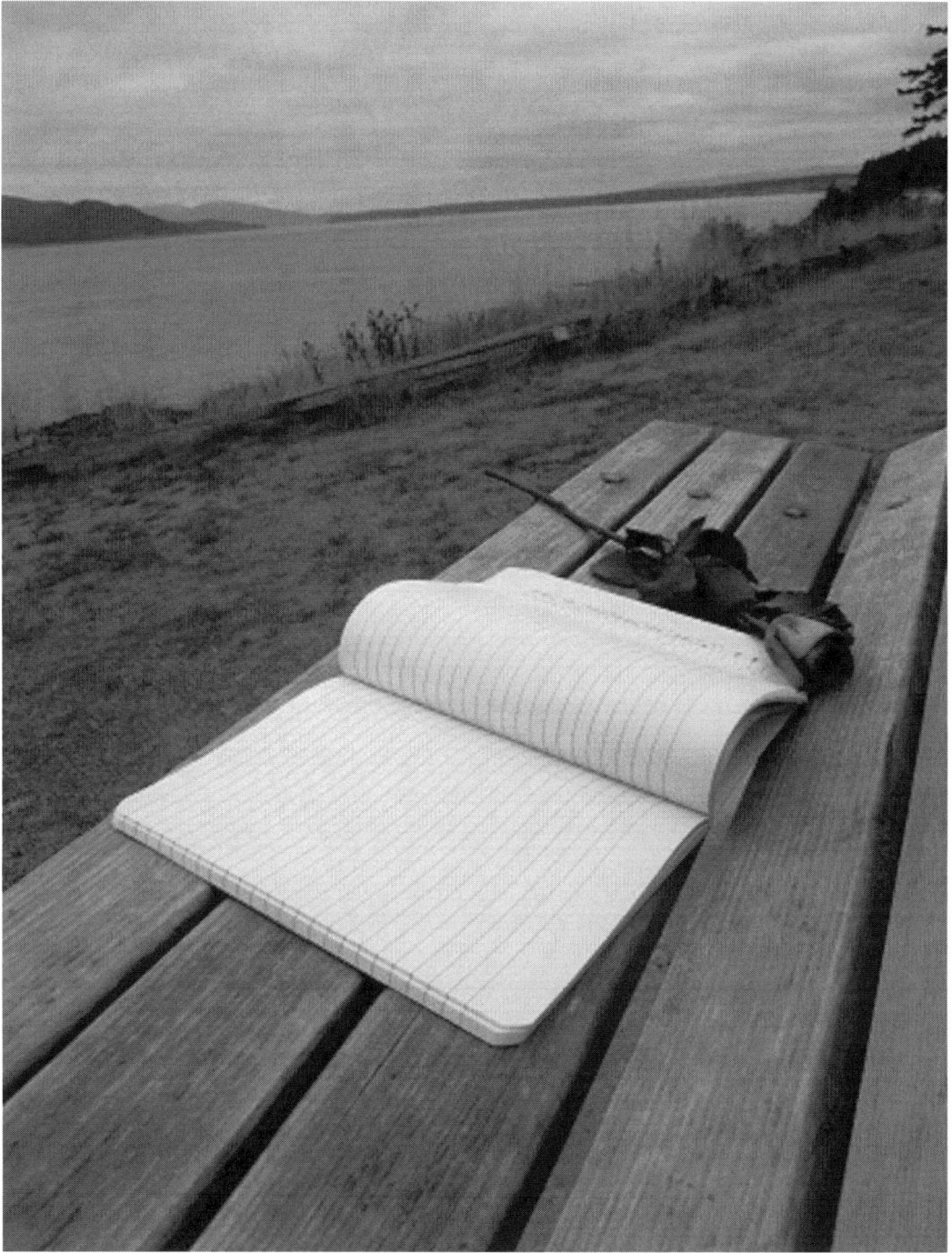

Chapters Close

Another page to end another chapter
But the fear & excitement of what the next chapter may behold
This chapter has to unfold

I must move on
It is time I leave you behind
You can't seem to move forward
And I need a future in mind

It is hard to say goodbye
But you already stopped
And if I stay
I too will be lost

Another page
This chapter much be shut
No looking back
There is a future at hand
This is where my next chapter starts

Childhood Dreams

As a child we were told we can achieve so much
If we believed and tried

I was a child
Who thrived to be famous
To sing, model & dance
I idled Sheryl Temple
And classical musicals
I dreamed of romance

One day I stopped believing
Got caught up in life and reality
Gave up on my dreams
And have been the person for everyone else but me

Followed the rules
Taking care of everyone else
And never took real chances
Childhood dreams became lost

What happened to dreams we dreamt
I have always kept goals
But only within reach
Life happens
Childhood dreams became a thing of the past

So much has changed
In all of us I know
But I won't be trapped anymore
God gave us gifts to use as tools to succeed
So believe and do something more

You too can achieve

My childhood dreams have been awaken
No longer do I yearn to be famous
Only to use my tools for good
Inspire others to keep believing
Always believe you could
And you will achieve more
Believing in childhood dreams once more

Don't Want To Be Another Barbie

I will not be another Barbie
Just waiting in the lobby
Beauty lies deep within

I aspire to be beautiful
Unique with more love to be given
I want to be more beautiful within

I will not be a carved image
I will not be another society Barbie
I was created to rise above
Inspired with so much love

I want to be beautiful
On the inside as well as out
I want to be heard
I need to be seen
On all levels between

There is more to me to be seen
So much more created in me
I will not be another Barbie

Believing In You, Believing In Me

I believe in you
Therefore I believe in me
There is so much out there
But only your eyes can see

My life is in your hands
My heart lies in you
My soul will only always belong to you too

You created life in your image
How can others not see your love to be so true
We are meant to be so much more
I will not dishonor you

I will strive to be better
More inspired by you
For I believe in you
So I must believe in me to

Better For You

Do I make you proud Father?
Do you really see me?
I love you & Jesus unconditionally

I may have moments
Sometimes selfish & stubborn
But in my heart I live for you
Always & forever

I strive to be better
My strength is loving you
Do I make you proud Father?
I want to do right by you

The Mirror

What I see before me
In the mirror starring back at me
I am my own worst critic
You can't see what I see

I am compelled to strive to be better
The mirror is my motivation
My determination to be the best I can be
The mirror is where I see me

What is it that you see?
Do you see my struggles?
My pain?
I'm in competition with myself
To be healthy
To succeed more again

I strive to make myself proud
To be a better person
Inside & out
I strive to make my angels above prouder than me

They motivate me to inspire
It starts within me
This is what I see
Looking back at me

What do you see?

Untamable

I am a free spirit
My love & faith are true
With a greater passion
I will see you through

They will not tame me
For I believe in me
And know you will see me through
I'm untamable

I'm untamable through you
I will conquer
I will thrive
I will meet this world alive

My spirit is strong
My passion is true
I live for you Lord
I am untamable for you

I Love Me

I choose to be happy
I choose to be single & free
Because you cannot handle the love & passion in me

I strive for greatness
My passion isn't pretend
I am proud to be me
For I love me

You will never find a woman like me
I have nothing to hide
Only strive to achieve & succeed
I love deep & passionately

I have so much love for the world around me
So I choose to be happy, single & free
For I love me

You only weighed me down
With your negativity
You were never true to me

I am happy
For I love me.

If I Had Wings

I wish I could fly
Grow wings
And sore through the sky

To look down from above
Only to see greater love
Not the mess
We seem to have around us

I wish I could fly
To be free in the sky
With nothing to stand in my way
Just storms to seek
And thrive through each day

If I could grow wings
I wouldn't stray
I'd be able to see the path around you
I would just fly above
And help guide your way

If I could fly
I would rise above
With greater love
And show you a better way

If only I had wings

Tears Of Happiness

Tears of happiness
Come much deeper within
God gave me courage
And determination

But his deeper love
Shine from above
Within the relationships down here
Always encourage & wait for me
To rise above
There is something much deeper to see

The love & support
With a sappy heart
I never ran

So much joy
Happy endings
Are only beginnings
Compassion overwhelms me
With happy tears
He has blessed me
And my life here

Surprise Melodies

There is a song
You never heard
It holds a deeper meaning

Surprise Melodies
Are not hard to find
They lie in laughter
Or even in a cry

Life is full of wonders
They are hard to find
When you take the blindfold off your eyes

Life is precious
It is beautiful
It is real
Life lies in the beholder
What it is you see & feel

Surprise melodies
The best music is unwritten
It is the song in you
That speaks more true

Surprise melodies
Gifts from Heaven
It is beautiful & soothing
I hope you feel it
And see it to be true within you too

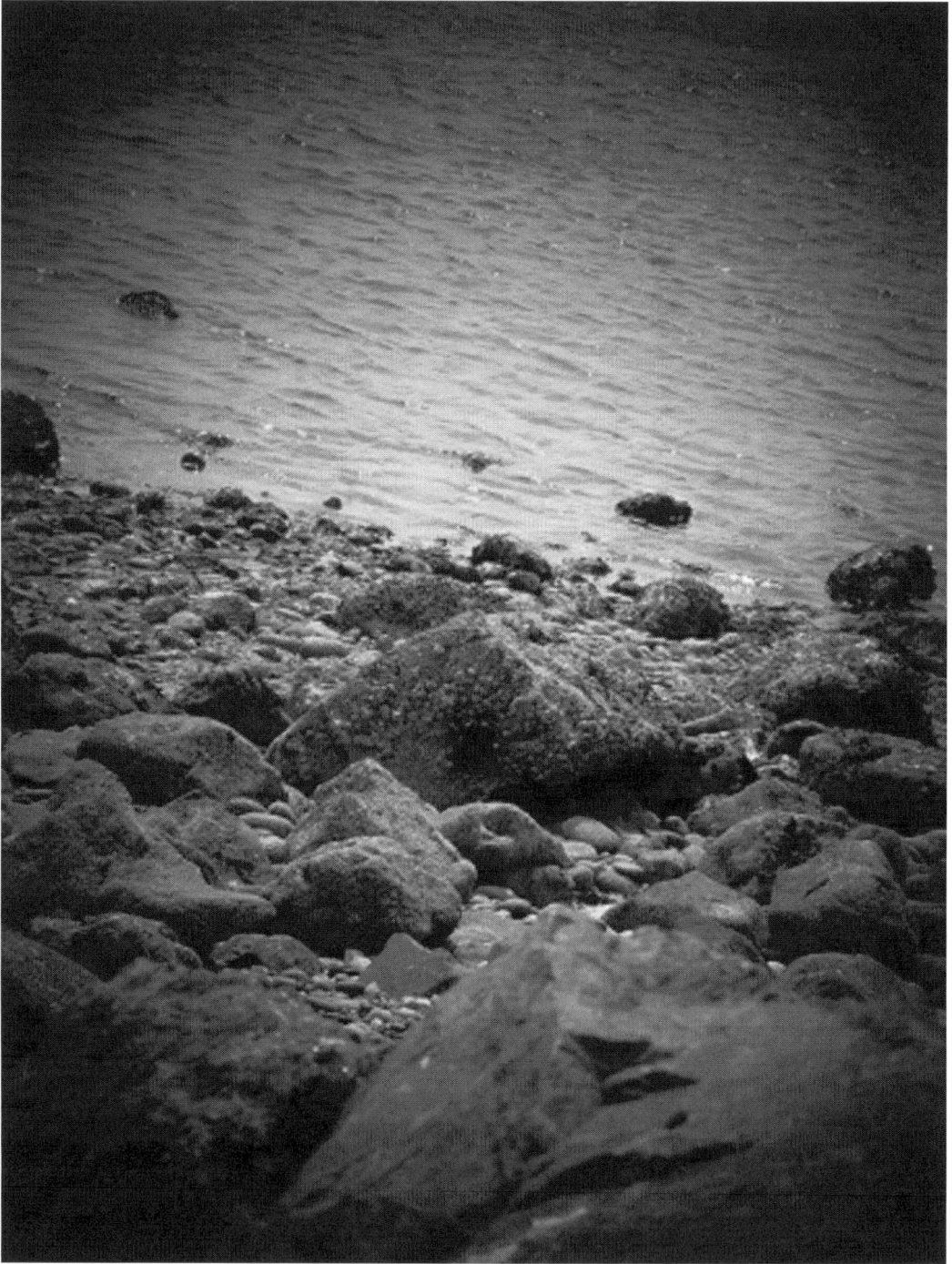

The Sea In Me

Next to the ocean is where I breathe
This is a deeper side to me
And at the sea is where I thrive
Where I feel most alive

Where the ocean is open & free
For the Lord is the anchor of me
Keeping me sailing smoothly
Through the storm I come strong
And at sea is only the beginning of me

A storm is where I find courage
The darkness can't take me
For Jesus is my Lighthouse
I push to my destiny
I will conquer the darkness
The storm has nothing on me

It is here on the ocean
Where he recognizes me
The ocean is my vision
The sea is where I breathe

My sails maybe blowing
But God is my anchor
And Jesus is my lighthouse
Through all of my journey

Eternal Beauty

True beauty lays within
Shining through faith & love
God's elegance & grace
Beauty doesn't lay just in the face

Life has so much beauty
Life is full of love
Look around with an open heart
Do you see the beauty of life?
That is what eternal beauty will find

I wish to feel God's amazing grace
Forever watching over me
For I believe in a higher power
I believe for what love he has for me
Jesus' eternal beauty
Is his love for you and me

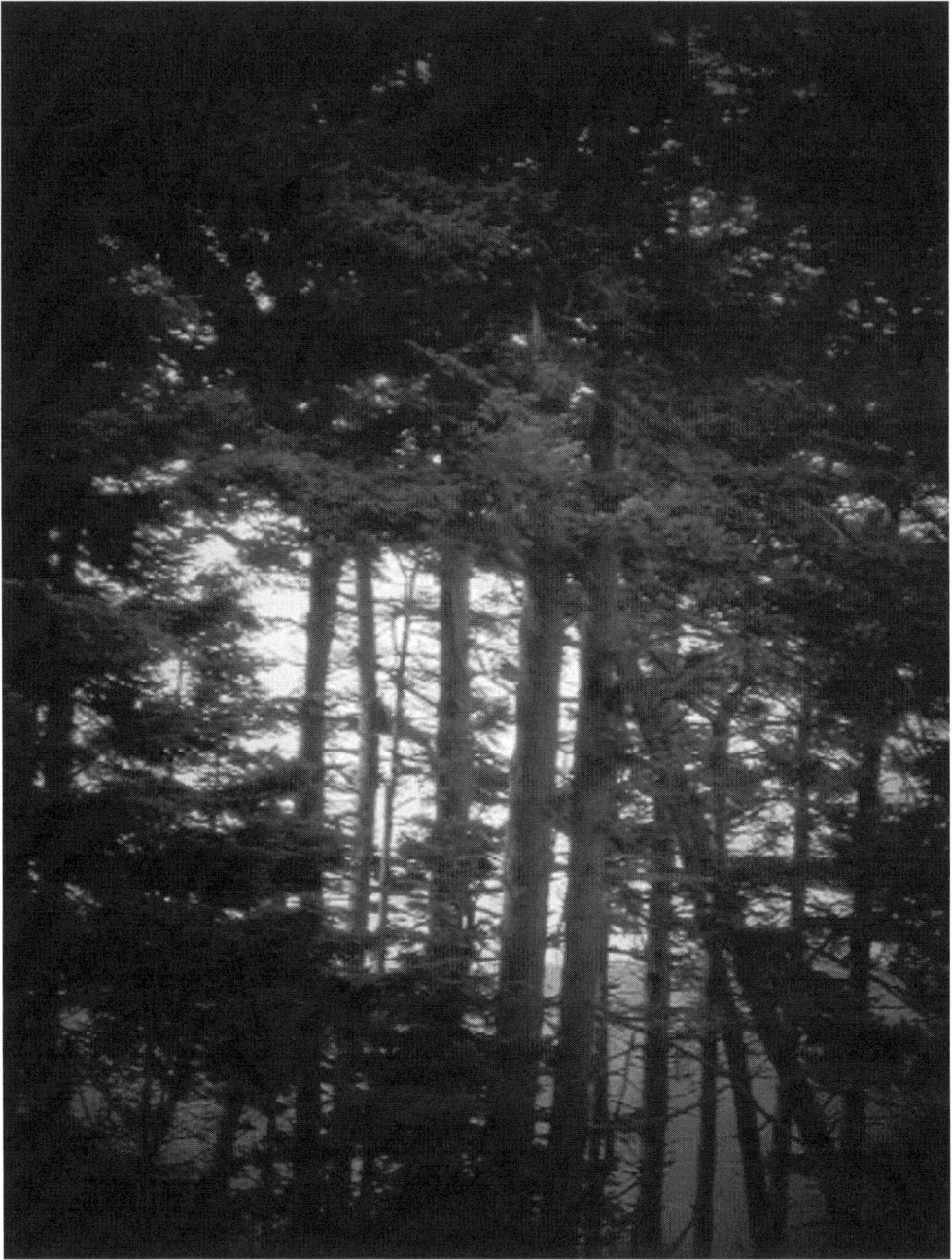

Walk Through Darkness

I am not afraid of the darkness
For I always have you
Darkness comes before me
Only for a short while
For you are the light which guides me through

I will walk through the tragedies
I will laugh at temptations
Darkness can't tempt me
I belong to you

Where you stand
Darkness will be in fear
For you have my hand

I will walk through darkness
I know you will always see me through
My faith & love are stronger
Then any darkness down here can do

I will rise above & conquer
Darkness will never know this love
I will walk with pride through darkness
And will one day meet you above

The Waves Of The Sea

The waves may push & pull
They may drag me whole
But the waves of the sea
Will never own me

I will conquer
I will swim
I will not abandoned him

I will strive to stay alive
The waves of the sea
Will never drown me

Here in the storm
Is where I must be feared most
The waves turn into giants
But they won't conquer me
The only become a part of me instead

The waves of the sea
Will always be a part of me
For I conquered the storm
The waves of the storm have never conquered me
I have always conquered them

Push Forward

Some will fight you
Some will hurt you
Some will entice you
But God will inspire you

Keep your head up
Don't look back
There is more coming
And you are stronger than that

Be true to yourself
Let God lead your heart
You have a bigger purpose here
God will not let you fall apart

Some will push & pull
The fake will be a test
But true compassion & a healthy love
Will be your greatest gift

Continue on your path
Only focus forward
The greatest gift will be given
When you have arrived
So push forward

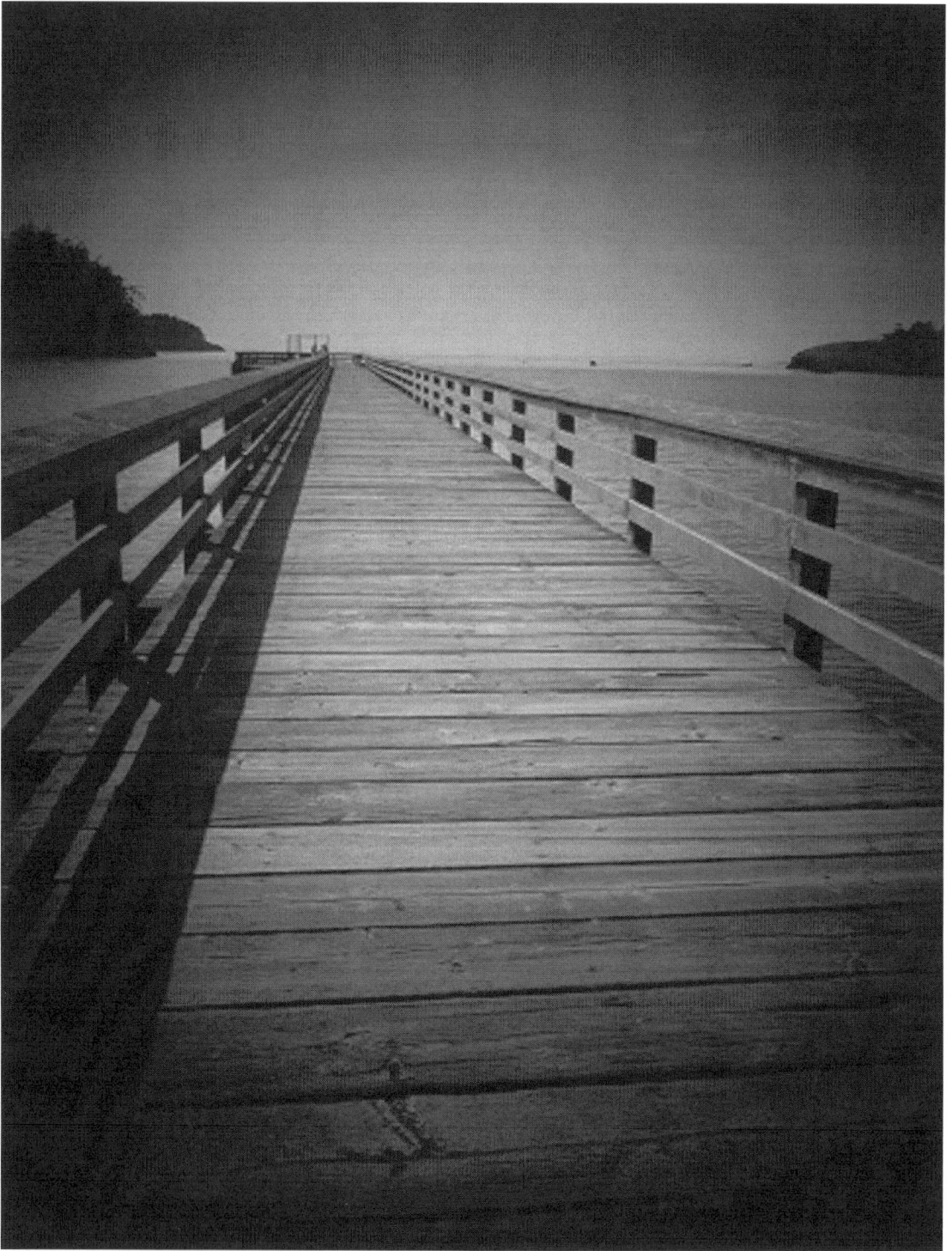

How Perfect Is His Plan

There is so much more to this life that lays before me
So much beauty that I can see
How perfect his plan must be

I am so proud to be your daughter
Continue to work in me Lord
I trust you
I believe in you
I have faith in how you see me

I will fight
I will grow stronger
I will always conquer with you above
How perfect his plan can be

I will sing
I will write
I will inspire
For my love for you my Heavenly Father
Will only inspire me to continue to stay true

You are perfect
You are amazing
I see so much beauty
In this life in front of me
Beauty in your creation Lord

The Marina

Looking down on the marina from above
So many boats and lives I see
We each have a purpose
A passion inside and drive to succeed

What leads them to the water
Where do they thrive
What is the mission
Where will they arrive

For each boat must have a journey
What stories they must hold
Near the open water is where I reside too

Do they feel what I feel inside
The pride of being closer to you Lord
I wonder
Do they to here feel more alive
With nothing to hide

So many boats
So many lives
As I look down from this cliff above
The marina I gaze and ponder
The water creates something more in each of us

So Girly

So girly I am
And proud of it
Grew up with too many boys as a kid

Pink is my favorite
Always dad's princess
But also a competitive sports brat

It is most fun being me
A tomboy in pink
I love only nice things
But I am the one who takes care of me

This world can be so much fun
When you love the outdoors & sports
And still can be a high maintenance girl

So girly I am
And very proud of it too
But I still can beat you

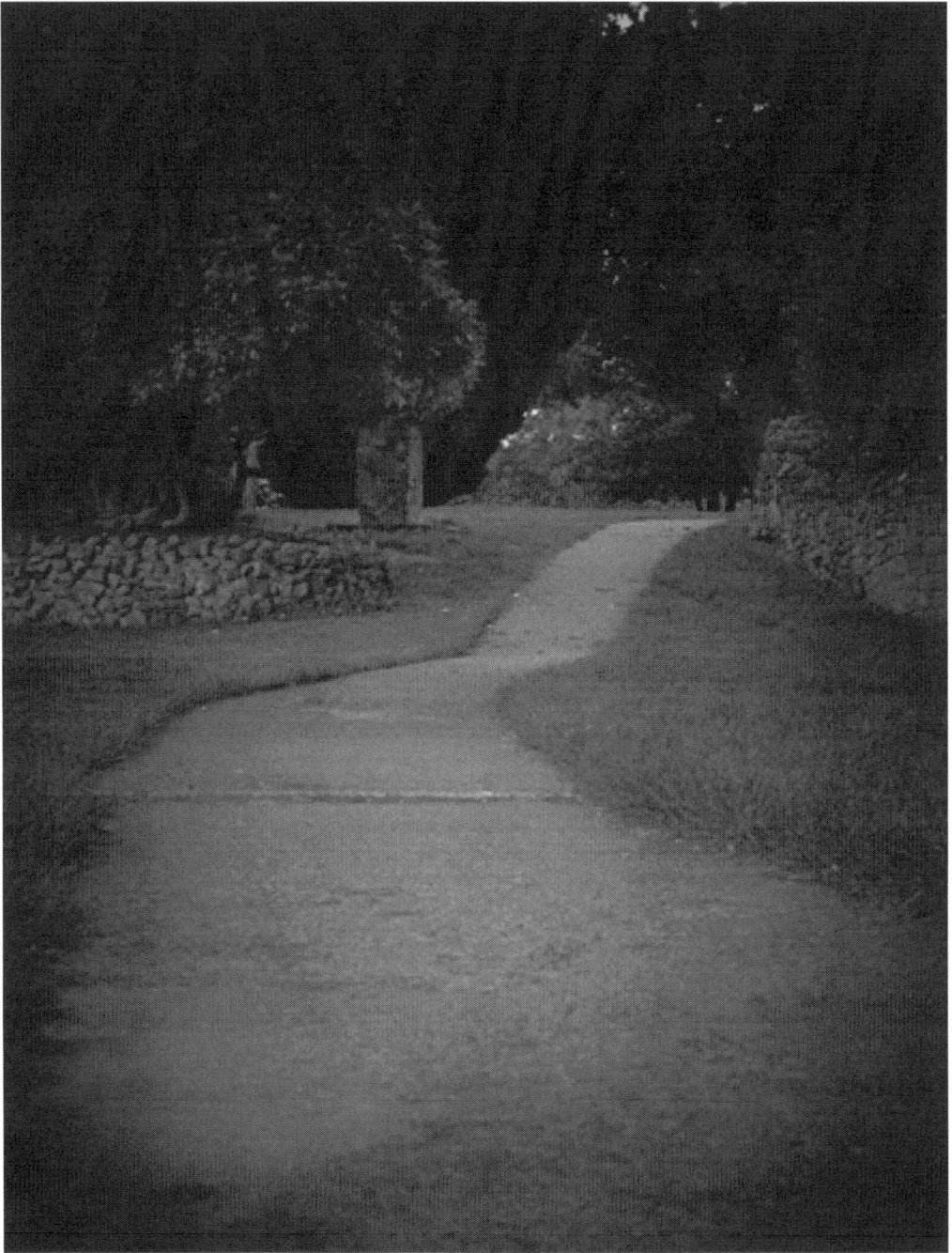

My Life Makes Sense To Me

The moment life makes sense
In aww of what I have learned
Peaceful knowing what is true

What is meant to be
Will always find a way
The hurt in not knowing
Has finally gone away

I am here for a purpose
My gifts are to be used for God
The moment life finally makes sense
I have finally arrived

I am finally here knowingly
My journey hadn't been easy
So hard to make sense
But I am finally here
I put everything in the Lord's hands

The moment life makes sense
My journey wasn't misleading
My faith has carried me here
It wasn't easy

Peaceful & free
I understand my journey
So much lost
But much more gained through my love in me
My faith & love brought me to peace
My life makes sense to me

Pieces Of Me
By Julia Anne Simpson

Pieces Of Me
By Julia Anne Simpson

Appreciation

To everyone taking the chance to read my book, I thank you and hope that it has inspired or motivated you to achieve your goals and dreams.

To my family & friends, your love, supports, and prayers are greatly sincerely appreciated. I love you all very much

To Phil Schwabe. A man who inspired a huge part of me that I thought I lost over 10 years ago. He challenged, inspired and believed in me, and I will never forget him.

To Taylor Lacroix. My best friend and soul sister, her support on all levels of what I have been pursuing to achieve and so much more.

To my Vi Family & Vi Community. If it wasn't for ViSalus I would not be publishing today. ViSalus is more then just another company looking to cure obesity and poor nutrition in the world. It is a better way of life. The "Pay It Forward" mission. I am proud to be a part of such an amazing mission.

My Faith. I am Christian and have an amazing relationship with God. For him and with him all things are possible and all things have a reason. Push through the negatives and find your positives. We were all created for so much more. Thank you Heavenly Father above.

There are so many people in my life that have touched me, supported me, believed in me, etc. You know who you are. And I am eternally grateful to have you in my life.

Thank You All!

Pieces Of Me
By Julia Anne Simpson

Credits

Photographers:

Jim DeFreece of Artscape
Pages: 178, 198, 228, 280, 282, 290, 301, 304, 308, 308, 328, 332, 336, 340, 350, 353, 378, 412, 418, 440, 548, 558, 568, 574, 712, Cover

G. Eric Engstrom
Pages 138, 192, 200, 274, 302, 420, 448, 576, 602, 706, 748, 750

Cassandra W. Photography,
www.cassandraWphotography.com
Pages: 60, 82, 90, 128, 132, 144, 218, 268, 540, 598, 630, 650, 676, 686, 699, 717, 738, 746

CMP - Oak Harbor, WA
Pg. 354

Editors:

Tony Alaya of Artfully
Pages: 186, 280, 290, 308, 328, 336, 382, 558, 574, 750, Cover

Kevin Devroy
Pages: 138, 146, 163, 178, 192, 198, 200, 202, 206, 220, 222, 238, 274, 282, 288, 292, 298, 301, 302, 304, 340, 350, 353, 360, 378, 412, 418, 424, 440, 576, 632, 678, 684, 706, 712

ViSalus: Life, Health & Prosperity
Pages: 19, 611-671, 782

To check out the mission behind ViSalus or to get "Your Challenge On"
JuliaSimpson.BodyByVi.com

For more photography and information about this author,
Go To: www.JuliaSimpson.net

Pieces Of Me
By Julia Anne Simpson

Made in the USA
San Bernardino, CA
09 November 2014